Professional Storyboarding

Professional Storyboarding

Rules of Thumb

Sergio Paez and Anson Jew

Focal Press
Taylor & Francis Group

NEW YORK AND LONDON

First published 2013
by Focal Press
70 Blanchard Rd Suite 402
Burlington, MA 01803

Simultaneously published in the UK
by Focal Press
2 Park Square, Milton Park, Abingdon, Oxon OX14 4RN

Focal Press is an imprint of the Taylor & Francis Group, an informa business

Library of Congress Cataloging in Publication Data
Paez, Sergio.
   Professional storyboarding: rules of thumb/Sergio Paez and Anson Jew.
   p. cm.
   Includes index.
   1. Motion pictures—Production and direction.   2. Television programs—
   Production and direction.   3. Storyboards.   I. Jew, Anson.   II. Title.
   PN1995.9.P7P25 2012
   791.4302'3—dc23
   2012029406

ISBN: 978-0-240-81770-5 (pbk)
ISBN: 978-0-240-81771-2 (ebk)

Typeset in Giovanni Book and Franklin Gothic
by Florence Production Ltd, Stoodleigh, Devon

Contents

Author Biographies

SERGIO PAEZ

Sergio Paez is a San Francisco artist specializing in storyboards, animation, and visual development for TV, feature film, and games. His animation credits in the United States and Europe include projects for Pixar, Lucasfilm, Sony, and Sega. Sergio's work is featured in The Art of Clone Wars published by Chronicle Books, in The Art of Darkwatch, published by Design Studio Press, and he was featured at the Totoro Forest Project Art Exhibition. With a strong foundation in traditional animation and illustration he has built his career on content creation and story structure.

In 2008 Sergio launched www.StoryboardArt.org, an online story community, with both a content creation and educational focus to further techniques in visual storytelling. Currently Sergio is working in San Francisco developing new media projects. You can see more of Sergio's work at www.SergioPaez.com.

ANSON JEW

Anson Jew is a freelance illustrator and storyboard artist based in Los Angeles. His credits include: *The Chronicles of Narnia: Prince Caspian, TMNT, Sky Captain and the World of Tomorrow, Anacondas: Hunt for the Blood Orchid, Scooby-Doo: Mystery Inc.* and *Wolverine and the X-Men.* He has storyboarded numerous commercials and video games and previously worked as an animator in the computer game industry (LucasArts) for nine years. Anson has spoken on the subject of storyboards at San Diego Comic Con and at Art Center and taught storyboarding at Otis School of Design.

Acknowledgments

We owe a great debt to the artists that came before us since they forged the way to creating the modern stories we now tell. I thank all the filmmakers, animators, illustrators, and storyboard artists of whose work and great skill I was always so envious. I now realize it was a gift they left for us other artists to follow and build on their work in the hopes that we too might achieve greatness as they have.

I care to acknowledge all those who in one way or another facilitated and supported me to achieve my dreams. To my parents and my brother André, without you I would have never gotten this far. To José Maria Guzmán Moreno, thanks for being patient to a young artist and sharing with me your storyboard knowledge. I am forever grateful to the world of story you unlocked for me. Finally, I pay tribute to the memory of the great Barbara Bradley, under whose guidance I achieved the most artistic growth. You are the generous educator, who passed to me the knowledge I needed to achieve my dreams.

Sergio Paez

Introduction

As I put my tablet pen down and shut down my computer my cell phone buzzes again for the third time. It's another text message from my friend Pete wondering where I am. Seeing as he made these dinner plans for us two weeks ago, I really should be more punctual. I rush off and arrive at the restaurant but the only thing dancing in my head is the dialogue from the scene on my desk. The questions keep ringing through my ears.

Shouldn't the character be sad at this moment?
Why am I cutting from a wide-angle shot to a close-up?
Is it better to use a two-shot here?
Does it make sense that she would slap the guy in the face at her work?

Throughout dinner, I absorb the idle chit chat and nod like a stoic robot. I look at Pete as his face turns into a composed square offset by the plants in the background behind him. I see vertical lines dividing my view into the rule of thirds.

This would make a cool long shot in that bar scene, I have.
"Wake up man, it's like you're day dreaming or something." Pete catches my blank stare.
"Sorry dude, it's this scene I'm working on. I just can't figure out how to get the staging right."

Pete doesn't get it. Most people don't. Once you get the story bug, it takes over your whole being and the only thing you can think about is trying to solve the visual problems in the most unique and creative way. Visual storytelling and drawing storyboards is another language of communication. Unfortunately, it's a difficult language to master and speak clearly, but once you solve the visual problems for your audience using storyboards, it becomes an addiction. After a while you start to think whether an average burger with your friend is really as much fun as manipulating characters in your scene.

Storyboards are comic book style drawings that establish the *emotional content* and *action* of a project. The goal of a storyboard is to communicate an idea. These drawings may only be looked at for a few seconds so you have to use every tool in your toolbox to get your audience to understand your ideas. Because of the quickness and relative cost efficiency, storyboards evolved into the blueprint for movies, TV shows, video games, and commercials. They form the basis of all other departments in the production process.

As important as they are, there is little information in books and other print material that covers storyboards and visual storytelling. Even art schools and traditional learning environments don't give you the necessary tools to improve your visual storytelling. Seemingly, the information of creating better visual stories gets passed down from artist to artist from within closed studio environments or only among professionals in the industry. Our aim here is to unlock the mystery of telling better visual stories using storyboards. Don't let your personal doubts or lack of experience hold you back. The best part about storyboards is that anyone can tell an exciting story once you know the basics.

Storyboards are essentially a short hand for the film and visual storytelling language. What we describe in drawings are aspects of cinematography: composition, camera angles, and staging. Even though we must master the tools of drawing, storyboards are not about drawing. They're about *communication*, not illustration. The end goal is to *tell a story*, and because of that, we need the tools to communicate our ideas visually. You don't have to be a master artist to tell a good story. You only need to understand *how* to communicate your ideas well to your audience.

While drawing skills are helpful, they are not a prerequisite to making storyboards. If you can draw stick figures, you can learn to compose a shot that communicates an idea for your story. For those seeking to become storyboard artists as professionals, drawing skills are indeed much more valuable. The traditional drawing skills of anatomy, proportion, composition, perspective, color, and design all apply when making storyboards. These arts skills require years of training. While lacking in story training, most commercial art schools nowadays do a decent job training graphic artists in traditional art skills. Art skills, just as storyboard skills, are a lifelong mental discipline that should be practiced constantly throughout your life. The focus of this book is not necessarily on traditional arts skills, but the application of specific tools to communicate visually through the use of storyboards. As we shall see, even understanding the basic principles of creating storyboards will allow those artists without exceptional art skills to communicate clearly and create winning stories.

ACHIEVING SUCCESS

There is only one secret to mastering a new art form: *practice*. No book can make you instantly better. No self-help tape will give you the magic recipe. It is up to you to learn new skills through repetition and practice. There are no prerequisites or age limitation; all you need is the desire to improve and the discipline to *practice*. I find it ironic that people always admire great artists or athletes for their "innate gifts" and "God-given talents." "You're such a great dancer . . . it must be from your mother's side," they always say. As if the fact that you dedicated 14 years of your childhood life studying acrobatic interpretive dance had nothing to do with it. The truth is, *everything I know about storyboards and visual storytelling was taught to me by somebody else.* You can truly learn to become a storyboard artist. The problem in the case of storyboards is knowing *what* to learn. The ability to quickly create storyboards that convey emotion, that show action, and that help to preplan productions relies on a specific set of techniques. Our aim is to show you the tools so you can become a storyboard professional and work on the movie projects you've always dreamed of.

THE HISTORY OF STORYBOARDS

Back in the very earliest days of film, there wasn't a whole lot of thought given to artistic expression. In 1895, Auguste and Louis Lumière perfected what is generally thought of as the first projected motion picture that could be shown to large groups of people.[1] The Lumière Brothers thrilled paying audiences with simple footage of workers strolling out of the Lumière Brothers' factory. These early audiences were impressed by the simple novelty of watching moving photographs. Ironically, the Lumière Brothers, believing that the novelty of moving pictures would wear thin on audiences, abandoned further development of motion picture photography and set their sights on trying to develop a process to create color photographs. Using moving pictures as a medium for telling stories hadn't occurred to them as a serious consideration.

By the time early filmmakers got around to telling visual stories, there wasn't much thought given to camera angles, camera movement, or editing. Most of the time early filmmakers shot their films as if watching a play, with the camera in a fixed position while the action played out in a wide shot until the scene was over. Only then would there be a cut to the next location and generally only using a wide shot and a static camera.

Over the first decade of the 20th century new techniques began to emerge. Camera movement, cross-cutting between actions, reverse angles, inserts, point-of-view shots, flashbacks, and other techniques began to take hold and develop into the beginnings of a common film language. One early film theorist and filmmaker, Sergei Eisenstein wrote at length about his theories on *montage*, about how several shots linked together in certain ways could create specific emotional effects.[2] His theories were very influential on later filmmakers.

EARLY STORYBOARDS

As directors got to the point where they were more serious about stories and storytelling, many filmmakers found pre-planning with artists' sketches to be useful. Eisenstein used them on *Battleship Potemkin*. Cecil B. DeMille used them for the 1923 version of *The Ten Commandments*. Artists would sketch out ideas for gags or design sets; however, these weren't what we would consider storyboards so much as concept sketches. It wasn't until a young upstart named Walt Disney came along with one of the first uses of what could accurately be described as a storyboard. It started with the making of a short animated film called *Plane Crazy*, the first of three shorts Disney produced after going independent (the other two being *The Gallopin' Gaucho* and *Steamboat Willie*).

STORYBOARDS FROM THE DISNEY STUDIO

One of the artists to stick with Disney's studio was the prolific Ub Iwerks, who is believed to have produced *Plane Crazy*'s first primitive storyboards.[3] It was basically six panels hitting the major action points drawn on a page comic book style, with the action descriptions written on a separate sheet of paper. Walt Disney would look at the boards and approve of things, suggest revisions, or cross out something if he wanted it cut. They were now seeing the film as it appeared as more of a whole. Up to that point, in most animated productions, each animator was assigned a scene and had to come up with funny gags around a single theme without much regards to how the gags worked within the context of the rest of the film. Now with storyboards, you could get a sense of the big picture; how each series of shots as working together as a sequence—more like what Eisenstein already established.

Plane Crazy (1928)

Plane Crazy, which also happened to be the first use of Mickey Mouse in a cartoon, and the second short, *The Gallopin' Gaucho*, were created as silent shorts and were rejected by MGM and sat in the film vaults collecting dust. By the time Disney did the third short, *Steamboat Willie*, he had decided to use synchronized sound after the success of the very first sound film, *The Jazz Singer*. *Steamboat Willie*, was such a huge success that *Plane Crazy* and *The Gallopin' Gaucho* were pulled from the vault, sound was added, and the success of these shorts allowed Disney to continue making animated shorts, eventually leading to the development of a full-length animated feature, *Snow White and the Seven Dwarfs*. A later short, *The Three Little Pigs* from 1933, was the first short to be fully storyboarded with many shots drawn on separate pieces of paper pinned to a board the same way it's done today in animation.

Aside from the artistic benefits mentioned earlier, storyboards have a much more practical use. In films, especially animated films, production is very expensive. Many people are involved in shooting film and if things are cut or changed after it's been shot, huge amounts of money are wasted. Storyboarding allows you to edit and change things on paper, before any expensive shooting begins, resulting in a net savings. It also allows many people to look at the development of the film and be sure that the story is working for maximum emotional effect. Because of this realization, storyboard use spread to both animated and live action film and is still widely used today.

WHO HIRES STORYBOARD ARTISTS?

Aside from animation and live action film, with the advent of new media platforms such as video games, web, and mobile applications, storyboards are more widely used now than ever. Despite this fact, the number of people who create storyboards for a living is relatively small. While there are certain industries that hire staff storyboard artists, most storyboard artists are freelancers. In most cases, freelance storyboard artists don't work on storyboards exclusively. They often work in other areas as well such as print, product illustration, comics, or concept art.

Independent Contractors vs Staffers

Storyboard artists can work either on a freelance basis or as part of a staff. Some industries work exclusively with staffers, while others work exclusively with freelancers, although occasionally, companies with art staff will hire out freelancers when they need extra work done. Staff positions for storyboard artists are found largely in animated feature productions and animated TV series, as well as in the gaming industry. Live action features, live action TV and the advertising industry use freelancers almost exclusively.

Staffers

Working as a staff storyboard artist means you work in the way most people think about a job: you get hired by a company as an employee where you have an assigned cubicle or office and you work 40 hours a week Monday through Friday. The standard corporate benefits would apply. Most of the tax you owe on your income is withheld for you. You have co-workers and supervisors that you get to know over the long haul. There are employee reviews and office politics. You work there as long as you can before you either quit, get fired, or get laid off. Because animation, unlike live action, requires that an entire show be storyboarded, full time staff storyboard positions mostly reside in the animation industry, TV shows, or the gaming industry. Staff storyboard artists' salaries vary depending on experience from around $40,000 to $150,000 a year.[4]

Independent Contractors (aka Freelancers)

Working as a freelancer means you are self-employed—you are your own boss. You demand your own pay rate. You decide if you are going to work or not. If you want health insurance, you have purchase it on your own (unless you're in a Union; more on that in Chapter 12). You have to keep track of your own income taxes and expenses.

Freelancers can be hired for gigs that are only a day long or that last for months. They may work at home via the internet or they may have to commute and work on-site depending on the job. Freelancers generally make it a policy to charge by the day rather than the hour, to avoid situations where you commute for two hours on a one hour gig, and then come home to find an offer for a full day's worth of work or more in your email inbox.

Generally speaking, a freelancer's rate is often higher than what a staffer makes. A decent freelance storyboard artist might charge nearly $700 per day. This may lead you to believe that freelance storyboard artists drive foreign sports cars and live in opulent houses in the Hollywood Hills. Oh, how we all wish this were true. The reality is freelancers often find themselves going for long stretches without any work, essentially unemployed, burning through their bank accounts to pay the rent until they land that next contract. This is one reason they have to charge more than staff employees.

Being a contractor is like being unemployed all the time in that you spend a lot of your non-working time trying to find work, via the internet or through phone calls or though some kind of marketing program. You are constantly sending out your portfolio and résumé, cold calling, schmoozing, or building up your online portfolio. Unlike a staffer, freelancers don't judge their success so much by what hourly rate they can charge for a day's work, but by how much work they can cobble together in a year. Their annual income tends to fluctuate depending how much work they can drum up. Unfortunately, most artists can't put enough work together to keep completely busy for an entire year (and those who can, can probably also afford to charge more). But if you manage to keep reasonably busy throughout the whole year, a professional storyboard artist can make a comfortable living.

Most storyboard work that is related to live action productions is freelance. This is for several reasons. For one, storyboards are not as universally used in live action as they are in animation, and when they are used, it is generally only for specific sections of the production like sequences heavy in special effects or action. Also, most productions involving live action, like feature films and commercials, are done on a project to project basis. For example, when live action feature films are produced, each film is its own company that only exists for the duration of the production of that film. Once the film is completed, the production company essentially shuts down and ceases to exist. This is in contrast to animated films, in which a single production company (like DreamWorks or Pixar) has several films in production at once, and where full time staff storyboard artists can jump from production to production once their contribution to a specific project ends.

The choice between a staffer and a freelancer is often not that difficult depending on the what kind of lifestyle you want to lead. In your career you may end up going back and forth from staff to freelance positions. In our discussion we will go through the benefits of each so you can make an informed decision about which areas of storyboarding you may want to pursue.

NOTES

1 B. Chardère and G. Borgé and M. Borgé (1985), *Les Lumière*, Paris: Bibliothèque des Arts.

2 Sergei Eisenstein (1949), *Film Form: Essays in Film Theory*, New York: Harcourt, Trans. Jay Leyda.

3 Frank Thomas and Ollie Johnston (1981), *The Illusion of Life*, New York: Hyperion, p.29.

4 See Chapter 12 for more information on rates. Also see published unions rates at http://animationguild.org/contracts-wages/

CHAPTER 2
Visual Literacy

Now we begin our journey into the mysterious world of visual storytelling and make our first strides to becoming a professional storyboard artist. To understand what it takes to create a storyboard image, we must first analyze what's involved in creating a visual story. Narrative stories use visual elements that are juxtaposed together in sequence and projected or displayed on a flat surface for the audience. (For the purposes of our discussion we will leave the topic of sound out for the moment.)[1] These visual elements can be anything we find in our real world or even in our imagination such as characters, deep sea vessels, or distant planets. The visual elements for these shapes are enclosed in a bounding box or picture frame that defines the edges of the composition. This frame can be the edge of the movie screen in a theater, the frame of your television set, or the edges of your computer monitor. It is important to realize that the visual elements are enclosed in a frame that allows us as artists to define the composition. Another point to note is that the resulting projection of these visual images is *flat*. The flat two-dimensional screen of the theater or television monitor emphasizes the necessity to create the illusion of depth on this two-dimensional surface. In a photograph, or a 3D rendering it's easy to see the illusion of depth because the resulting image more closely relates to how our physical eye sees the world. As we shall see in a drawn storyboard, we must take the depth cues from the real world, and emphasize or de-emphasize them as we see fit.

SCREEN REFERENCE

When talking about storyboards, we often refer to the images as if they were already projected "on the screen." We will refer to terms such as "screen direction," or "camera left," "camera right." These terms refer to the physical camera and the final projected image on a movie screen. Also terms may come up that reference the actual shooting of a live action movie such as "camera height" and lenses. We will go into the deeper meanings of these terms later, but since these industry terms are tossed around often, it's important to understand what they mean in reference to a single storyboard image. When we discuss creating storyboards, imagine the flat storyboard panel as the final projected image in a movie theater or on a TV screen. Since many of the projects will end up in one of these formats anyway, it's good from the start to imagine any work we do as closely resembling the final projected image. Throughout this book, we will refer to storyboard images as if they are part of the final projected movie or an actual film production.

THE STORY POINT

In discussing storyboards one topic that comes up is fulfilling the *story point*. The story point is simply the purpose of the shot or scene. It answers the question "why?" Our goal as a story artist is to solve visual problems and answer the "why" question. Why did the character enter the scene? Why is the character afraid? Why did the bank explode? The story point is the reason we draw a particular storyboard panel. Each panel needs to have a specific reason why it's drawn and answer a question of what *story point* that image reveals. We will discuss the story point more in depth later, but for now realize that every panel, you draw should have a purpose for the story.

EMOTIONAL RESPONSE

A goal in any piece of artwork is to evoke an emotional response in the viewer or audience. This is no less important in a visual storytelling medium, such as storyboards. In fact, it can be argued that it's even more important in storyboards and visual storytelling since we need to control the added dimension of *time*. Emotions can build from the beginning of your story to the end to create a moving visual experience. In this sense we usually talk about emotions as *beats*, the stepping stones in a story to create the overall emotional response. Understanding what techniques evoke these emotions and when to use them is a skill that's built through experience. It's not enough to create pretty pictures. These pictures need to be designed to move an audience *emotionally* and truly engage them in your story. We will discuss emotion more later, but let's begin with the basics of evoking a visual emotional response.

VISUAL APPEAL

Another concept that needs to be clear within our images is the idea of *visual appeal*. Appeal, as defined by the great Disney animators Frank Thomas and Ollie Johnson, is that innate ". . . quality of charm, pleasing design, simplicity, communication and magnetism" in the image. They go on to discuss appeal:

> A drawing that is complicated or hard to read lacks appeal. Poor design, clumsy shapes, awkward moves, are all low on appeal. Spectators enjoy watching something that is appealing to them, whether an expression, a character, movement, or a whole story situation. While the live actor has charisma, the animated drawing has appeal.[2]

Learning how to create this visual appeal in storyboards requires understanding the basic concepts of design and command of visual shapes. As artists gets better with their drawing, it becomes easier to develop the images to have more aesthetic appeal. Although there are many artists with great skill, this doesn't necessarily mean they can create storyboard images that have this visual appeal. Sometimes the simplest of lines and shape can evoke great appeal and give valuable story strength. It is important to understand that this concept exists. Sometimes when you look at your drawings, and something feels off, it might actually be that the drawing lacks *appeal*. Maybe the arrangement of the shapes in your composition is too cluttered. Maybe the facial expressions looked over-worked. Sometimes just understanding and rationalizing this concept can help you avoid creating a dull storyboard panel.

FIGURE 2.1

COMPOSITION WITHIN YOUR PICTURE FRAME

Now that you understand that the goal is an emotional response, and that your images should have visual appeal, we can discuss the tools to help achieve these ends. As a storyboard artist you should always start out with a compositional boundary or picture frame. This helps determine the elements that go within the composition and how they are arranged within the box for maximum *visual appeal*. By manipulating the elements in the composition, you can direct the audience's eye to where you want the eye to look. This will direct attention to the *focus*, or *story point* and help communicate the emotional beat. We will discuss aspect ratios later, but for now, it's important to point out that most visual stories follow a horizontal rectangular composition. (Figure 2.2)

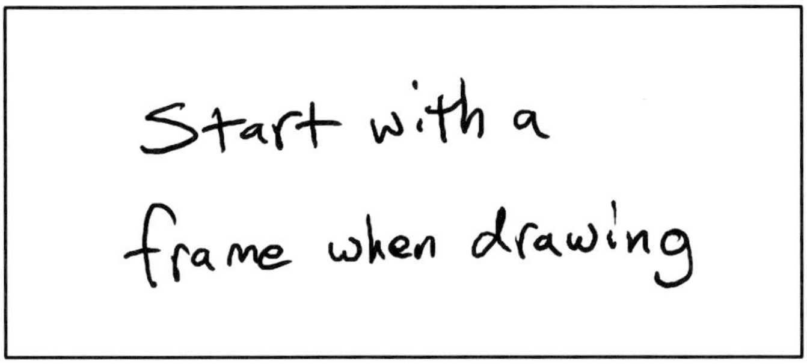

FIGURE 2.2

WORKING WITH SHAPES

Before we talk about complex shapes like automobiles or the human figure, let's break down the visual elements into the most basic abstract shapes. Later we will be able to imagine these shapes as people, trees, or explosions, etc. For now, though, let's take a look at how these shapes work in isolation, and then later juxtaposed together to create an emotional response in our compositions.

Lines

Lines in your composition will give a different emotional reaction to the audience depending on how you use them. Traditionally, the more horizontal and vertical lines there are in your composition, the more static your image will be. The more diagonal lines you have, the more dynamic your composition will be. Use this to your advantage when communicating an action scene, or a subtle drama.

FIGURE 2.3
Horizontals gives the feeling of calm-static.

FIGURE 2.4
Verticals also feel calm, but feel somewhat more active than horizontals.

FIGURE 2.5
Diagonals feel more active than either verticals or horizontals.

Let's look at how these lines can divide the picture frame. (Figure 2.5)

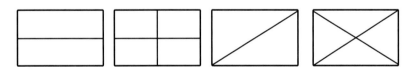

FIGURE 2.6
Lines that divide space evenly are boring.

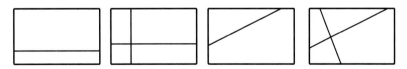

FIGURE 2.7
Move the lines so that the spaces are unequal to create visual interest.

FIGURE 2.8
Parallels give us a sense of stateliness and order.

FIGURE 2.9
Asymmetry gives us a sense of chaos and disorder.

FIGURE 2.10
Noble static composition.

FIGURE 2.11
Dynamic composition.

You can create the feeling of symmetry or asymmetry, depending on what your story requires. So often I see young storyboard artists create static and symmetrical images by default. Because of this, it's important to force yourself to create a pleasing asymmetrical image first and then adjust the composition according to your story requirements. If your story calls for a noble king to enter into the frame, you might want to use horizontal and vertical lines to represent his nobility or power. If on the other hand, the story is about a disorganized business executive, you may want to make the lines in your composition, asymmetrical creating the feeling of uneasiness and disarray. The point to realize is that this is an important artistic choice to arrange the lines and elements within the composition.

The Rule of Thirds

The rule of thirds is a guide to help you avoid symmetry in your composition. Draw lines that divide the frame into thirds both vertically and horizontally. The intersections of the lines make good places to put your visual elements. You can align objects with the lines themselves. (Figure 2.12)

FIGURE 2.12

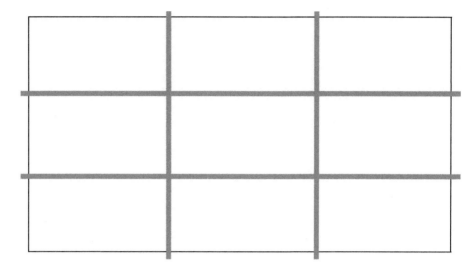

Symmetry tends to split your composition and make it seem overly stiff and formal. (Figure 2.13) Unless this is your intent, avoid putting areas of interest along the halfway line.

FIGURE 2.13

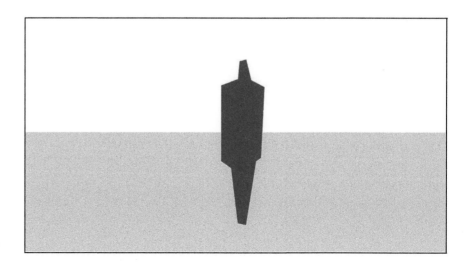

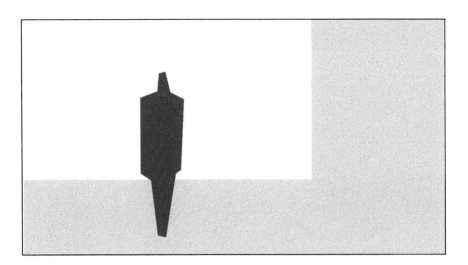

FIGURE 2.14

In most cases, you should put the most interesting elements of your compositions into the area where the picture divides into thirds. (Figure 2.14)

Design of the Shapes

As humans, we have been conditioned to have specific visual stimuli evoke certain emotions in us. With knowledge of this, these visual stimuli can be manipulated by the artist to invoke these feelings in the audience.

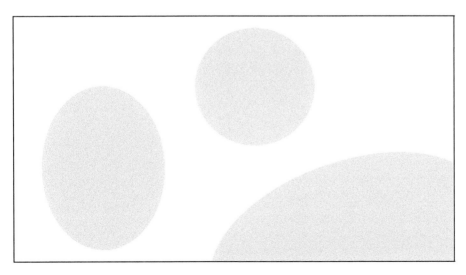

FIGURE 2.15
Circles, ovals, and curves evoke feelings of friendliness, fun, and happiness.

FIGURE 2.16
Squares, rectangles, and right angles evoke feelings of formality and order.

FIGURE 2.17
Triangles create feelings of aggression and dynamism.

Use the design of the shapes in your compositions to create the feeling you want for your audience. These visual elements add great richness and depth to the story. Often, the audience do not realize they are being manipulated, but even the design of the shapes can influence the audience's emotions. In a storyboard image every element is important, especially the design of the shapes in your composition.

FOCAL POINT

Good composition directs the audience's eye to where you want them to look on screen. Every storyboard needs a focal point or center of interest. This focal point can be anywhere within the picture frame, but it's important to choose beforehand where your focal point will be. Creating storyboards is about describing story beats, and manipulating the audience to look at where you need them to look. In order to make your story point clear to the audience your focal point also needs to be clearly designed within the picture frame. Every element of the composition should also emphasize the center of interest. You might deliberately angle tree branches pointing in the direction of your focal point. You can also design the angles of tables and chairs to point and accent your center of interest. (Figure 2.18)

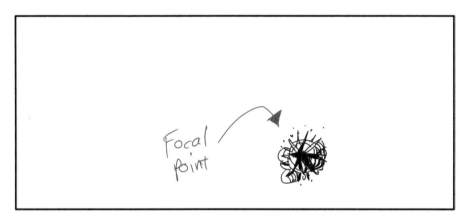

FIGURE 2.18

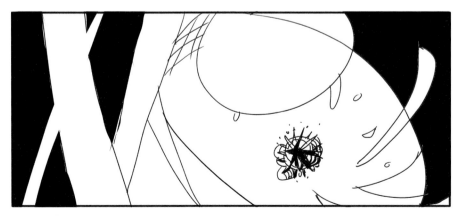

FIGURE 2.19
Design the elements of your composition to emphasize the focal point.

STORY TIP

If your story beat is confusing, or the composition starts to get cluttered, it could be that your focal point is not clear. Begin removing elements of your composition until you find a clear focus to better serve your story beat.

In any storyboard image, you can only have one focal point at any given time. Often compositions get cluttered with too much information, and the focus is not clear in the image. This might be a case of trying to describe too much information all at the same time. Just as you should only relay one story beat at a time, you should only have one focal point at a time in your image. This doesn't mean you cannot have supporting elements that help balance the composition. A storyboard image might have two areas of focus, a *primary* focal point and a *secondary* focal point. A storyboard might even have three centers of interest: *primary*, *secondary*, and *tertiary*. Even though there are multiple centers of interest, there is always an order of importance. You must decide where the *primary* focal point is and keep that element as the most important in the frame. The secondary and tertiary focal points should always support the primary focal point.

FIGURE 2.20
Primary focal point.

FIGURE 2.21
Secondary focal point.

FIGURE 2.22
Tertiary focal point.

DEPTH

One elusive concept for young artists to achieve is a sense of depth in a storyboard. The default tendency is to create a flat image with little perspective or depth cues. As artists we often talk about a scene as having *deep space*, versus *flat space*. Deep space is a scene with a clear and expansive sense of space. A flat space scene is one where characters might be up against a wall or in front of a staged backdrop limiting the distance our eyes can travel within the scene. Each spatial choice has a benefit when trying to describe dramatic or comedic moments and specific story points. These depth cues are a conscious choice to create a specific effect for the audience. It is often more difficult to achieve a scene with a lot of depth using deep space. Story artists should not be limited by their tools and the default should not be only what you are physically able to draw. The good news is that once you are conscious of different tricks to achieve depth and limit depth when necessary, it becomes easier to produce a convincing storyboard image. Let's discuss some tools for creating depth.

FIGURE 2.23
Deep space.

FIGURE 2.24
Flat space.

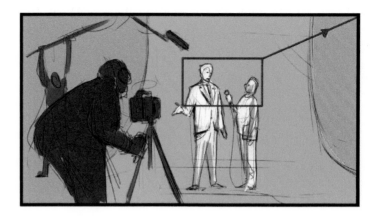

FIGURE 2.24
Flat space.

Perspective

Perspective is one of the most useful tools to create the illusion of depth. You should use a perspective grid in almost every frame you draw. The grid is a quick and easy shorthand to establish the camera height and to give a sense of depth within the frame. A drawing without a perspective grid leaves room for interpretation and might indicate a camera height that you don't intend. Perspective can be a complicated and intimidating subject, but what we will describe here is a specific use of perspective as applied to storyboard images. Just as in any other topic of classical drawing, the more you know about perspective the more versatile as an artist you will be and the better your drawings will look. There are many great resources on the topic of perspective, and we highly recommend you study them all. Check out the Resources section at the back of this book for more detailed information on perspective. Here we will discuss a shorthand to perspective as applied to storyboard images.

PERSPECTIVE BASICS

Parallel lines appear to converge as they recede into the distance toward a point (*vanishing point*) on the horizon. This optical illusion is clear when looking at photos of railroad tracks or a row of cars going off into the distance. The objects will appear to get smaller and converge to a single point in the distance. The horizon line represents the eye level of the viewer *and the height of the physical camera as placed on a movie set*. You can have an infinite number of vanishing points on the horizon line, but in any composition you can only have one horizon line. There are three types of perspective, *one-point perspective, two-point perspective,* and *three-point perspective*.

ONE-POINT PERSPECTIVE

Start by drawing a horizon line through your picture frame. Choose a point on that line to be a vanishing point. Radiate lines from that vanishing point below the horizon line. Now draw lines parallel to the horizon to create a grid representing the ground plane or the sky plane. This creates a one-point perspective grid you can use to position objects in space. The sides of your objects will converge to the vanishing point. This grid is a handy reference that you can use to create the illusion of depth.

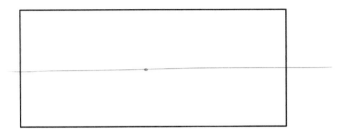

FIGURE 2.25

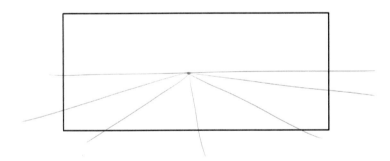

FIGURE 2.26

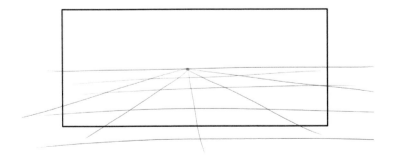

FIGURE 2.27

TWO-POINT PERSPECTIVE

Create two vanishing points on the horizon line leaving a space between the two points. By drawing lines radiating down from both of the points the lines intersect creating a two-point perspective grid. Two-point perspective gives us a more dynamic way to show two sides of an object. Plant your objects on the grid with the lines of your objects converging to the vanishing points. This orients the figures in space relative to each other, and supports the sense of depth.

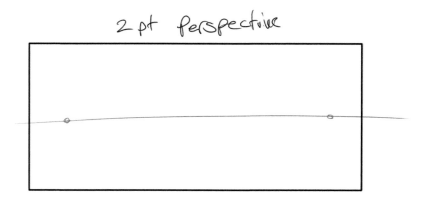

FIGURE 2.28

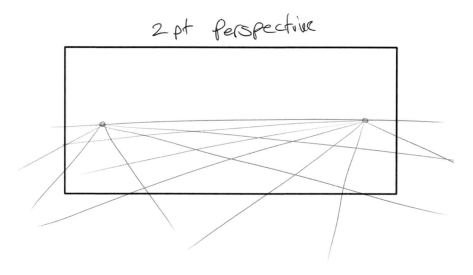

FIGURE 2.29

FIGURE 2.30

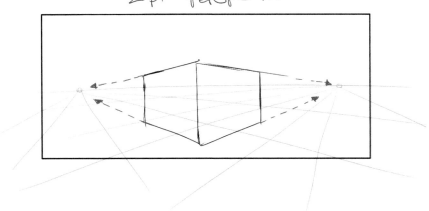

FIGURE 2.31

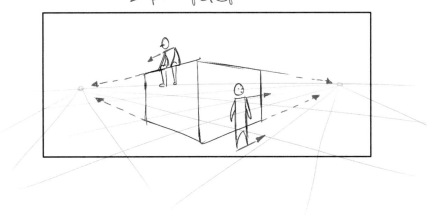

THREE-POINT PERSPECTIVE

Start with a two-point perspective, and add a third vanishing point projected vertically upward or downward from the horizon line. Vertical lines, such as the sides of a building, will converge on the third vanishing point. This helps the sense of depth by exaggerating the distortion of the objects relative to the camera height.

FIGURE 2.32

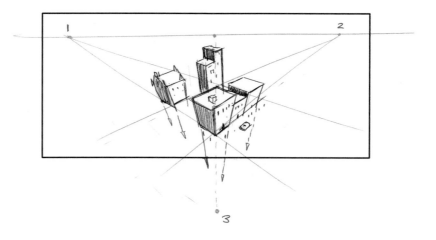

FIGURE 2.33

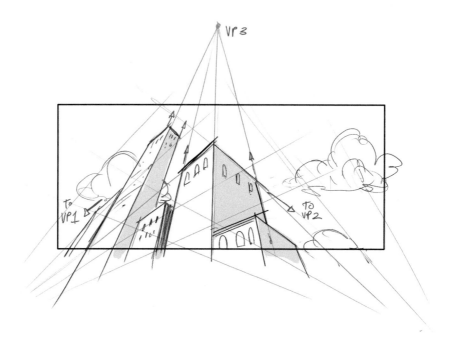

Learning perspective can be challenging, especially if you have little experience in drawing. Again, the only solution for this is practice. Looking at references from life and from photography can help guide you as well. One-, two-, and three-point perspectives are the foundations of building a realistic scene, and they are a guide to plant your figures and objects on that perspective grid. This works even if your perspective isn't 100% accurate. What is important in a storyboard is to give the illusion of depth and a size change in the objects because of the perspective. In every shot you draw, you should be able to identify where the horizon line is, and why you placed it there. The horizon line represents the height of the camera. Nothing should be arbitrary, especially the height of your camera. These are conscious decisions you will make to manipulate the audience. Knowing perspective is extremely helpful, especially when we begin talking about different camera lenses in later chapters.[3]

CHEATING PERSPECTIVE

You don't have to draw the horizon line and the grid lines with a ruler. In a quick sketch your vanishing points and converging lines might not exactly line up. What's important is the overall sense of objects converging to the vanishing points. Often your vanishing points and horizon line may be outside of your picture frame. You may even have instances where the vanishing points go off your drawing table or digital canvas. A roughly sketched grid of converging lines is enough, even without the horizon line and vanishing points inside the frame. With time and practice, you should be able to draw a solid grid of perspective simply by knowing where your vanishing point and horizon line *should be* in relation to your subject.

TIP

Draw the perspective grid in every frame to help you create the composition and to establish the camera height.

FIGURE 2.34

FIGURE 2.35
Learn to draw your perspective grid freehand just by imagining where your vanishing points and horizon line should be.

HANGING PERSPECTIVE

Hanging perspective is a storyboard artist's secret weapon. *Figures and objects of the same height will be cut off at the same place on the horizon line even if they're located at different distances within the scene.* Objects will seem to "hang" on the horizon from this intersection point. This is a quick way to plant figures and objects of the same size within the picture frame just by knowing where your horizon is. Start with the figure that you want to be your reference subject. Other figures will be based on this first figure. In this case, the figure is cut off at the waist by the horizon line (Figure 2.36). Now you can add more figures in the foreground and the background and "hang" them at the waist along the horizon line. With very little effort, you have a scene full of characters that all give the illusion of depth in correct perspective (Figure 2.38).

The same rules apply for hanging perspective even if the objects are above or below the horizon line and not intersecting it. *The proportional distance of your subject figure from the horizon line will be the same for all objects or characters of the same height.* A good measuring stick is to use the height of the character's head and the proportional distance of these head heights from the horizon line to establish multiple characters in correct perspective. In a storyboard it is not necessary to correctly rule out head heights or any other rigid measuring point. As long as the illusion of perspective is drawn correctly it is enough to sell the scene. With practice, you should be able to draw an image that has depth and multiple characters freehand with no rulers. As long as you understand the concept of hanging perspective and size changes you can create the illusion quickly and effectively.[4]

FIGURE 2.36

FIGURE 2.37

FIGURE 2.38

FIGURE 2.39
Figures "hanging" from the torso.

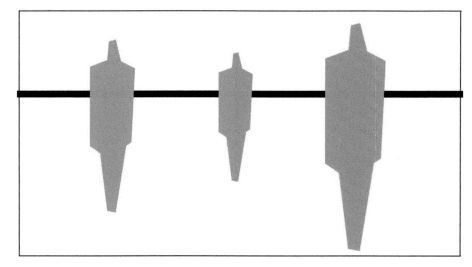

FIGURE 2.40
Figures "hanging" from the knee.

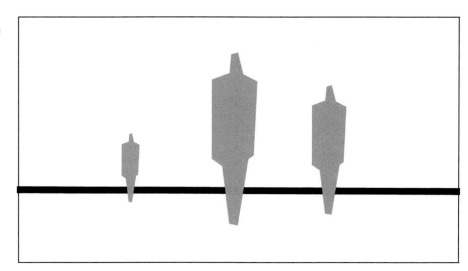

STORYBOARD MAGIC: THE GRID TRICK

Having a perspective grid in your storyboard is an incredibly powerful tool not only to add depth and describe the camera height but also it can be just as useful to change the nature of the shot completely. Simply by changing the direction of your perspective grid, you can indicate a different camera angle without redrawing your subject. Take a look at the drawings below. By changing nothing else but the grid, we suggest a down shot in the first frame, and an upshot in the second. Add some background elements to complete the illusion and you have a convincing storyboard panel. The perspective grid is your friend.

FIGURE 2.41

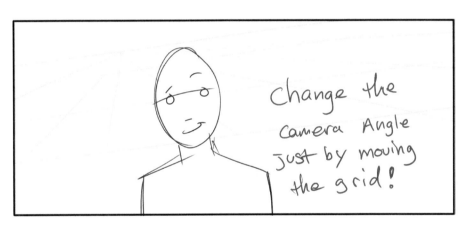

FIGURE 2.42

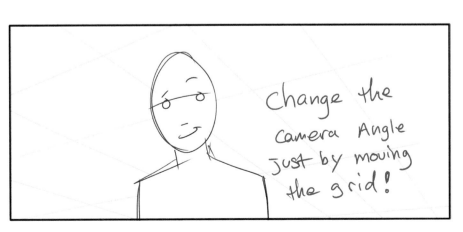

FIGURE 2.43

FIGURE 2.44

Contrast

Contrast, we will define here as the difference or similarity between objects. Contrast can help define the focal point of a shot as well as create depth. The eye is attracted to what is different. A light object will stand out if everything else is dark. Play with the amount of contrast between objects to affect the emotional response of the viewer. By contrasting shapes or isolating a color you can easily create a focal point within your image. You can juxtapose different objects and elements in shape, color, value, size and almost any attribute you can think of.

- Big vs. small
- Triangular shape vs. circular shape
- Dark vs. light
- Sharp focus vs. soft focus
- Moving vs. still

FIGURE 2.45
The circular shape stands out in a sea of angles.

These gray boxes below have different levels of contrast and, therefore, have different emotional weight to the viewer. The first set of boxes gives a feeling of calm and unity. The second contrasting shapes are more dramatic and tense. Value and color contrast is also a way to help achieve depth. Light images feel closer to us. Dark images recede. With color images, warm colors feel closer and cool colors recede.

FIGURE 2.46

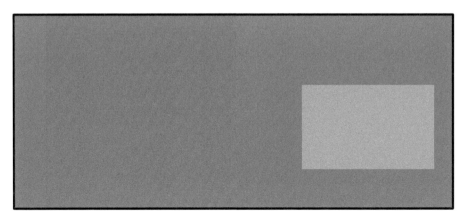

FIGURE 2.47

Things that are close to us appear to have a broader range of light to dark than things that are farther away from us, due to atmospheric perspective. The range of light to dark is much lower in objects that are far away. As humans, our attention seems to be drawn to the areas with the greatest amount of contrast.

FIGURE 2.48
Foreground vs
background contrast.

Foreground, Middle Ground, and Background

When composing your shots, always try to incorporate a foreground, a middle ground, and a background. The more you can show these elements, the more depth your composition will have. Our natural tendency is to flatten things out and draw images that are on one plane. Force yourself to break that tendency. Even in a close up shot, you might be able to add a foreground or background object.

FIGURE 2.49

Overlapping Forms

By not intersecting lines of an object, we perceive one object to be in front of another. This overlap creates the illusion of depth. Overlapping forms can exist within the human figure, or with different objects within the scene. (Figures 2.50 and 2.51)

FIGURE 2.50

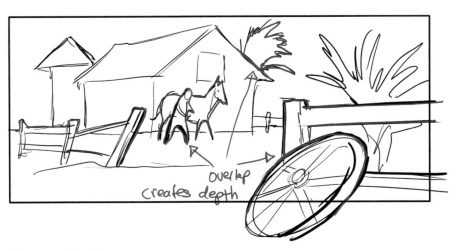

FIGURE 2.51

Change in Size

With a single object a change in size from one frame to the next creates a sense of depth. Objects that grow appear to come closer and objects that shrink appear to move further away from us. This change in size of the objects within the scene adds visual interest and depth to the shots. This is one of the reasons why it's preferable to stage compositions so that objects will grow in size within the frame instead of using profile shots (Figures 2.52 and 2.53).

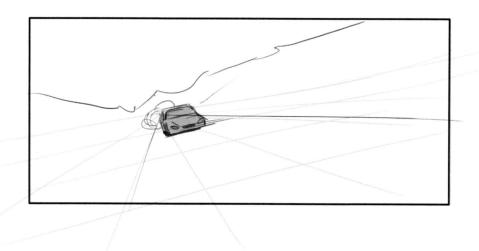

FIGURE 2.52

FIGURE 2.53

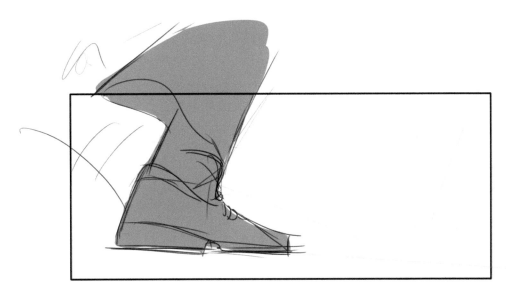

FIGURE 2.54

FIGURE 2.55

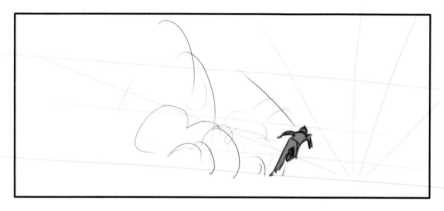

FIGURE 2.56

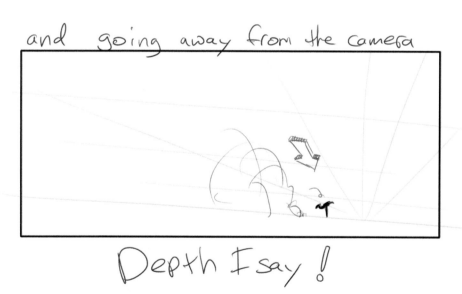

FIGURE 2.57

Character Walking

No Depth   boring!

FIGURE 2.58

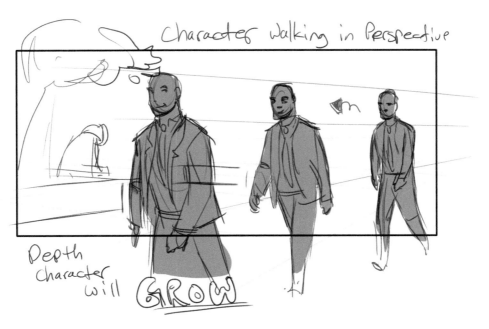

Character walking in Perspective

Depth
Character
will GROW

FIGURE 2.59
Avoid profile shots and stage your compositions so that characters and moving objects will change size within the frame.

NOTES

1 Audio plays a huge role in designing a visual story and its importance should not be underestimated. Our concern here is with visual storytelling, and the techniques involved in creating the storyboards. It's important for a story artist and a filmmaker to understand the role of audio and sound design in the product as a whole. Sound can often influence the visuals, and vice versa.

2 Frank Thomas and Ollie Johnston (1981), *The Illusion of Life*, New York: Hyperion, pp.68–69.

3 We highly recommend you study and learn your perspective as much as possible. For more detailed resources, see the Resources section in the back of the book.

4 For a brilliant description of perspective and hanging perspective see Andrew Loomis (1944), *Figure Drawing for All It's Worth*, New York: Viking Press, pp. 34–37, 45–49.

CHAPTER 3
Drawing for Storyboards

Storyboards are an informational tool. They are a quick shorthand for storytelling meant for a small audience generally consisting of directors, actors, cinematographers and other film professionals. They aren't meant to be published, adored, or admired as beautiful works of art and are only used within the duration of a production. Thousands of drawings may be produced for a particular project. Storyboards are frequently redone, changed, or discarded altogether. Storyboards are disposable art—a rough draft of the movie. Because of this it is important to utilize a series of drawing tools to create a complete looking image in the quickest possible amount of time. One advantage for the modern artist is to use digital tools to create storyboards. Digital tools and computer work speed things up considerably, but a thorough understanding of drawing shortcuts is still important. It may be the case where there is enough time to create a highly polished and complete illustration that can be used as a storyboard image. What is more often the case, is deadlines are extremely tight and without the use of drawing shortcuts it might be impossible to finish the assignment. Building a library of shortcuts will help you draw effective and quick storyboards. Forget about the unnecessary detail, and draw what is important to communicating the action. You should be able to draw a car, boat, house, person, or tree, with simple recognizable shapes that you draw within seconds. Simplifying a drawing also helps with *clarity*. If the drawing isn't clear, all the fancy drawing in the world won't fix it. A story drawing must be *clear*, first and foremost, to communicate the idea. Let's discuss an approach to reaching maximum efficiency and shortcuts in your drawings.

YOUR DRAWING ALPHABET: SICO SHAPES

Everything you draw can basically be broken down into drawing a few elements: *S-curves*, *straight lines*, *C-curves*, and *ellipses*. Once you master drawing these elements confidently and fluidly, the quality of your drawings will improve significantly. Practice these over and over with the kind of finesse you would if

FIGURE 3.1

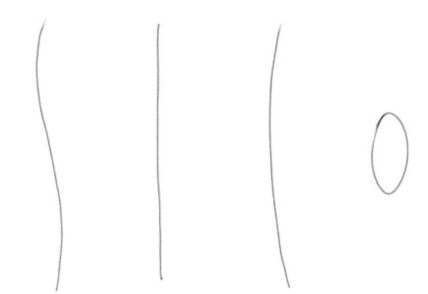

you were trying to master your golf stroke or your forehand in tennis. Ghost your stroke just above the surface of the paper several times and let the pencil tip lightly drop on to the paper as you try to master a single smooth, wobble-free line. Practice and master doing this from a single angle. If you want to draw your line or curve at a different angle, don't change your stroke, spin the paper instead.

These exercises might seem basic and boring, but you have to learn how to skate before you can play hockey, right? Find the time to draw while chatting at dinner with a friend or while in front of the TV.[1] Get into the habit of carrying a sketchbook everywhere you go and using it every opportunity you have. And by everywhere, I mean *everywhere*! If you're in line at the movies you should be drawing. On the bus? That's drawing time. Out with your girlfriend? DRAW HER! If you have nothing to draw you can always spend 10 minutes on these SICO exercises. The point is from now until your death bed, *you will carry a sketchbook and use it*. It makes no difference whether the drawings are good or bad. The idea is to move your hand and build the pencil mileage that will help you produce great work later on.

S-Curves

Mastering the S-curve will take you a long way in creating fluid, expressive drawings. Practice drawing them as described above, but especially practice drawing S-curves that have a subtle gentle curve to them. It may be so subtle that you're almost drawing a straight line. Try to trace over an S-curve you've already drawn as smoothly as you can in as graceful a stroke as you can. Then practice drawing reverse S-curves.

FIGURE 3.2

Straight Lines

Draw two dots on a page and practice your accuracy by trying to draw a straight, freehand line that passes through both dots in a single stroke. Practice drawing a series of straight parallel lines. Draw slowly at first, then build up your speed. Think of this exercise as Zen meditation, which is also good practice for the art of patience. With time, you will be amazed how close you can achieve near perfectly straight lines drawing freehand. The trick is to build up your hand and eye coordination so the drawing strokes react as you want them. Don't believe me? Take my challenge—try drawing straight lines 10 minutes per day for a week. By the end of the week you will be like a robot drawing perfectly mechanical straight lines.

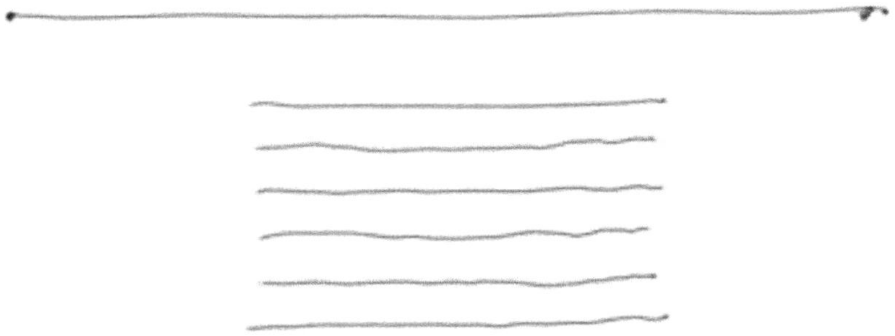

FIGURE 3.3

C-Curves

Practice drawing C-curves as you would S-curves, especially focusing on the subtle curves. You can practice the more severe curves by drawing three dots on a page and trying to draw a smooth, graceful line that passes through all three.

FIGURE 3.4

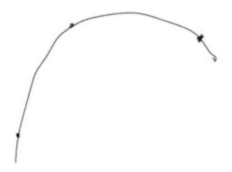

Ellipses

Practice drawing smooth, even ellipses at various sizes. Try to close the shape as cleanly as possible. An ellipse is a very difficult shape to master especially because of the different perspective views. Treat drawing ellipses, much like drawing straight lines above. Practice drawing the shapes a few minutes a day for a week and you will be amazed at your improvement.

FIGURE 3.5

Compound Shapes

Draw shapes with 3 to 5 sides using only S-curves, C-curves, and straight lines as the sides of your shapes. Combining these shape techniques will help greatly when you create your storyboard images.

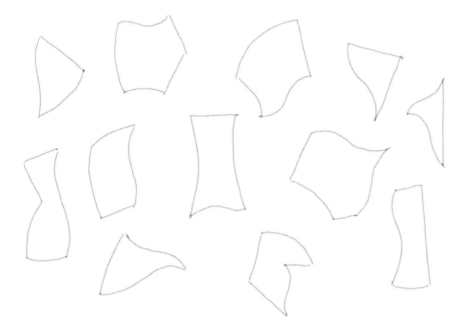

FIGURE 3.6

THE ART OF THE ROUGH

If storyboards are disposable art why make a rough of a rough? In many situations, such as story pitch boards, you wouldn't. But if you were doing an agency board for a commercial, or 2D television animation show to be sent overseas to be animated, your boards need to be clean or *on model*[2] enough to be understood by people who weren't intimately involved in the initial prepro-duction process. Also, it will often come down to the individual preferences of the director whether they like tight storyboards or not. In any case, it should be clear to you why you are doing the rough. Rough drawings are used by all kinds of illustrators, graphic designers, and animators, but for different reasons. Animators, for instance, use their roughs to help them map out action, stay on model, and establish realistic volumes. But as a storyboard artist, these are secondary or tertiary concerns in the rough. Your primary concern is placement of the characters within their environments in the clearest, most dramatically satisfying way possible as they relate to the story point. Spending a lot of time making a single character drawing look just right is a waste of your time, and more importantly, your director's time. The thing you should be concerned about is fulfilling the story point using your drawing skills. So when you are doing your roughs, you should expect that you will be doing a lot of rearranging of the characters before taking the drawing to finish. This means that you should be able to draw, erase, and redraw your figures quickly and painlessly. Don't overinvest time or effort on your figures at the rough sketch stage. It's a tremendous waste of time and effort and can be heartbreaking if you get too attached to your work. See the work you are doing within the proper context of how it's going to be used within the production. "Easy to draw, painless to erase" should be your motto in regards to roughs.

One way to think about your roughs is that you are arranging and photographing uncarved marble slabs on a soundstage to represent your characters, props, furniture, etc. Once the placement of these elements is complete and working properly across the entire scene, then and only then should you go back and carve out more complete drawings out of your rough slabs.

FIGURE 3.7

Notice in my analogy, that I said "marble slabs." Not piles of feathers, or large masses of chicken wire. Marble slabs are distinct in size and shape with easily discernible boundaries and edges. They are clearly subject to the laws of perspective and there is no ambiguity about them. Look at these three rough drawings. (Figure 3.8)

The first is the type of rough you might expect from an animator or a comic book artist. This is far too much investment of time and effort for use in storyboards. Storyboards aren't about pretty figure drawings, they are about fast communication. Taking time on a figure drawing within the context of a storyboard won't get you admiration. It is more likely to get you fired.

The second rough is far too indistinct and ambiguous. You can't tell where the top of the head starts and the bottom of the feet ends. You really can't tell how wide the figure is either. Without any of these visual cues being clearly defined, it will be difficult within the context of a storyboard to distinguish the size and scale of the character. In medium and close shots it would be hard to distinguish different characters from one another as well. A director should be able to look over your roughs and be able to tell exactly what's going on.

FIGURE 3.8

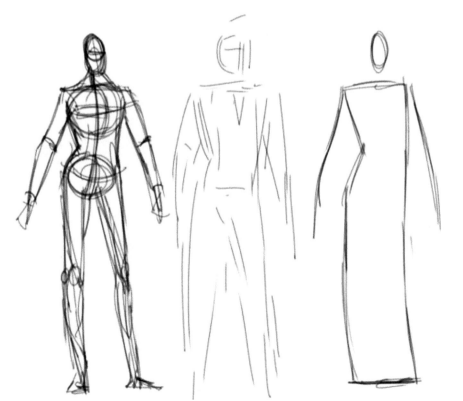

FIGURE 3.9

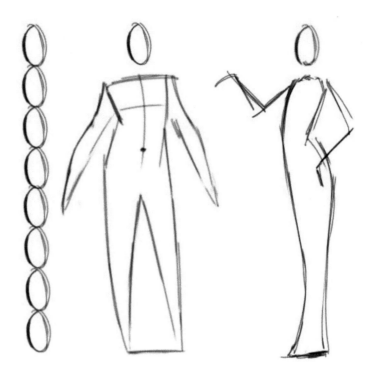

This third rough is better. You can easily see the boundaries of the character and how tall they are. The body type and pose are clearly defined. At the same time it is "quick to draw, and painless to erase" and redraw if necessary. Notice that even though the drawings are very simple, you can clearly read the poses and even see perspective and foreshortening in some cases. With some minor adjustments, you can even distinguish body types and gender. All this information is here even without the surface features like faces, clothing, shading, or rendering of any kind. Another benefit of this type of rough figure drawing is that it forces you to put more emphasis on the whole body. There is a tendency among beginners to express every emotion through the face. This puts an undue burden on your ability to draw accurate facial expressions, and is limiting as far as storytelling. If your figures can express the emotions you want at this rough level through body language alone, you know that any facial expression you add later will just be icing on the cake.

One way to master these kinds of figures is to draw the figure without a head or arms, and adding those parts last. Learn to master these simplified figures and it will save you many headaches later. Even at this very rough level certain rules about the figure still apply. It's to your benefit to draw your characters at correct human proportions, even at this rough level. In animation, each character is usually based on body shapes and a number of heads tall. For live action film there is a standard roughly based on real proportions with variations allowed for age and body type. In general, the standard adult human is depicted as being eight heads tall.[3] With these proportions, certain body landmarks fall in some easily remembered places. The crotch appears at the halfway point—four heads down. The shoulders start roughly a head and a half down from the top of the head. The pectoral muscles end at two heads down. The navel is three heads down. The fingertips end five heads down from the top of the body when hanging straight down. The knees fall just above the six heads mark. For more information on figure drawing see our resources listed in the back of the book.

DRAWING SHORTCUTS

Look at these images. Can you identify each of these objects? (Figure 3.10)

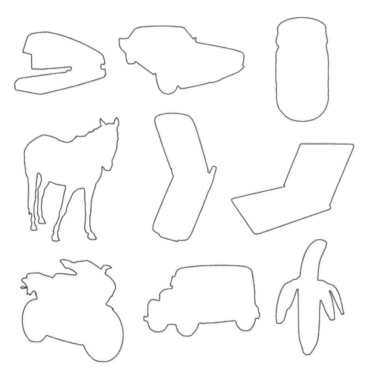

FIGURE 3.10

Can you get a sense of each object's thickness, roundness, or flatness? It's not so difficult, right? This is despite the fact that there is no shading, or any kind of interior visual cues to be seen. We often underestimate how much information we can see just by observing an object's silhouette. Save the detail for your oil paintings.

TIP

"Communication not illustration" is the name of the game when drawing storyboards.

Simplify

As a storyboard artist, you can take advantage of silhouettes by drawing shapes. Notice that most of these objects can be broken down into easy to draw primitive forms—cylinders, cubes, etc. Take away some of the picky details and these forms aren't hard to draw. Learning to do this will speed up your drawing time and help your images read instantly. Start by blocking in the form. (Figure 3.11)

Add structure. (Figure 3.12)

Finish with some details. No need to over render for the purposes of a storyboard. (Figure 3.13)

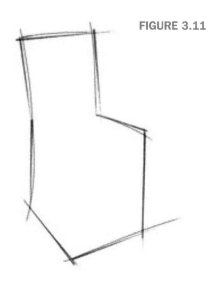

FIGURE 3.11

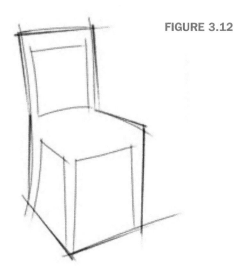

FIGURE 3.12

FIGURE 3.13

Characters

As we mentioned above, when you draw a human character simplify the bodies, hands, and faces, for maximum clarity. What is important is to communicate the pose or expression, not the detail.

FIGURE 3.14

Star People

Can't draw? No problem, make a "star man." It's the most basic expression of a character without drawing a stick figure. With a little bit of practice you can get all types of body positions and even expressions. (Figure 3.15)

Another method is to use a simple block for the male form. You can taper the sides a bit, but the shape is still basically rectangular. Add arms and a head and you have a simple but complete figure. (Figure 3.16)

For a female, try a diamond shape for the upper body. The lower shape should be more rounded. Add arms and a head with some longer hair and you have a symbol of a female character. Just a few lines are enough.

FIGURE 3.15

FIGURE 3.16

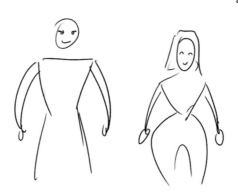

Poses

For posing your characters, try this shortcut. Break the human shape into four components: 1) head, 2) torso, 3) hips, and 4) limbs. Start with the head and work your way down. Position the figure in the frame with the head first. Drawing the torso and the hips separately allows you to offset the shapes for flexibility and to create the illusion of weight. Practice drawing figures by using the body divisions in this order. The faster you become at drawing recognizable poses, the better you can communicate your ideas with your storyboards.

FIGURE 3.17

Hands

Draw a box and add five sausages to it. With these basic shapes you can make hand gestures quickly and easily.

FIGURE 3.18

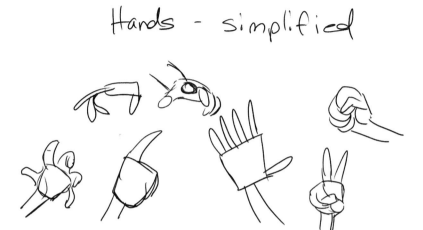

Heads

A head can be as simple as a circle. Imagine a head as a sphere in space. Add vertical and horizontal axis lines to describe the angle of the head. Move the axis lines off-center to point the face in any direction you choose. If you add a carrot for a nose you can use this shape to point the head in the direction you want the character to look. You can also distinguish a male and female face by using the sphere as a base and then modifying the shape. The rounded, upper part of the face is an oval. The lower part of the face is wide and angular to give the face a more masculine appearance. The female face should be curved with no hard angles.

FIGURE 3.19

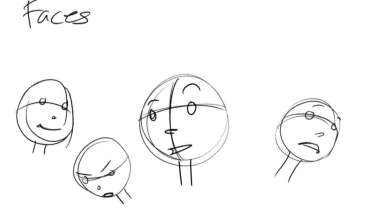

FIGURE 3.20

FIGURE 3.21

Eyes

The shape of the eye and the placement of the eyebrow can indicate expression and the direction in which a character looks. Pupils seen from the front are round. Pupils seen from the side are oval. Use this oval to point the pupil in the direction you want your character to look. If you are in a real rush with your deadline, you can often get away with without drawing a full eyeball and just drawing the pupil to direct the look of the character (Figure 3.22).

Eyebrows are essential for showing expression. All you need are the pupils and eyebrows for a fast and effective way to create expressions (Figure 3.24).

FIGURE 3.22

round   Oval

eyes - short cuts

FIGURE 3.23

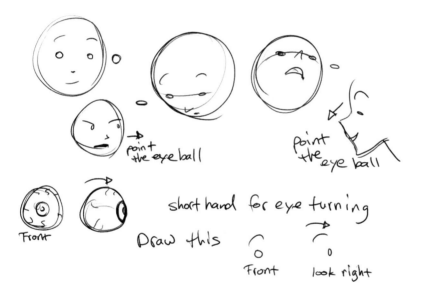

point the eye ball

point the eye ball

Front

short hand for eye turning

Draw this

Front   look right

FIGURE 3.24

NOTES

1   Watching TV is a time stealer and a lazy activity. In my opinion, you should only be watching TV while studying films or animation, or shows related to visual stories. Even still, your sketchbook should be with you at all times so that you can be actively drawing while watching TV. Drawing well takes years of practice. So hurry up and fill every moment of your life with drawings especially while watching TV.

2   Drawing storyboards "on model" mostly relates to animation storyboards. This refers to drawing the characters of the project accurately as shown in the character designs called "model sheets" for the project. See the discussion of storyboard types in Chapter 8.

3   See Andrew Loomis (1944), *Figure Drawing for All It's Worth*, New York: Viking Press, pp. 28–9.

CHAPTER 4
Cinema Language

A storyboard artist is a sprinkle of fine artist, a dash of filmmaker, and a smidgen of writer all kneaded into one crispy bread loaf. A key ingredient in the mix is the filmmaker part and for that we need to understand the cinema language. The cinema language makes direct reference to a camera when discussing shots and visual storytelling. The concept of a camera is what determines the point of view of the story. In this chapter, and the discussions that follow, we will be constantly referring to the camera as the principal device for determining the flow of the story. Think of yourself as being part of the story and being able to view the events through your personal camera lens. As a storyboard artist, we look through the camera lens of our minds and capture what we see in a drawn image. In the beginning, these camera and cinema concepts may seem overly technical, but once you understand the principles behind the film language it unlocks all of the excitement and challenges of a storytelling project.

Pay close attention to these cinema principles, for if you memorize and understand these techniques you can draw on them when necessary to enhance your images. Do you remember when you first learned to drive a car? The radio was off—two hands on the wheel—eyes peeking like a hawk at each mirror— each movement in your body was consciously rationalized in your head to safely maneuver through town. How about when you drive now? I bet it's a more like the music is full blast—you talk on your phone while chewing on the French fries in the passenger seat. You don't have to *think* anymore about the compli- cated process of driving a sophisticated automobile. The same goes with storyboards and the cinema language. With practice, it will become as natural as driving a car. The exhilarating part happens when the film language is second nature, and you can worry about the story content of the project you're working on. Remember, to achieve this level of mastery requires practice and discipline.

ASPECT RATIOS

As mentioned before, the default framing box for a storyboard image is a horizontal rectangle. This rectangular composition box has a specific ratio between the horizontal and vertical length of the framing box called the *aspect ratio*. The aspect ratio determines how wide the image is by denominating the horizontal width versus the height. For example, the aspect ratio of 2.35:1 means that the horizontal width is 2.35 times the height. Using different aspect ratios will affect the composition of the storyboards. For this reason, one of the most important things to determine before beginning any project is what the aspect ratio will be. Once a project has decided on the aspect ratio there are usually no changes in the format from then on. This way, the storyboard artists can use the particular framing box for the compositions and move on to other visual storytelling concerns. Each project will call for a different aspect ratio, so here are some of the most common formats.

1.33:1

Also known as 4:3 aspect ratio. This is the Television 16 mm film and 35 mm Academy aperture. This is the most common format for television productions, although the trend is now moving to a widescreen format. Films like *Citizen Kane*, *The Wizard of Oz*, and *Gone with the Wind* were shot in 1.33:1 aspect ratio before the widescreen format was popular. Most TV shows from the 1970s, 1980s, and 1990s were shot using this aspect ratio.

FIGURE 4.1

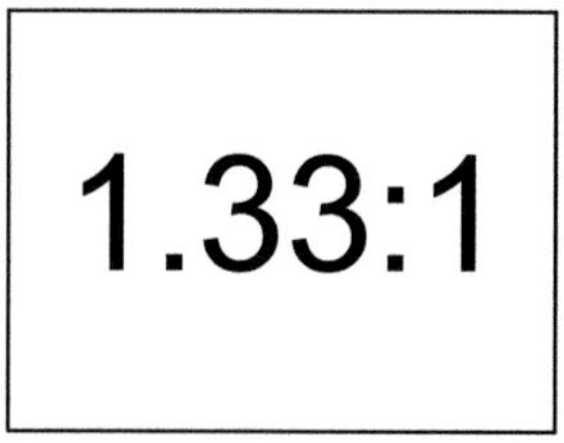

1.66:1

This is a common European widescreen standard and native for Super 16 mm film. From the late 1980s to the early 2000s, Walt Disney Feature Animation animated their features in the 1.66:1 ratio as a compromise between the 1.85:1 theatrical ratio and the 1.33:1 ratio used for home video.

FIGURE 4.2

1.78:1

Also known as a 16:9. This is the most common widescreen format for video games and commercial advertisements. Films like *The English Patient* were shot in 1.78:1.

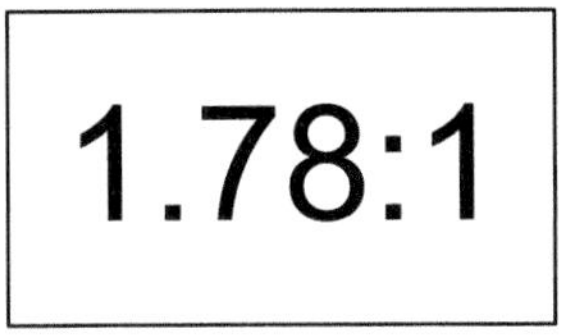

1.78:1

FIGURE 4.3

1.85:1

1.85:1 is the US and UK widescreen standard for theatrical film.

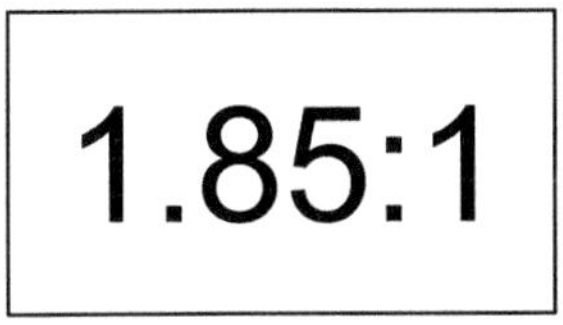

FIGURE 4.4

1.85:1

2.35:1

Also known as 35 mm anamorphic projection, Panavision, or Cinemascope. Films such as *Star Wars* and *Lawrence of Arabia* were shot using 2.35:1 aspect ratio.[1]

FIGURE 4.5

2.35:1

SHOT CHOICE

After choosing an aspect ratio, you can choose how your compositions will look in your various camera shots. This *shot choice* refers to the camera angles and the camera's location relative to the subject of the story. It will be shown later how these compositions, and *shot choices* affect the emotional content of the scene. There are three basic choices:

- Wide shot
- Medium shot
- Close up shot

Within these three choices there are an almost infinite number of variations. We will go over some of the most common.

Extreme Wide Shot (EWS)

The point of an EWS is often to show the environment. If subjects are on screen, they are so small that they are generally interpreted to be part of the scenery. The EWS is most often used as an establishing shot.

FIGURE 4.6

Wide Shot (WS)

Like the EWS, the subjects in the WS are very small on screen. This is generally used to place the character within the environment, yet the character is too small to focus heavily on their actions. The difference from an EWS is that in the WS, the subject is prominent enough to be established as the main focus of the shot rather than the environment. A WS is tight enough to discern action, but distant enough that the environment is still a prominent element of the shot. Often, the shot is about the interaction of the character with his environment. A WS is also often called a *long shot*.

FIGURE 4.7a

FIGURE 4.7b

Full Shot (FS)

The FS is the tightest the framing can be but still allowing the audience to see both the head and the feet of the character. The focus here is clearly on the character. The FS is usually used in shots where broad body language or the action of the character is highlighted in the scene.

FIGURE 4.8

Cowboy Shot

This medium FS includes the subject from the top of the head to mid thigh. Generally speaking, this shot highlights action or gesture expressed through the arms and upper body, like handshakes or casual hugs. The name of the shot comes from the popularity of this type of framing in American Western movies.

FIGURE 4.9

Medium Shot (MS)

A MS includes the figure from the top of the head to the hips. This shot allows for lots of expression from the face, but also allows for broad gestures and actions with the hands and upper body. Slightly more intimate than a medium FS, a hug, for example, might feel more meaningful to the audience if shown in a MS than in a medium FS.

FIGURE 4.10

Close Up Shot (CU)

The most intimate shot is the CU. It starts at the top of the head and ends at the base of the neck. It is usually used when trying to communicate very important personal information about a character.

FIGURE 4.11

Choker Shot

The choker shot objectifies the character somewhat, cropping off the head above the forehead and ending at the chin. Surface features of the character's face begin to take prominence, although it still captures a lot of emotion. This shot was originally made popular in many film noir movies.

FIGURE 4.12

Extreme Close Up (ECU)

An ECU is a shot from the bottom of the lips to the top of the eyebrows or closer. This is a special case shot that really objectifies the subject, reducing them to mostly their attitude or surface details on the face.

FIGURE 4.13

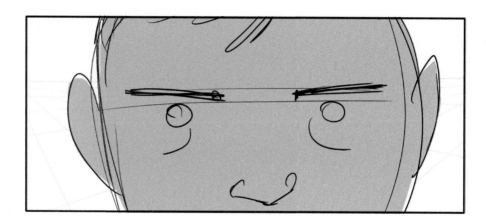

Over the Shoulder Shot (OTS)

As the name implies, this shot is as if the camera is looking *over the shoulder* of an actor in the foreground. The shot can be used as a CU or MS, but there is always a foreground element of the character's head or shoulders. This helps remind the viewer that both characters are interacting and that the foreground character is there listening.

FIGURE 4.14a

FIGURE 4.14b

Point of View Shot (POV)

A POV shot is a camera angle that reflects the viewpoint of a character. This type of shot often comes after a CU of the character and then we cut to their POV. Most often, this shot is a medium or WS, but it can also be a CU to punch in on a detail the character sees.

FIGURE 4.15
POV shot.

Reverse Shot

A reverse shot is one which is shot from the opposite viewpoint of the previous shot. It is important to be mindful of screen direction[2] when doing a reverse shot.

Reaction Shot

Often, a character's emotional reaction to new information being revealed is of significance to the story. A reaction shot cuts to that character's reaction, whether or not that character is actively participating in the action in question. This type of shot is usually a medium or CU.

FIGURE 4.16a

FIGURE 4.16b
Reaction shot.

Insert Shot

An insert shot refers to revealing a piece of information within the context of the scene. For example, two characters may be talking about driving, and we cut to an insert shot of one character pulling out his car keys from his pocket. This type of shot is most often represented in a CU, but depending on the context can also be a medium or WS to reveal new information.

CAMERA POSITION AND HEIGHT

As was mentioned above, when talking about storyboards filmmakers and artists reference a physical camera even in animated film productions. The point of reference for storyboards is a physical movie set where a camera is placed in front of actors. With advancements in digital technology the camera can literally be anywhere you can imagine. Regardless, it is common to refer to storyboard shots in relation to a physical camera and its placement on a set. Following this line of thinking, the horizon line drawn in a storyboard is the height of the camera and the height of the camera will affect the emotional importance of the subject. Adjusting the height of your horizon line is often referred to creating a *high angle* versus a *low angle* shot.

High angle shots are defined as shots in which the camera is placed above the subject's eye level. High angle shots tend to focus the viewer's attention on the environment or situation, making it more prominent than any individual character. This is often used to make a character seem less in control of their situation. An *overhead shot* is a shot that looks straight down on the action so that no horizon line is visible in the frame. It is often used to diminish subjects and make them seem insignificant. The *bird's eye view* is a special type of high shot that is high above the action, as if from the point of view of a bird. This gives a broad view of the environment and its layout.

FIGURE 4.17
High angle.

FIGURE 4.18a
Bird's eye view.

FIGURE 4.18b
Bird's eye view.

FIGURE 4.19
Overhead shot.

Low angle shots are shots in which the camera is placed below the subject's eye level. These shots tend to make the subject seem more powerful or in control because as a viewer we are looking up at the subject. Low angle shots can naturally spotlight an individual by the fact that the closest subject to the screen will naturally have their head higher than any other subject in the shot.

STORY TIP

You place the camera where you place your audience.

This camera position also tends to speed up action since the scaling effects of perspective are more pronounced when the camera is placed low in the shot. The *worm's eye view* is a specialized type of low angle shot that has the camera shooting from ground level. Speed and perspective seem more exaggerated and extreme from this viewpoint, and the scaling effects of perspective are very pronounced.

FIGURE 4.20
Worm's eye view.

CAMERA POSITION AFFECTS EMOTION

The camera can be placed anywhere in the scene relative to the subject. Different camera positions relative to the subject can have different psychological effects on the viewer. Use this to your advantage, by emphasizing the emotional importance of the character within the scene. The difference in camera height can be very subtle. By moving the camera height (horizon), slightly above or below the character, you give a different feeling of importance to the audience. It is important to realize that *you place the camera where you place your audience.* Imagine the camera as the direct point of view of your audience. In this sense, you can keep the audience closer and more involved in the action by placing the camera closer to the characters or dialogue. Many times it does not make sense to cut to a WS when your characters are involved in dramatic dialogue. This has the effect of pulling your audience out wide from the conversation as well. Intense action is better felt when the camera is in the middle of the scene. If you want to feel dynamic action, place the camera next to cars screaming down the highway, or along the airplanes flying up in the clouds in an intense dogfight. If you need the audience to be engaged with the action, keep the camera close to the subject.

FIGURE 4.21
Even slight differences in camera height affect the emotional importance of the character. These two storyboards illustrate how a difference in camera height (horizon line) show lesser or greater importance to the character on the right.

FIGURE 4.22

Eye Line

In terms of the camera placement when looking at a character, the more frontal and direct the look of a character is to the camera, the more engaged the audience will be. We talk about this as being the character's *eye line*. Remember, the camera is a representation of the audience's viewpoint. A character staring directly into the camera should be treated as if the character is looking directly at your audience. This involves the audience with the character in the maximum possible way. As the character's eye line moves further away from directly looking at the camera lens towards a profile view, the less engaged the audience will be with the character's reaction respectively. Films like *The Silence of the Lambs* used CUs with the characters looking directly at the camera to create this audience connection. Young storyboard artists will default to near profile views of the characters in medium or CU shots. A more engaging view of the character would be a 3/4 frontal view of the character with the character's eye line looking slightly off to the right or left of the camera lens. Remember, we always want objects coming directly towards and going away from the camera lens as much as possible. This includes the eye line of the characters as well. Keep the audience interested in a conversation by composing the character's eye line just slightly off-center of the lens.

FIGURE 4.23
Frontal shot engages audience most.

FIGURE 4.24
3/4 shot, but too close to profile.

FIGURE 4.25
3/4 frontal shot works best.

Pivoting Motions of the Camera: Panning and Tilting

Panning refers to horizontal pivots of the camera, left vs right, and tilting refers to vertical pivots, up vs down. These movements feel like the movements of the head on the neck as it looks around. Pivoting the camera horizontally is called *panning*. When we swivel the camera from right to left the motion is called "pan left" and pivoting from left to right is known as "pan right." Pivot movements like pans and tilts are easily distinguishable from moving camera shots in that you see virtually no changes in the perspective of objects relative to each other. There is little *parallax* between objects. The term *parallax* is an apparent change in the position of an object when the camera looking at the object also changes position. The perspective of objects will appear to change and move at different speeds creating the illusion of *parallax*. Imagine traveling in a car while looking out of the window at the landscape. The objects in the foreground will appear to move much faster than the hillside in the middle ground, and the mountains in the background may appear to have no motion at all. This creates the illusion of *parallax* between different planes in relation to the camera. We will discuss how to represent the illusion of parallax in storyboards later.

Because turning one's head is a very deliberate act of shifting attention, it feels more natural for corresponding camera motions like pans and tilts to be "motivated." We need to feel that there is a reason that our attention is being directed in such a specific way. Pans and tilts are usually motivated by some action that catches our interest like a bird flying across the screen or a person walking. Otherwise, the audience will feel as though their point of view (the camera) is drifting aimlessly. The exception to this rule is if the shot is from a character's point of view (POV shot). The camera being subjective to the character, is understood to be "under control" of the character, and thus out of the audience's control. Also, generally speaking, every pan or tilt should begin with a static beginning position and end with a static ending position. In other words it's not favorable to cut into a pan or tilt, nor should you cut away in the middle of a pan or tilt.

Moving Camera Shots

The movement you see in pivot moves and zooms[3] is the entire image moving relative to the picture frame. The movement in a traveling camera move is of objects moving relative to each other (parallax). Moving camera shots will display a certain amount of parallax between the objects within the field of view. Any type of moving camera shot can be combined with a panning and tilting motion of the camera as well.

DOLLY

A dolly or tracking shot (also called crabbing, trucking, or tracking left/right) is a moving camera shot, where the camera is placed on linear or curving tracks and rolled through the scene. Imagine viewing a scene from a slow-moving railroad cart. Dollies refer to horizontal movements of the camera.

PUSH IN/PUSH OUT

A Push In/Pull Out (also called Truck In/Truck Out shot) refers to the camera moving toward or away from the subject. Imagine the camera sliding closer towards the subject. Trucking/Pushing refers to forward and backward motions of the camera.

BOOM

A boom shot is a moving camera shot in which the camera is placed on the end of a boom arm attached to a fixed anchor. The boom arm can pivot as well as rise up or down on the pivot angle. Imagine viewing a scene on the end of the seesaw as it rises up. A boom arm can also be placed on a dolly and pushed through the scene to add a greater dimension of camera movement.

CRANE

A crane shot is similar to the boom shot except a movie crane has a much larger field of view and its pivot arm can extend out as well as rotate. A crane can also travel on tracks and can be pushed through the scene. This creates a large and sweeping camera movement that can begin on a CU or MS and end on an EWS or vice versa. Booms or cranes refer to vertical movements of the camera.

STEADY CAM

A steady cam shot is a camera that is mounted to the cameraman enabling the cameraman to follow the action throughout the scene. Imagine yourself as the camera as you walk with the actors through the action of the shot. A steady cam shot can create an extended moving camera shot with multiple setups in a variety of compositions within the shot. The camera can also raise and lower on the steady cam arm to create a lower or higher angle shot.

Other Specialized Shots

DUTCH TILT

A Dutch tilt is simply tilting the horizon line or camera so that it is not perpendicular to the ground plane. This creates the effect of a shot that is leaning to one side. It adds an off-balance feeling for the audience. As a compositional device, even tilting the horizon a few degrees can add visual interest to the angles within the shot. (Figure 4.26)

ZOLLY (OR THE "HITCHCOCK EFFECT")

A Zolly is a specialized effect in which a zoom[4] and a dolly are employed simultaneously, but in opposite directions (for instance, a zoom in and a dolly out), in such a way that the framing of the subject does not change, creating an emphasis on the change created between the background and foreground elements. This effect was popularized by Alfred Hitchcock in films like *Vertigo*,

FIGURE 4.26
Try tilting the horizon line in your shots for more dynamic effect.

and has been used in later films like Martin Scorcese's *Goodfellas*. This camera move gives an unnatural feeling to the reality of the scene.

SLEEPER/CORKSCREW

A sleeper is a shot looking down at the subject as the camera rotates. Hitchcock used a sleeper at the end of the shower sequence in *Psycho*.

Unique and memorable camera shots have been created by combining a variety of techniques to create a complex camera move. The opening shot to *Touch of Evil* is a famous extended tracking crane shot. The opening shot to *Boogie Nights* was accomplished by starting the shot with the steady cam operator standing on a crane and then lowering the cameraman as he steps off the crane and walks into the shot following the actors.

Knowing what the camera is capable of doing and what types of shots produce the desired effect is a key consideration when producing storyboards for any medium. Even computer animated projects will reference a camera and camera lenses, and it's important to know the difference each camera effect will produce. It's sometimes impractical or time consuming to draw all the perspective changes over time in a traveling camera move, so for purposes of storyboards especially in live action work, moves are usually presented with block arrows.

CAMERA LENSES

In addition to understanding how the camera moves it is important to understand the visual effects different camera lenses produce. Again, most productions will reference a physical camera *and physical lenses* when talking about shots and storyboards. It is not necessary to understand technical photography, but the general difference between lenses is important when discussing storyboard shots. Lenses are denominated in millimeters and different lenses will have different *focal lengths* or *depth of field*. This focal length is the distance at which the subject can be in sharp focus and it varies depending on the type of lens. We will discuss how to draw and indicate different lens types in storyboards later. For now let's identify the various lens types.

Long Lens (Narrow-angle Lens)

Long lenses refer to lens measurements from 40 mm to 120 mm or more. Long lens shots are typically shots that are filmed at a distance from the subject, but the image is magnified through the use of the lens. Because of this, space is compressed and the perspective seems flat making objects appear close together in space. The *depth of field*, or potential range a subject can be in focus, is narrow with a long lens. This drives the background and foreground elements out of focus. This can create a feeling of claustrophobia. Long lenses can also be used in action scenes where characters need to fight each other. Using a long lens will make it appear as though the characters make contact but in reality they are physically far apart.

Short Lens (Wide-angle Lens)

Short lens shots or wide-angle shots refer to lens measurements from 15 mm to 40 mm. A wide-angle shot can be used to show a location in an establishing shot. The lower the lens number, the more distortion the lens creates. This is often unfavorable for doing CU shots of characters, but a wide-angle lens is being used more as a stylistic choice in comedies or independent movies. A wide-angle lens will also exaggerate the speed and size change of a character or subject. These types of shots are often used in CUs of action sequences such as car chases or a martial arts kick towards the camera.

Fisheye Lens

An extremely short lens (18 mm or less) creates an exaggeration of perspective and distortion of the image that is similar to looking through a bowl of water. This will exaggerate greatly the size change of the subject matter. This can give a comedic feel to the scene or in a suspense movie, add an uneasy visual feeling.

Zoom In/Zoom Out

A zooming shot uses a lens that can change from 50 mm to 100 mm, for example. The resulting effect is a magnification of the subject and it appears the subject grows on screen. This effect is caused by the lens and not by any change in the distance from the camera to the subject. A zooming effect is used sparingly in modern films since it gives an unnatural movement with little parallax. This type of camera effect was used extensively in 1960s and 1970s films as a stylistic choice.

Rack Focus

Rack focus is the selective use of focus to emphasize one subject over another within the same shot. The depth of field of the camera lens is physically changed during the shot to blur out one element and focus on another. This type of shot helps in directing the viewer's eye to what is important in the scene.

FIGURE 4.27

FIGURE 4.28

DRAWING DIFFERENT CAMERA LENSES

Most of the time in drawing storyboards, specific camera lenses will not be called out by the production. In this case, you can draw a general representation of a WS versus a CU and leave the lens choice to the final cinematographer. Other times though, directors might specify a 20 mm lens or an 80 mm lens for particular shot. Again, these are generalities that no one will check to make sure that the image you create is an exact representation of a 20 mm lens. What is important is to draw the difference between a wide-angle versus a short-angle lens when necessary. For indicating the difference in lens choice, we go back to the wonderful and useful tool of perspective.

You can vary the size of the lens you use in your drawing simply by adjusting the distance of your vanishing points on your horizon. The further apart your vanishing points are the longer the lens (narrow angle) will appear. The closer together your vanishing points are the shorter the lens (wide-angle) will appear. On a 35 mm film camera, a 50 mm lens is approximately what the human eye sees. Use this as the basis for your shots and then adjust the distortion wider or narrower accordingly. As a general rule of thumb, you should not have more than one vanishing point inside the picture area. Having two vanishing points within your picture area represents too short a lens for most camera shots as it will have too much visual distortion. (Figure 4.29)

Drawing a Long Lens (40–120 mm)

Start by keeping your vanishing points very far apart. Add the perspective grid as a guide to plant your objects in your scene. With a longer lens, there is a short focal length, which means the foreground and the background will most likely be out of focus. One additional way to sell the shot is to create the foreground and background on separate layers and draw them fuzzy or blur them out of focus using digital tools. The subject in the middle ground will appear more in focus creating the illusion of a longer camera lens. (Figure 4.30)

Drawing a Short-angle Lens (18–40 mm)

Keep your vanishing points relatively close together on the horizon line. The closer your vanishing points are the more fisheye distortion you can create. You can even add three-point perspective to further the illusion of a short-angle lens. This type of lens will reveal more information in the foreground and background, and the size change of your moving characters will be exaggerated as they come closer to the camera lens. If the character is sitting with their arms at the table, you can draw an extremely large foreground hand with a smaller body and head towards the middle ground of the shot. This will give the illusion of a wide-angle lens. Since the focal length is larger than in a longer lens, the objects in your foreground and background might all be in focus. Indicate this with a hard edge line from your foreground elements to your middle ground elements. (Figure 4.31)

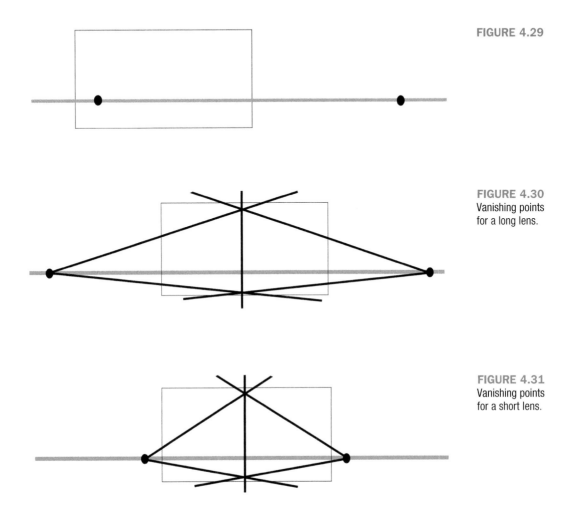

FIGURE 4.29

FIGURE 4.30
Vanishing points
for a long lens.

FIGURE 4.31
Vanishing points
for a short lens.

SCREEN DIRECTION

Up to this point, we have discussed the basic tools of drawing, composition, camera moves, lenses, and shot choice. We also mentioned before the principle of *clarity* in storyboards. It is a good idea now to revisit the principle of clarity and reinforce what is important in a storyboard. Creating a storyboard is often like creating a tasty and well put together sandwich. A sandwich has many layers including the bread, lettuce, tomato, roast beef, and mayonnaise dressing. Sometimes a sandwich tastes better by leaving out some ingredients, and other times a sandwich gets more delicious by adding new layers of tasty condiments. In this sense, think of creating a storyboard image by putting together all of these principles in various sandwich layers. Sometimes you will use a camera move together with a wide-angle lens and some drawing shortcuts, other times you may have a static shot with high contrast. There's a lot to keep track of in filmmaking and creating a storyboard. Aside from creating an appealing image that directs the viewer's eye and touches an emotional response, a storyboard image must be *clear*, and instantly identifiable to the viewer. The principle of clarity seems easy enough to understand, but when combining multiple "sandwich" elements of filmmaking together in a single image it is important not to lose sight of the story point and clarity. This becomes increasingly important in talking about screen direction and moving characters in your scene along with your camera.

Most of the time in a scene, the characters and the subject will be moving around the set creating the opportunity for a variety of shot choices. For every shot, you decide the direction from which the camera is viewing the scene (camera position). Where the characters are placed in a composition is defined as being on the left of the frame or on the right of the frame. We talk about this in terms of the final projected image being "screen right" or "screen left." If you establish a character on "screen right," you should maintain that character on the right side of the screen throughout the scene (unless you have a reason to switch positions, which we'll talk about later). This helps your audience identify the character according to their screen position. When you begin a scene the decision to place a character on the left or the right can be arbitrary. You might begin a scene with a wide establishing shot where character A is placed on the left and character B is on the right. As you continue the scene for the purposes of clarity, it is important to maintain the established screen positions of the characters. As you cut in using closer shots in the scene, maintaining character A on *screen left* and character B on *screen right* in your compositions will improve the clarity for your audience. The audience will continue to identify and expect to find character A composed on screen left and character B composed on screen right. The importance of this screen clarity will be shown, as we talk about the characters and the camera moving through the scene.

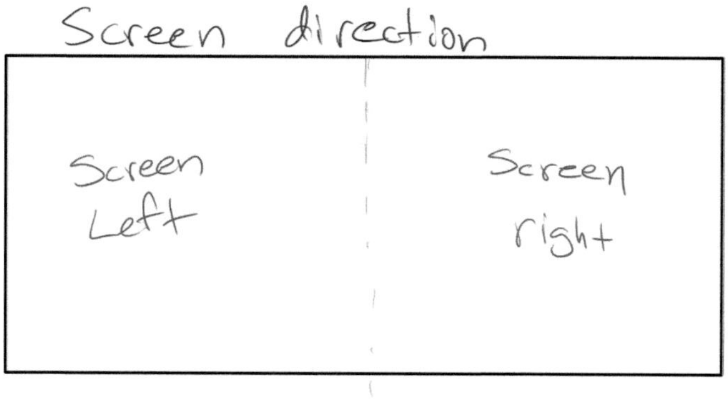

FIGURE 4.32

FIGURE 4.33

THE 180° RULE

The 180° rule or "line of action" is a cinematic convention that helps orient the viewer by maintaining a consistent screen direction between shots throughout a scene. "The line" is an imaginary line that is drawn from one character to the character they are interacting with. If the character is moving, the line will be drawn along the direction the character is traveling or facing. The rule states that all successive shots in a scene should only be viewed from one side of this imaginary line within a 180° radius to avoid confusing the audience (Figure 4.34).

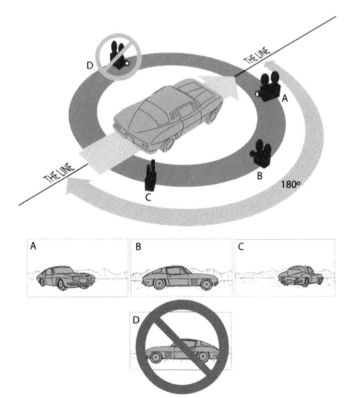

FIGURE 4.34

FIGURE 4.35
A 180 rule set up with
2 characters. Moving
the camera to the other
side of the line will
appear to make the
characters flop
position.

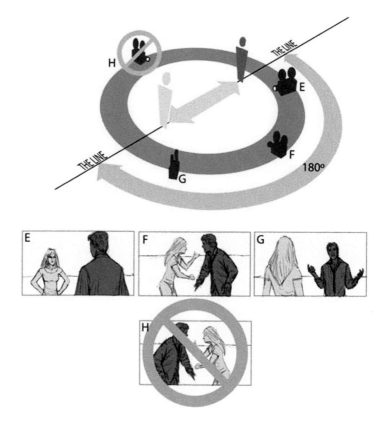

As with all guidelines in filmmaking there are exceptions to this rule. Let's leave these exceptions out for the moment. Leaving the camera within this 180° safe zone basically keeps each subject moving or facing a consistent direction with each successive shot. You can place the camera anywhere within the 180° area and your character position and screen direction will be the same for your audience. Selecting a new shot from the opposite side of the line without showing any kind of transition is called "jumping the line" and results in the jarring and confusing effect that the characters have suddenly traded places. If the character is in motion, they appear to suddenly flop direction. To avoid confusion, the camera should stay on one side of the 180° line.[5]

180° Rule with Three Characters

Three characters create three imaginary axis lines (Figure 4.36). The 180° rule applies to all three axis lines. To avoid confusion you do not want to cross any of the three lines from one frame to the next. Here you can combine screen direction with the 180° rule. What helps in this situation is to group one set of characters favored to one side of the screen. This essentially removes one of the

180 Rule with 3 characters

FIGURE 4.36

3 Axis
lines
created

Camera placement

FIGURE 4.37

axis lines and character A on screen left will be talking to characters B and C positioned on screen right (Figure 4.38). The axis line in this case is drawn between character A and a combination of characters B and C. This type of grouping also works well with multiple characters or large masses of people. Favor different groups on different sides of the screen and treat groups or masses of people as if they are one collective object. In dealing with multiple characters, you can also use geographic clues to associate one character with a particular background. A famous example is the Mexican standoff in Sergio Leone's *The Good, the Bad and the Ugly* where three characters face-off in a gun duel for the final climactic scene. Sergio Leone intercuts between all three characters using successively tighter shots, maintaining clear screen direction. Also behind each character are different geographic landmarks to maintain clarity for the audience.

FIGURE 4.38
Favor one group on either side of the screen.

FIGURE 4.39
If you cut to another angle maintain the screen direction.

An interesting thing to note is that screen direction is more important than physical geography. It may be the case on a physical movie set because of location limitations, a character's position may physically have to change in order to maintain proper screen direction. From shot to shot characters may have to move closer to or further away from the background, for example. What is more important than maintaining physical geographic accuracy is screen direction accuracy with the resulting shots. In most cases, as long as you maintain characters on the correct side of the screen the audience will not notice minor shifts in the geographic location where the characters are standing.

Breaking the 180° Rule

Above all, clarity is key. *Don't break the 180° rule, unless you have a good reason.* The reason for flopping screen direction should support the emotional beat in your story. The history of filmmaking is full of examples of stories where screen direction is constantly flopped disregarding the 180° rule.

Most of the time this decision is not arbitrary. The filmmakers have intentionally chosen to cross the 180° line because of an emotional beat within the story. Even so, there may be times when it's necessary to place the camera on the other side of the 180° axis. You can cross the 180° line by following these guidelines:

> **STORY TIP**
>
> Don't break the 180° rule, unless you have a good reason.

CUT AWAY TO A NEUTRAL SHOT

A neutral shot is a shot that doesn't include any of your subjects, or a shot that has a centered object in a neutral position relative to the screen direction. A neutral shot between two characters in conversation might be a dead center CU of one character's face. In this CU the character is looking straight ahead, not favoring one side of the screen or the other. Another example of a neutral shot would be to cut away to a CU of an object in the scene and then cut back to the conversation where the screen direction has changed. Be careful using neutral shots as a way to change the screen direction. It may still look jarring to the audience if you cut away to a single neutral shot and then cut back to the conversation and the character positions have changed. The more neutral shots you can show in between a screen direction change, the less jarring the change will be to the audience.

MOVE THE CHARACTERS

You can physically move the characters from one side of the screen to the other in the same shot to change the screen direction. If the audience views the change of character position on screen they will not be confused by the newly established screen positions.

MOVE THE CAMERA

By moving the camera across the 180° line in the same shot you can change the character positions. Because the audience see the movement around the characters they are not confused by the change in character positions.

MOVE BOTH THE CHARACTERS AND THE CAMERA

You can also move both the characters and the camera to create a new screen direction and 180° line. This type of screen direction change is trickier to handle, but adds visual richness to the scene by showing both the characters and the camera move within the set.

If two characters are interacting with each other, but are moving in the same direction (such as inside a moving car), it can be problematic in terms of doing reverse shots. That is to say, if you established your scene with a shot from an angle showing one character talking to the other (camera I) and you want to shoot from another angle to get a reaction (say camera K), how do you do it without crossing the line (BB)? One way to do this is to shoot from a neutral angle (camera J) or restrict your shots to an area that crosses neither line (quadrant AAA). In cases like this, the 180° rule can usually be suspended temporarily for the duration of the verbal exchange, but reverts back once the talking is over. But in cases like this, it also helps to keep the shots close on the characters so that the audience stay focused on the characters and not the direction they appear to be moving.

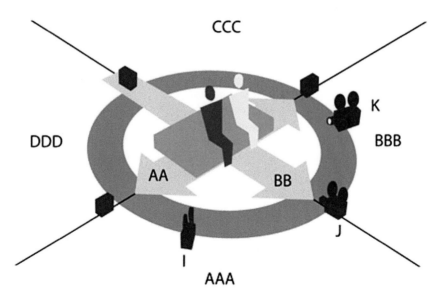

FIGURE 4.40

NOTES

1 The anamorphic standard has subtly changed so that modern anamorphic productions are actually 2.39, but often referred to as 2.35 anyway, due to old convention.

2 See Screen Direction below.

3 See Zoom In/Zoom Out below.

4 See Camera Lenses below

5 This is a general guideline that has many exceptions and is disregarded all the time in modern filmmaking for various reasons. For the purposes of simplicity and clarity it is best to begin by following this 180° rule and then make variations once you are confident that your scenes are coming across clearly.

CHAPTER 5
Story Structure

Properly organizing your story into clear and interesting events is an art in itself. Understanding the cinema language will give us well composed shots and properly structured shot choices, but we still have to put these elements together to create an interesting flow to our sequence of shots. As a storyboard artist if you tie this together with drawing skills, composition, film language, it is a lot to keep track of. It can get overwhelming when attempting to make sense of all these tools. But story design, just like composition design, is a tool that has guidelines you can follow to get to your destination. I like to think that we all have an inherent sense of what makes a good story and we have to channel these feelings into something a broader audience can understand. Let's begin by defining a *story*.[1]

WHAT IS A STORY?

A story can really be almost anything. A collection of jokes, a photo montage, or a recap of an event can all be loosely labeled a *story*. A *story* in regards to visual storytelling and cinema has a deeper meaning and requires more thought around its structure. For the purposes of visual storytelling a story can be defined as:

> A progression from point A to point B.

This progression insinuates that there is *change* from point A to point B. The difference in change from A to B doesn't have to be very big. But the absence of any change means there is no action and therefore nothing to document with images. A story can even go from point A back to A, but we need *change* during the journey in order to document the story. This definition can include almost anything that includes change. The changing seasons, societies moving closer together, or subatomic particles as they dance through the universe, can all be subjects of a story. More often than not the subject of a story will be human experience as the main focus of this progression from point A to point B. Human existence has so much depth and history and its familiarity to us all creates almost infinite possibilities for visual stories. This being the case, we can further define a visual story as:

> The emotional journey of a character in their pursuit of going from point A to point B.

With this definition, the term *character* can come to mean almost anything including societies, seasons, and atoms as mentioned before, but emotion is most commonly applied to human beings. This being the case we will keep our discussion focused to emotional journeys of human characters.[2] Describing the emotional journey of a character in images, and the correct placement of these images in sequence is what creates the story structure.

Let's break down story structure into its basic elements. All stories have a *beginning, middle,* and *end.* How you get to each of these pieces is what makes your story interesting. More likely what drives your story is the subject or *protagonist* trying to reach a goal (the protagonist can be a person, object, or abstract ideal). There will be forces working against the protagonist that create *conflicts* and visual interest for your story. The story *begins* when the protagonist decides on what their goal is (the start of the progression from point A to point B). The *middle* part of the story is the visually documented events along the journey. The *end* part of the story is reaching the imaginary point B. The end does not necessarily mean that the protagonist has achieved their goal, but that in pursuit of their goal they create events that we can visually document.

A story with a beginning, middle, and end is traditionally broken down into a *three-actt* structure.[3] Each *act* in a story serves as a marker point in the journey of the protagonist. Act I is the beginning, Act II is the middle, Act III is the end. Within the protagonist's journey in the story there is a point of maximum conflict or emotional intensity called the *climax.* This climax will usually fall towards the beginning of the third act in the traditional three-act structure. The story ends with a *resolution* in the third act that ties the story elements together from Acts I and II and closes the story for the audience. A story will end when the protagonist either runs out of time or runs out of choices. There are an infinite number of ways to use this structure for storytelling with deep complexities. For the purposes of clarity let's further identify terms used in story structure.

Story

This is the whole story structure put together. Whether you're talking about a 90-minute feature film or a 1-minute commercial, you can usually divide and subdivide the story into some form of the following:

ACTS

The story is usually divided into three *acts* as mentioned above. The first act is the set-up and identification of characters and the problem. The second act is the process of dealing with the problem and the third act is how the problem is finally resolved.

SEQUENCES

Each act is a collection of *sequences*. A sequence is a collection of closely related scenes that form a unified whole, generally to drive home a particular story point of the act.

SCENES

Each sequence is divided into scenes. A scene is a collection of dramatic beats unified by character, location, time, or theme. Each scene needs an objective. The scene objective must relate to the overall objective for the arc of the story. Each scene must cause change to occur. Each scene causes change or *turning points* in four ways:

- Surprise—wow the audience with unexpected reversal information.
- Increase curiosity—what's going to happen next?
- Insight—fills the gap of the set-up from previous scenes.
- New direction—changes the course in the film after established events.

SHOTS

Once a story begins to be expressed in the language of cinema, each moment can be expressed through a series of camera set-ups, known as *shots*.[4] Shots are unique to film (although comics can also be said to have shots), in that a novel, a play, or a screenplay can have a story, acts, sequences, scenes, and beats, but only film can have shots. As a story artist each shot is defined by a number of decisions you have made, which include:

- Which subjects is the camera looking at?
- How high off the ground is the camera?
- Which direction is the camera pointed?
- Is it a wide-angle or long-lens shot?
- How is the image cropped?
- What part of the action is being shown at this moment and when does it start and stop?

In a given shot, the answers to these questions become easier to identify once you ask yourself the following questions:

- What does my character want and why should we care?

and

- What do the audience need to see *right now*?

Your knowledge of how the cinema language and shot choice affect the emotional thrust of each shot will be crucial to your success in storytelling.

BEATS

Each shot is a collection of *beats*. Beats are collections of actions that describe a single thought. If you were at a movie describing the action to a blind friend, how would you describe it? Each sentence you use would likely describe a beat. A *beat* is the smallest unit of action within a visual story. For example, within a shot there might be many *beats* to signify the different moments or breaks in action.

Let's take, for example, a character taking a sip of water and then looking to the right. I would consider grabbing a cup as beat 1, drinking as beat 2, and then looking to the right as beat 3. This is a simple example, but "beat" is also used to signify major actions or important moments. You may have heard the term "beat board" before. This is a series of drawings that are not necessarily in continuity, but only capture the major moments or "beats" that drive the story forward.[5]

You may want to think of this in terms of music. In a piece of music, you have many notes that form the song. The music "beat," you might say is, the rhythmic tempo that you can feel at the beginning of each measure. Not every note is a "beat" but you can hear the difference in notes as the beats drive the music forward.

ACTIONS

Each shot is usually expressed as a series several actions by characters in the shot. Each action a character takes begins somewhere and ends somewhere else, relaying a pertinent piece of information. Live action storyboards are usually drawn down to the level of shots or actions. Animation storyboards often take that a step further to the level of gestures.

GESTURES

Each action can be divided into a number of gestures. Gestures are about *how* an action is taken. Gestures are acting. Character decisions are revealed through acting. Since animation is generally dealing with imaginary characters interpreted through the work of many artists rather than a single actor, it is helpful to build a sense of the character at the gesture stage through storyboards.

The progression of the above terminology in story structure is as follows:

> Gestures create actions, actions create beats, beats create shots, shots create scenes, scenes create sequences, sequences create acts, acts create the story.

Aside from the above terms there are specific elements of story structure that also play a role in creating the story.

Protagonist

The protagonist is the subject of the story.

Motivation

This is the driving force inside the protagonist, motivating their decisions to act. The protagonist conceives of an "object of desire," which creates this *motivation* to act.

Conflict

These are the forces working against the protagonist. There are three levels of conflict:

- Inner conflict—self.
- Personal conflict—friends, family, acquaintances.
- Outer/extra-personal conflict—society at large, the Church, government, etc.

Antagonist

The antagonist is the personification of the major force working against the protagonists. This can be a villain, a nemesis, or even the weather.

Inciting Incident

The inciting incident is an event that propels the protagonist into an active pursuit of the "object of desire." The inciting incident radically upsets the balance of forces in the protagonist's life. The inciting incident either happens directly to the protagonist or is caused by the protagonist. The inciting incident throws the protagonist out of balance then that arouses the desire to restore the balance.[6]

Plot

A plot is the action of the story, usually external conflict. A story can have many subplots.

Climax

The climax is the point of maximum emotional intensity or conflict. Without the climax you have no story.

Resolution

This is the final winding down of the story. The resolution serves as a beat for the audience to gather their thoughts and ponder their emotional journey in the film.

STORY CHARTS

When discussing a story as an overall project, the story can be divided up in the following way:

- *Plot*—The action of the story, usually an external conflict. A story can have many subplots.
- *Character*—The infusion of human nature in the story. This can be an internal conflict.
- *Theme*—The larger idea. The character's relationship with the larger world. The world changing around you.

These elements will also have a progression from A to B. There should be a notable change although the change does not have to be that big. This progression represented visually will have the three acts blocked out in a growing progression from left to right. The curves of the acts grow in size until reaching an apex in Act III of the climax and then the curve takes a slight dip as we reach the resolution. We can think of this curve as the emotional journey of the audience through the story. Within each act, there is also a mini-climax, or a turning point that results in an apex followed by a slight dip as it begins to rise again in the subsequent act. In the three-act story structure these act turning points are usually major decisions or events for the protagonists in the journey towards the ultimate climax. Also note that the inciting incident is near the beginning of the story chart as this is what sets the story in motion, and usually happens within the first act of the story. Blocking out the story structure this way helps organize the various elements so we do not get confused in a complex story.

FIGURE 5.1

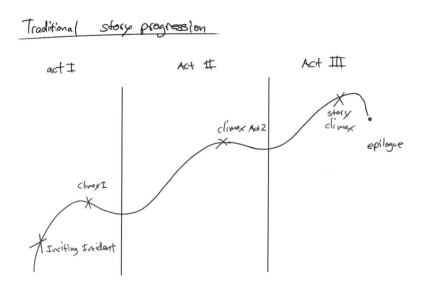

INCORPORATING DESIGN IN YOUR SCENES

Visual design and story design have to come together to tell a great story. By understanding the emotional beats in the story at a particular point within the story you can design your shots with a visual motif to better communicate the emotional beat. You can use certain camera moves for more intense parts of the story, or design more angular shapes around the villain character during the climax. This should all begin at the storyboard phase of the production. Thinking about story structure while creating your storyboards will reinforce the bigger picture of the story as you design your shots. By incorporating certain camera moves or compositions, this will affect the emotional weight in the story and can help reveal deeper meanings about the character or even foreshadow events yet to occur. In a story that has a large reversal, you may want to maintain slow and steady camera moves until the reversal happens. Which, after the particular camera movements might change according to the chaotic nature of the reversal. This design should also be reflected from sequence to sequence and eventually throughout the whole project. Just as there is a progression in story structure, there should also be a progression in visual design, which begins with the storyboards.

As storyboard artists, we do not always have the liberty to make story changes to the script. What we do control is the visual elements that are presented as the story beats are revealed. This manipulation of the visual elements can be very powerful in influencing the content of the script. What would otherwise be a dull dialogue exchange between two characters, a storyboard artist can turn into an emotionally rich scene by injecting dynamic visual design, which reflects in the character and camera movements as the scene plays out.

RHYTHM

Another element within the control of the storyboard artist is the rhythm of the shots and the pacing of the cuts. By *rhythm* we mean to describe how fast or slowly a scene develops from beginning to end. In essence we are the first editorial pass of constructing the scene with images. Scripts are often vague when it comes to rhythm, and it is up to the story artist to first interpret the correct pacing for the emotional beat of the story. This is a very powerful tool, especially when building tension towards a climax or strong emotional moment. Instead of revealing all of the climactic events at once, the story artist can inject cutaways and reaction shots from surrounding characters to increase the tension. These story moments are often not written in the script but are necessary for the story artist/filmmaker to create and construct an entertaining and dynamic scene.

CHOICE

An axiom of story structure is that *true character is revealed through the choices they make*. The harder the choices, the more depth we see in the character. These character choices need to be strong! A character choice between coffee or tea is not what we're talking about here. An insignificant choice has no emotional weight. Choices made under pressure reveal true character. True choice is dilemma. The decision for Michael Corleone to kill his own brother in the *Godfather II* was powerful. Michael Corleone chooses to enforce his strict Mafia law over the life of his own brother. The giant in *The Iron Giant* chooses to sacrifice himself in order to save the townspeople. These are decisions made under pressure that have great significance and emotional weight in the story. By knowing the importance of choices, we can discuss another axiom of story structure:

> Expectation *should not* meet result.

If you set it up . . . *give an original payoff.* Any type of story scenario is a matter of revealing information to the audience and creating an anticipation for the audience to watch until the end. This is essentially the "set-up" stage. The payoff is the point where you reveal the information and create a moment of tension or choice for your character or protagonist. You will have to "set up" the situation or scenario and give a "payoff" of your set-up. The key guideline to keep in mind is that *expectation should not meet result*. To keep things interesting your characters and the events that happen should not be predictable. As your story progresses build the intensity in the events or scenarios as your reach your climax. Use your characters, or active story elements, to drive the tension by decisions and conflicts you introduce in the story. Conflicts can be internal to the characters, such as inner feelings of self doubt, or exterior, such as a man battling a torrential storm at sea. These conflicts and how your characters or objects react to these conflicts are what keep the action interesting. The last thing an audience wants to see is a story where they predict the final outcome of the set-up and in the end, their prediction comes true! It's one of the greatest let-downs for an audience. If you go into a story knowing what the ending will be there is no tension. There is no reason to continue watching. The job of the storyteller is to create a curiosity in the audience and give them a new and original pay-off as their reward for watching all the way until the end.

NOTES

1   Story structure is a deep and complex topic. In this book, only a general overview of story structure is touched on, and how it applies to creating storyboard images. We strongly encourage any prospective story artist to continue to study story theory, story structure, and writing, as a supplement to this book.

2   Interesting topics of study for the basis of human stories are both psychology and praxiology. Psychology attempts to discover the reasons behind human choice and their resulting actions. Praxiology is the study of human action as such and the choice of man using means to achieve ends. For a discussion on praxiology, see Ludwig Von Mises (1998), *Human Action*, The Scholars Edition, Auburn, Alabama: Ludwig Von Mises Institute.

3   There are many different forms of story structure. The traditional three-act structure is the most common found in traditional Western visual storytelling and is, therefore, the subject of our analysis here. For a deeper understanding of story structure and its variations, see the Resources section in the back of the book.

4   This refers to shot choice as discussed in Chapter 4.

5   For beat boards, see Chapter 8 on Storyboarding.

6   Robert McKee (1997), *Story*, New York: Harper-Collins, pp.1181–207.

CHAPTER 6
Emotion

FIGURE 6.1

By now you've heard us talk about emotion and refer to the emotional beat as some elusive element to achieve in your stories. Emotional importance is the foundation for all action in the story. Figure out "why" things happen and "how" they happen will be easy. The end goal of all action should be motivated by a strong driving force in the characters or environment, grounded in emotional feeling. The importance of emotion cannot be overstated. Audiences are paying to experience emotions. They pay to suffer emotions that they would normally do anything to avoid in life. An audience believes in the story as long as we don't give them a reason to doubt. Meaning and substance produce emotion. This meaning needs to be built up within the protagonist throughout the story so that when their object of desire is near there will be more emotional weight with the audience. This creates that heart-beat-skipping, edge-of-the-seat feeling with the viewers. Even the most glamorous and spectacular medieval battle becomes boring if there is no meaning attached to the results of the outcome. Remember to give the audience what they want, but not in the way they expect.

Emotion always trumps logic. When we talk about screen direction and technical issues of filmmaking keep in mind that emotion is the important goal in the scene. The audience wants to suspend their disbelief and be scared, sad, frightened, etc. So if you come across technical issues with character placement and screen direction don't get too caught up in technicalities and forget about resolving the underlying emotional beat. If you disregard logic in a way that doesn't talk down to the audience, you can get away with having some holes. As a storyboard artist your power of visual manipulation without calling attention to it makes a huge difference in the outcome of the story. *Make the audience feel an emotion without them sensing that they are being manipulated.* Keep in mind that when an emotional experience repeats, the power of the second event is cut in half.

Make the mental, physical. Create *visual* storytelling. The old adage of "show not tell" always applies. What is the character thinking and why? Is what the character is saying the same as what they are thinking? Dig for subtext[1] and a deeper meaning within the character. Think of how to make these emotions, visual for the audience. Use the tools of visual design and story structure, and show elements that will reflect the character's emotion. The default is to show an expression. But, be creative and invent ways to show a character's anger in the pose. Maybe they shift their tie or harshly beat some eggs for breakfast. Turn the emotions into visual cues that will relate with the audience.

JUXTAPOSITION OF SHOTS

Is it really that difficult to solicit emotions from your audience? If you hold on an image long enough, this will evoke an emotional response with anyone. Remember that the audience want to experience emotions. If you hold on an image of a flag waving in the wind, the audience will conjure feelings of patriotism, nationalism, or nostalgia depending on their personal experience. If you immediately cut to a shot of someone's face, the audience will project those feelings they have in their mind onto the character in the shot. This is essentially another axiom of filmmaking discovered by early Russian filmmakers Lev Kuleshov and Sergei Eisenstein and their theories of montage and editing.[2] The Kuleshov Effect is a film editing (montage) effect demonstrated by Kuleshov in the 1910s and 1920s. Kuleshov edited together a short film in which a shot of the expressionless face of Russian actor Ivan Mosjoukine was alternated with various other shots—a plate of soup, a girl, a little girl's coffin. The film was shown to an audience who believed that the expression on Mosjoukine's face was different each time he appeared, depending on whether his face was juxtaposed with the plate of soup, the girl, or the coffin, showing an expression of hunger, desire, or grief, respectively. Actually the footage of Mosjoukine was the same shot repeated over and over again:

> [The audience] raved about the acting . . . the heavy pensiveness of his mood over the forgotten soup, were touched and moved by the deep sorrow with which he looked on the dead child, and noted the lust with which he

observed the woman. But we knew that in all three cases the face was exactly the same.[3]

Eisenstein just as Kuleshov felt the "collision" of shots could be used to control the feelings of the audience and create movie metaphors. This concept of telling the story "in the cut" can help bring the all-important emotional element to your audience. Viewers bring their own emotional reactions to a sequence of images, and then will attribute those reactions to the actor, creating the important emotional response bringing meaning to a scene. Manipulating the shots to evoke an emotional response with the viewer is a wonderful tool in the hands of a storyboard artist.

An easy solution to show someone sad is to see them cry. A more sophisticated solution to show sadness would be to juxtapose a man's burning house with a shot of his expression looking at the house. No dialogue is necessary or even acting. The audience will apply the emotions they feel in the moment to the character they see on screen. In this way, emotion can be spelled out visually, and this is the power that a storyboard artist has in manipulating the script. There may be no dialogue to describe how a character is feeling, but by juxtaposing certain images relating to the character you can create deep meaning and emotion in the scene. This is the greatest weapon a storyboard artist has in developing a scene. Even with poorly written dialogue, a storyboard artist can emphasize emotion with the shots and turn the scene into a sophisticated and rich visual experience.

NOTES

1   See Subtext in Chapter 9.

2   Sergei Eisenstein (1949), *Film Form: Essays in Film Theory*, New York: Harcourt, Trans. Jay Leyda.

3   V. I. Pudovkin (1974), "Naturshchik vmesto aktera," in *Sobranie sochinenii*, volume I, Moscow: I.B. Tauris Publishers London/New York, p.184.

CHAPTER 7
Staging

One of the downfalls of most young storyboard artists is a weak use of staging. *Staging* refers to the arrangement of characters or objects within your scene and the corresponding character and camera movements. Choreographing your shots and characters in an exciting way creates efficiency with the scene and will bring even the dullest script to life. Interesting staging can cover up bad dialogue and give needed visual interest to unappealing characters. Arguably one of the most important skills for a storyboard artist to master is staging.

First, let's talk about staging in a single shot. Depending on how close an object is to your camera, or how it is framed by the other objects, will affect the emotional response of your audience. One basic rule of composition is to never have two objects with equal importance in the frame. Two things with equal importance divide the interest of the viewer and make the picture look flat. Give one object more visual weight by making it bigger. Use this compositional staging to support the emotional beat of the scene. (Figures 7.1 and 7.2)

If the idea is to show the audience how a character feels after being rejected, pick the right camera angle and arrangement of objects to emphasize that point. To better show the character's isolation and sadness, use a high angle and distance her from her friends. Sometimes the best way to sell a character's expression or attitude is to not show their face at all. Yet people always think of the face when they think "expression." Expression is conveyed by the staging, the environment, and the character's whole body language. You can't say "loneliness" or "isolation" better than putting the character small and alone in the middle of the frame with lots of empty space around them. (Figures 7.3 and 7.4)

Staging as it relates to the scene has the same effect by enhancing the drama and creating visual interest. A default set-up for a dialogue scene would be to simply cut between alternating shots of each character speaking. The resulting effect is essentially shots with "talking heads" in each frame with no corresponding character or camera movement. This is a dull and basic solution to what can

FIGURE 7.1
Flat and even staging. Both characters compete in the composition for visual importance.

FIGURE 7.2
A better alternative. One character is bigger and more important in the frame.

FIGURE 7.3
Trying to show sadness? This staging is a bit weak.

FIGURE 7.4
This staging is better. The character is isolated and alone, emphasizing the emotional beat.

emphasize emotion in staging

otherwise be an exciting visual opportunity. Even in a scene with two characters talking to each other, you can have one character sitting down versus the other standing to create variety in the staging. Something as simple as having one character turn their back to the other as they speak can also create visual variety with the shots. These actions combined with the character movement and the corresponding camera movement across the set will add visual richness to the scene. In addition, moving the characters around the set can create the opportunity for efficient scenes by combining lines of dialogue in the same shot, which would otherwise be filmed as an individual shot. It is this staging movement that can also highlight the important emotional moments in the dialogue. For example, a witness character might get up out of his chair and walk across the room as the interrogator reveals the outcome the crime.

Be creative and original with your staging, and do your research. Watch movies for inspiration, and how filmmakers might handle difficult staged scenes. Know your subject matter. Imagine a scene in an auto body shop. You would need to know about car repair, and how a mechanic would act and talk. You would also arrange the machines and tools in the garage to create visual interest and opportunities for camera movement. During a conversation with a client, a mechanic might slide out from under a car, get up and reach for some tools in the back of the scene. Imagine all of the wonderful foreground elements you can add passing in front of the camera as a mechanic walks through his garage. All of these elements can be used for visual and emotional advantage by the storyboard artist.

SECONDARY ACTION

A character can be engaged in an action that supports the story point, or contrasts their emotions or dialogue. This can be as simple as someone moving to the back of the room. The point is to create a motion or action of the character, giving the opportunity for unique camera set-ups. Try a scene with two fast food workers talking about weight loss while serving unhealthy food. The set-up in a fast food restaurant contrasts the point of the story creating a visual irony. The characters could be anywhere talking about weight loss, but the "secondary action" of serving fast food creates the opportunity for unique camera set-ups. In addition, having the characters serve greasy French fries, while talking about cutting calories, may visually enhance the futility of their weight-loss goals. The opportunities for camera movement are much greater in the kitchen of a fast food restaurant than they would be if the characters were sitting on a park bench. The camera could track with the characters as they move from the register to the French fryer, to the grill.

What about a scene between two politicians as they reveal insider information? You could put the characters in a closed boardroom as they debate the issues. But how about placing the politicians competing in a game of golf while debating the congressional bill? Having the characters play golf gives them some secondary action during the scene, but it is the *way* they play their golf game that might enhance the story. One character might psych out the other by standing close behind him as he chooses his club. When you construct a scene, think of how you can approach the story point with the most interesting use of staging and secondary action to enhance the story. Give yourself some action to visually stage out. Don't go overboard though; make it appropriate for the scene in question.

USE DEPTH TO SUPPORT YOUR STAGING

A general rule of thumb is to use deep space for drama, and flat space for comedy. When you're staging a dramatic scene, an action scene, a mysterious scene, a scene of tension, an emotional acting type scene, etc. it will work better if you create depth within your staging. Place the camera in such a way as to avoid symmetry and to create diagonals within the frame, avoiding straight lines within the composition completely. Whenever possible, use a darker and more limited palette without a lot of bright colors. For a comedic scene, flat staging tends to work best. Think of a one panel comic strip or an on stage comedian. There is usually a limited amount of depth behind the character, which would otherwise distract from the funny performance. With these characters, their movement is either directly in front of the camera or moving parallel to where the camera is placed. Creating a sense of flattened space cues us that something is funny and enhances the feeling whenever you're trying to present a comedic idea. Bright colors seem to cue us that something is funny while muted and darker hues seem to tell us that something is serious and dramatic. When you board an action scene (or any other type of dramatic scene) and make the mistake of drawing flat staging, it always ends up detracting from the feeling that you are working hard to convey. Distance can also play an important part in both of these types of sequences. When you put the camera far back enough, even the most extreme action can become humorous. On the other hand, putting the camera far back from the action when a scene is supposed to be dramatic can really hurt the tone of the scene. Being far back from the action has the effect of making you look at it in an uninvolved, dispassionate way.

By combining depth choices, and camera and character movement that reflect the emotional beat within your scene, your staging will be visually exciting to the audience. You may even be able to create an efficient series of shots that only require two or three camera positions to deliver multiple pages of dialogue. With proper staging you only need to cut when it's absolutely necessary. Each shot in turn will have more meaning, since each shot becomes new information revealed to the audience instead of cutting for cutting sake.

CHAPTER 8
Storyboard Types

There are few main types of storyboards with different techniques required for each one. If you understand the fundamentals of visual storytelling you can apply these skills to any type of storyboarding challenge. The main differences will be the technical requirements of each storyboard type. Each type of storyboard will require strong drawing skills and a thorough understanding of the cinema language.

BEAT BOARDS

At the early stages of a film, or on certain kinds of jobs (such as agency boards for commercials) you may be asked to draw storyboards as *beat boards*. Beat boards don't necessarily reflect how a project might actually be shot, but they do convey the major story points of the project so the story can be roughly imagined in a visual way. Often, storyboard artists will flesh out storyboards based on a set of beat boards and fill in the gaps. A key characteristic of beat boards is to create single panel storytelling images that convey meaning and emotion. These are usually the most climactic moments of the story represented in one illustration. The level of detail may vary depending on the project needs but for the most part, artists usually have more time to add details for a particular beat board. The classic American illustrators such as Norman Rockwell and Dean Cornwell were masters of capturing a whole story in one image. Of course, as storyboard artists we do not have time to take photo reference or labor for weeks over one image, but thinking in terms of storytelling illustration may help create winning beat boards. (Figures 8.1–8.3)

FIGURE 8.1

FIGURE 8.2

FIGURE 8.3

CONTINUITY BOARDS/SHOOTING BOARDS

Continuity storyboards or shooting boards are storyboards that describe every shot and every beat within the shot. With these storyboard images you have a complete flow of each camera angle that is suitable to hand off to the cinematographer to use as reference to shoot the movie. An edited video reel

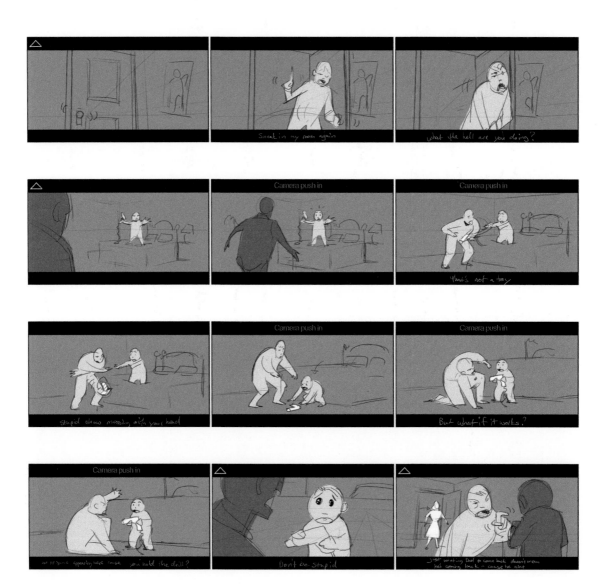

FIGURE 8.4
An example of continuity boards.
Images courtesy of Metanoia Films Little Boy

with temporary dialogue and music, called an *animatic*, can be created using continuity boards. TV and feature animation productions will also produce continuity boards for use with an animatic or as the blueprint for the animation. To make for better hook-ups, fewer arrows are used and instead more poses are added to describe the action. (Figures 8.4–8.7)

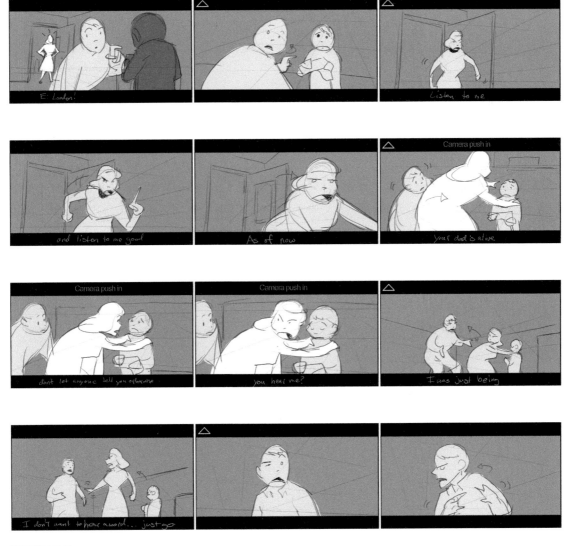

FIGURE 8.5

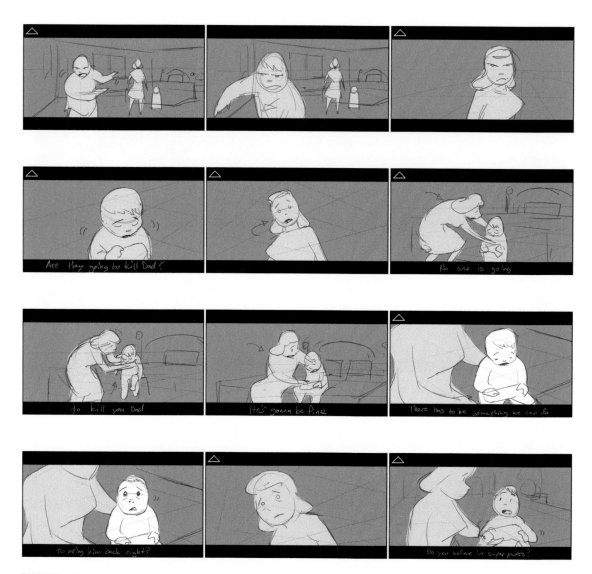

FIGURE 8.6

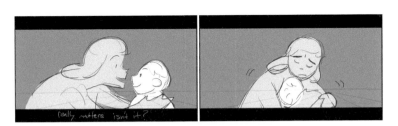

FIGURE 8.7
Images courtesy of Metanoia Films *Little Boy*

LIVE ACTION BOARDS

A live action movie production will use storyboards as a reference for planning the compositions and scheduling necessary set pieces and equipment. More action heavy movies will use storyboards to their full advantage and plan every camera angle and action. In most situations though, live action storyboards are only used as reference since many of the camera angles will be finally decided upon by the director and cinematographer on the set. Staging indications may also change when the actors perform on the set. Because of this live action boards are most commonly used as inspiration, and not thought of as the final composition or staging for the movie. This pushes the storyboard images to be more conceptual and rendered. Live action boards may look like finished illustrations requiring more time and detail to be added to the drawings.

The story artist will usually work from a completed draft of the script or work directly under the notes of the director. The job requirement for the story artist is usually one of execution only since there is little opportunity to deviate from the script or director's notes. The level of detail necessary will vary with each production since every director will have their own requirements. It might be necessary to create continuity boards for a live action project, but more often shortcuts are used to create fewer drawings. Live action boards usually have arrows for camera and stage direction instead of multiple poses showing each beat.

Almost all live action work is done freelance. Live action feature film storyboards are often the most coveted kind of storyboard work among freelancers, because the jobs generally tend to be longer term work. Jobs can last from a few weeks to several months, especially on big budget effects films. That means less time devoted to searching for work and more time drawing. However, these gigs are mostly union jobs, and finding work if you're not a union member can be frustrating, if not near impossible. (Figures 8.8–8.10)

FIGURE 8.8

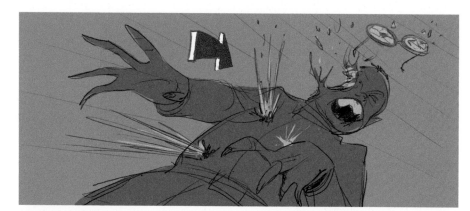

FIGURE 8.9

FIGURE 8.10
Images courtesy
of Metanoia Films
Little Boy.

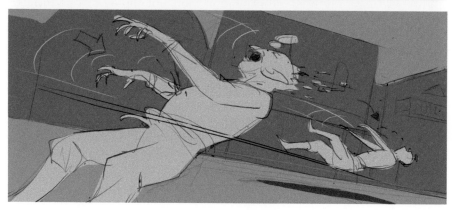

FEATURE ANIMATION BOARDS

Feature animation boards are unique in that the drawings are used extensively as the tool for molding and designing the story. The story department in feature animation is one of the most important since decisions made in the story department will affect the whole production. Storyboards may be produced all throughout the production with story adjustments being made even near the last few months. The real emphasis with these drawings is story design and construction. There may be a finished script, but the story artist has more freedom to make dialogue suggestions and change story details to enhance the story. There is an effort in feature animation to work as a team to produce the best story possible under the close guidance of the director. Drawings are produced with the intention of creating an animatic reel. Thousands of images will be produced over the course of the production as scenes will be worked and reworked until they feel right. The level of detail may vary greatly since even last minute thumbnails may make it in the animatic reel. The true valve of the drawings is not their beautiful execution, but the communication of the story point. Nevertheless, a feature story artist position is incredibly demanding requiring both top notch drawing skills and story knowledge. Arrows are rarely used to describe the action as each beat and camera move is documented with multiple poses. It is not a priority to create drawings that are "on model" since the animators will create the final look of the characters. Story beats and acting are important though since the drawings serve as the emotion foundation for the animators.

FIGURE 8.11

ADVERTISING STORYBOARDS/PITCH BOARDS

The traditional approach to advertising boards is creating highly rendered images to be able to pitch or sell the idea to the client. Storyboard panels may look like finished illustrations with full colors or tightly rendered shading. Arrows can be used to describe the action since the emphasis here is on slick and classy presentation. Story design may also be less of a priority than the image presentation. With advertising boards you may work from a rough script or outline describing the images necessary to produce.

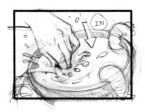   

FIGURE 8.12
Example of advertising boards for a TV commercial.

TV ANIMATION BOARDS

TV animation boards are similar to continuity boards but with the added element of drawing "on model" characters and environments. A story artist for TV animation establishes a tight blueprint for the rest of the production to follow. Since much of the animation work is produced overseas, it's necessary to draw accurate and exciting poses for the animators to follow. In certain cases, overseas studios will simply enlarge the storyboard images and use these images as the key poses for animation and layout. In addition, the camera work and layout elements need to be indicated in the panels. Deadlines are usually tight and there is little opportunity to deviate from the script. Certain shortcuts can be used in TV animation, but with digital storyboards the work is getting more complex almost resembling feature boards.

VIDEO GAME STORYBOARDS

Video games can be very complex requiring storyboards for both in game action and cinematic cut scenes. The level of detail will vary depending on the production but the boards are often a cross between continuity boards and TV animation boards. The cinematic cut scenes are mini movies that can require the same care and attention as feature boards.

Staff positions in the gaming industry exclusively as a storyboard artist are rare. More likely, storyboards would be one of many different art tasks you would be asked to carry out as an in-house staff illustrator or designer. In the games industry such a person would have to be able to excel at painting, designing characters, environments, and props, and be expected to effectively adapt to a variety of styles. The gaming industry is non-union, and mostly works with in-house staff. Sometimes storyboards are outsourced to freelancers, or the cinematic sequences are outsourced to a digital effects company (who might in turn outsource to freelancers for the storyboards). (Figures 8.13–8.16)

FIGURE 8.13

FIGURE 8.14

FIGURE 8.15

FIGURE 8.16

PREVIS

Previs is short for "previsualization" and is a method for using rough 3D animation to block out the scenes in a script. 3D artists with story training will take script pages and create animated movie files representing the shots of the film. The finished result can vary from highly complex animations with lighting indications and effects to rough and simple cameras flying through the digital set. The advantage to previs is the clear timing and scale of the shots with accurate camera lenses. More large scale productions are using previs to conceptualize the scenes instead of drawn storyboards. Currently, there is still a high cost and time investment with previs since every element in the composition needs to be modeled and rigged in 3D in addition to the camera and character animation. Because of this previs is normally reserved for the most complex action sequences of the story.

Creating a previs sequence usually requires the help of multiple 3D artists and is normally executed by small to midsized pre-production studios. Previs teams may also work together with traditional storyboard artists to create drawings first before committing resources to expensive 3D assets. Since the advent of previs, there is an ongoing debate with previs artists and traditional storyboard artists as to which method is more effective. Hollywood directors seem to love previs since they get an immediate representation of the finished scene. The 3D animations can be cut together in an animatic like the final live action footage. The debate begins from the veteran story artists who understand that any scene can also be created with drawings no matter how complex. The reality is that previs is another tool for visual storytelling and the result should always be the same: *tell the best story possible*. The story principles we have been talking about all apply. No amount of fancy 3D animation can save a poorly conceptualized scene. A story artist should understand that previs is a useful tool and is now a part of the visual story telling industry. It's not the focus of our discussion to cover the details required to becoming a previs artist. Understanding the techniques of visual storytelling will give you a solid foundation for becoming a previs artist should you choose to enter the discipline.

CHAPTER 9
Storyboarding

At this point, you understand the level of complexity in creating a storyboard image. Before you decide to give up and never pursue a story career, know this: *There is no greater thrill than creating your own stories and showing them to an audience.* Once you get the story bug you can never go back to other art disciplines. Storyboarding is essentially filmmaking and filmmaking is visual storytelling. The passion grows in you like a crazed obsessive–compulsive junkie. At least storytelling is a more healthy addiction than crack or alcohol. Don't believe me? I dare you to make someone laugh with your storyboards. You will never want to do any other types of drawings. As a story artist not only do you use your craftsmanship, but you involve a thinking process designed to emotionally move your audience. You have to think about all aspects of your project including how your images and scenes fit into the bigger picture of the story. You are a mini director in the sense that you take control and ownership of your scenes and you need to construct them in the most exciting visual way possible.

This may be one of the most challenging things you ever do. As a newcomer the amount of information you need to learn is daunting. The reality is, through practice, much of the information you need to know is naturally absorbed in the working process. Just as Robert Henry brilliantly states, "No knowledge is so easily found as when it is needed."[1]

If you're reading this, it's assumed that you already like to draw and tell visual stories. The rest of the process is not hard work if you really enjoy it. It's a long journey to master all of the techniques as a storyboard artist, but it's this journey that will make your professional career a joy. Begin by mastering the drawing and compositional aspects of creating an interesting image. This task alone will take many years to master. (Yes, I said *years*, but don't get discouraged—it's fun!) In the meantime, you can think about creative solutions to visual scenes you want to tell the world. Most young storyboard artists are already oversaturated with movies, stories, and images. You may already have a natural sense of what makes a unique and interesting story. It only takes putting these life influences together with the techniques we are talking about to create rich visual storyboards. Learn your film history. Watch the great movies of the past and continue to enjoy new releases and stories as they come out. This is the fun and exciting part about having a career as a storyboard artist. It is your job to be on top of the latest storytelling and filmmaking techniques. Don't limit yourself to movies either. Comic books, paintings, and other forms of visual storytelling can be an influence and inspiration in your work. Look at a career as a storyboard artist as a journey that will challenge you for the rest of your life.

Is your passion strong yet? *Use the force, Luke* . . . ahem, in other words, train like a Jedi. Imagine Yoda on your back as you build your story muscle. Eventually you might be able to lift an X-wing out of a swamp . . . or at least lift a dull script to new heights. *Now that your passion is strong*, let's discuss a method and process to creating storyboards that you can use as the foundation on your Jedi journey. As you progress as an artist, discover your own voice and methods for solving problems. This is what will distinguish you from others in the storyboarding discipline and will make you a valuable asset to any production.

THE STORYBOARD PROCESS

For the purposes of this method we will assume you understand all of the fundamentals covered above as far as drawing, composition, shot choice, etc. (You do, right? If not, go back and practice!) First you should find out all the technical details of the project. Find out what aspect ratio your project will be in and collect any relevant character designs or background designs necessary for you to complete your job. These reference materials should be provided by the producer or head of the project. If there are no reference materials, find some of your own through research on the Internet or your own reference library. You should also find out the final image delivery format for the project, whether they are scanned images on paper or digital JPEG files. Most projects will have an outline or a script, which is the basis for creating images on the project. If there is no script, direction will most likely come verbally through the director or producer. Take good notes, and ask any questions about things you do not understand before you begin any drawing. Below is a typical process for tackling your storyboards.

Script Analysis

Every production is different as to the level of input a story artist has in regards to the script. Story departments on animated feature productions use story artists almost as idea creators/writers. These specialized story artists write the story through images and come up with ideas and gags visually. The script on these productions can sometimes be only a loose outline, and it is the job of the story artists to construct an entertaining scene that makes sense.

Outside of animated feature productions, for the most part the storyboard artist must simply execute the script and doesn't have freedom to change the content. Although this may seem like a restriction, a storyboard artist has great power to manipulate the scene visually and arrange the dialogue and beats in the most entertaining way.

The first thing you should do is read the entire script. You should understand the section of the script you are working on and how it relates to the rest of the story. Read and re-read the script until you get to a point where you understand everything that happens without having to refer to the page. You should know the sequence of events that happen in your scene as well as *the who, what, where, when,* and *why.* More importantly, you should know how all the characters are feeling internally about what's happening, and how they are outwardly acting upon those events.[2] You should understand the overall themes that the screenplay is trying to get across and how this relates to the particular scene.

BREAK THE SCRIPT DOWN INTO BEATS/TAKE INVENTORY/ GATHER REFERENCES

With a good sense of the big picture, you should be able to break the story into beats. This helps you prioritize what is important to show in a scene and what to leave out. At this point, it's also a good idea to visually scan the script and take inventory of all the people, places, and props that need to appear over the scenes you are drawing. Do you know how to draw all the things that appear or have adequate reference materials to help you? Make sure to do all these things before drawing a single panel. Is there a scene you know of similar to the one you need to board? If so look at it as reference and inspiration, but not to copy. Make yours unique.

SCRIPT NOTES/PLAN VIEWS

With all this information gathered together, you can now organize and plan how you are going to express the story in film terms. To this end, it may be helpful to mark up the script with notes and thumbnail sketches. You can figure out just how you are going to describe the information in the story and when. You can figure out what shots work best for a scene at a given moment. Would a close up work well here, or a wider shot? A high angle or a low angle? Should a reaction shot be inserted here? Do we need another establishing shot to show the audience where everybody is? Marking up the script and drawing little thumbnail sketches in the margins can help you get a clearer picture of where you are going. It's also helpful to draw a plan or architectural view of the scene to help you figure out the staging of things before moving on to actually drawing the boards. In this flat architectural view, you can arrange furniture and plot out the entrance and exits of your characters from the scene in relation to the camera. You can also show this plan view to your director to make sure they are on board with your camera choices.

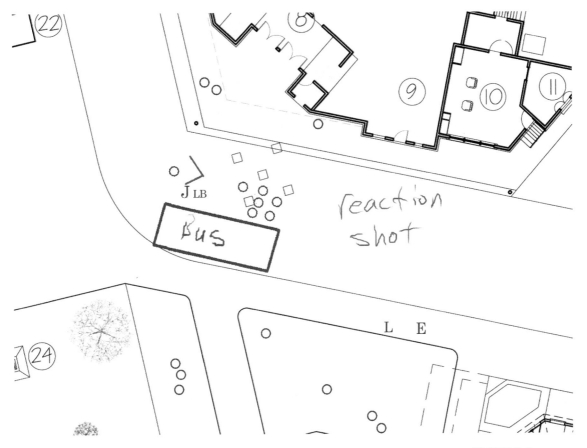

INTERPRETING THE SCRIPT

As you read the script, call out key words in the description and dialogue that represent actions that you need to draw. Take the following description and line of dialogue, for example:

EXT. RONDA PLAZA—EVENING

The General, Javier, and the local clergy are mingling in the town square. The townspeople look on from street level and others from the Plaza windows. The General addresses the crowd.

        GENERAL ROBLES

      I welcome you here to our civil meeting.
      The Republic thanks Father Michele and
      our great El Javi de Ronda for joining
      in support with us today.

The first line in the above example, calls out the location and time of day of the scene. Whether the location is an interior or exterior is denoted by the abbreviations *EXT.* or *INT.* This is followed by the time of day, in this case, evening time. The paragraph that follows describes the characters involved in the scene and the set-up of the action to be shot. Dialogue is written in block format, beginning with the character's name and followed by the lines of speech.

Action cues as they relate to drawing storyboard images can be found both in the descriptive paragraph and in the lines of dialogue so pay close attention to every word in the script. We know from the above script example that the scene begins outside in a Plaza area during the evening. Naturally, we will have to establish the location and time of day visually by at least showing an establishing shot of the crowd gathered around General Robles. Visually showing it is evening time is easily accomplished by showing lit street lights or a dark night sky in these compositions.

Depending on the needs of the scene, it may require more than one establishing shot from different angles to show all of the characters and the crowd involved. Also note that the script specifically calls out "townspeople" observing from the street level and from the Plaza Windows. These phrases mean the storyboard artist needs to draw at least one shot from street level of the townspeople looking on, and another shot of those observing from apartment windows looking down at the Plaza. There is no specific number of townspeople called out in the script above. In this case, this detail needs to be confirmed from the director how many extras are in the scene, or the decision can be left for the storyboard artists to decide. This set-up should conjure all types of memories of civic speeches we've seen on TV or witnessed in person. If necessary we can even look for video reference of these types of town gatherings. A typical set-up for this would be a speaker behind a podium using a microphone system to speak to a crowd. Right away, we can visualize where the characters will be arranged in relation to the speaker. This also brings up the question, what does the Plaza look like? If there are concept designs and images of the Plaza it's necessary for the storyboard artist to reference these when drawing the boards. If not, it's up to the storyboard artist to use their best judgment and research skills to find or create a believable civic Plaza for this particular set-up.

As General Robles speaks, he specifically calls out Father Michele and Javier. This again is another script cue for the storyboard artist to include a possible reaction shot of Father Michele and Javier. Also insinuated in the description above are necessary reaction shots of the onlooking crowd. The number of reaction shots, as well as the various shot choices for this scene, will depend on the emotional beat needed. When breaking down the script in this way call out important details and visual landmarks to help guide you. Look for places to add secondary action that support the story. Remember to fulfill the story point. Be able to identify a change in story or character from the beginning of a scene to the end.

It is often said that a picture is worth a thousand words. For the storyboard artist, sometimes a few words in a script add up to *a thousand pictures.* Scripts are written without camera indications or staging details. It is assumed that these elements will be handled by the director and cinematographer, or in our case by the storyboard artist. This being the case, a script writer might include a brief paragraph that goes:

```
EXT. FARM—DAY

The Riders come over the hillside as the
army battle ensues.
```

What! That's it? With only one sentence, this one line can trigger hundreds of storyboard images required to fill the needs of the scene. What would make cool action for the battle? Are there horses involved? Archers? It is the job of the storyboard artist to establish the scene and draw out the necessary action as described. This might be one of the most crucial battles in the whole story in which case a lot of time and detail need to be spent in arranging the staging and choreography of the opposing sides. The storyboard artist essentially fills in the blanks of the script and creates the dynamic action that will eventually be shot and captured on film.

FULFILLING THE STORY POINT

The most important thing when drawing your storyboards is to identify and fulfill the story point of the scene. As we mentioned before, every scene and every image has a specific reason for being incorporated into the story. This "story point" needs to be crystal clear to the audience in the storyboard images. Most of the time, you can read the script and interpret the desired story point. If you don't understand the meaning of the scene consult with your director about the proposed story point. Make sure you understand beforehand what the story point of the scene is before creating any images as this will affect the content of your scene. You will save yourself a lot of revisions, if the story point is clear in your head. The story point can be as simple as *"Bob grabs his lunch from the kitchen counter."* The fact that the character, Bob, needs to grab his lunch might be important to the story as a whole and is necessary to establish in your particular scene. If you know that it's important to show Bob grabbing his lunch, you would avoid unnecessary camera set-ups and staging. You would create a scene that is the most efficient and unique visual solution to showing Bob grabbing his lunch from the kitchen counter. Anything else that distracts from the story point should be cut, and is not worthy of your time and draftsmanship. Every image you draw as a storyboard artist needs to be weighed against the story point as something that supports the story point and never detracts.

SUBTEXT

Subtext is the meaning behind the dialogue being spoken by the characters. Live action actors will always look for subtext in the dialogue in order to add emotion and meaning to the performance. Likewise, for the storyboard artist, it is necessary to read into the dialogue and identify the subtext. Even if there is no apparent double meaning behind the dialogue being spoken, think hard about why a character would say the lines of dialogue written in the script. With careful thought, you can usually find a meaning behind the dialogue. Identify the subtext in the dialogue and who is the focus or sympathetic character. This information will help when staging out the shot. Integrate your staging to reflect the acting in the dialogue. Adding subtext to the scene can create a powerful visual statement without adding or changing the dialogue. The subtext is a method of adding layers of depth to the scene in a subtle way. The character may not say outright what they are feeling, but you can show the feelings visually when you draw your storyboards. Take these lines of dialogue, for example:

ALICE

It's so good to see you. You're all grown
up and dashing.

JIMMY

Thanks Ma'.

At first glance you might think this is a happy reunion of a mother and son. You might stage this in the entryway of the house as the two characters hug. If on the other hand, you understood from the story that Alice is a widow and recovering drunk, these lines of dialogue take on a whole different meaning, where the subtext is important. Let's assume that the relationship between Jimmy and Alice is a tumultuous one. As Alice says her lines, what she might really be thinking is, "It's so painful to see you because you remind me of my dead husband." Here the meaning and the staging of the scene will change completely. You might stage the scene so that Alice has her back turned to Jimmy and she says her lines while glancing at a picture of her late husband. Jimmy too might have subtext in his line adding a layer of sadness or sarcasm to his delivery. This needs to be shown visually with Jimmy's pose or body language. Again, all of this needs to relate to the underlying story point of the scene.

THUMBNAILS

Let's assume you have identified the story point, subtext, and elements needed to draw your scene. The next step in the storyboard process is to create a thumbnail first pass of the scene. A thumbnail version of a storyboard is a fast rough draft sketch to see how your shot choices and your compositions are working before you begin adding detail. These are normally tiny drawings, no bigger than 1 or 2 inches, with many drawings filling up a single sheet of paper. You can use these drawings to quickly lay out your whole scene, as well as to show your director for initial approval. There is no need to polish your drawings in a thumbnail. In fact, fancy drawing distracts from what is important– the story point and the shot flow. In thumbnails all you need are quick and simple drawings that convey the basic information about camera angles, composition, and staging. No amount of shading will sell a shot or make up for your story flaws. Any good client or director will see right through it. Forget about the drawing and start communicating!

FIGURE 9.2
Thumbnails drawn by hand on an 8.5 × 11 sheet of paper. These are simple line drawings with little shading or tone.

Why thumbnail? If you don't thumbnail then you are just settling for the first idea off the top of your head. This works occasionally, but most of the time you want to dig deeper than your first idea. Up front planning will save you a lot of pain in the end. Be organized and *think*! Thumbnailing is about discovering the emotional beats, through shots and staging. You are making choices that affect emotions, and trying to find the most efficient way to get there. Explore every possibility until you discover the best way to sell that particular idea or emotion. Forget about the details of drawing and lose yourself in thinking about how to be original and fresh. This is a process in which you might draw, cross out, and redraw ideas. Each drawing should only take a minute or so to draw. The idea is to organize your thoughts on paper before you begin your finished storyboards. In a storyboard assignment that might take you a week, you may spend up to three days simply scratching out thumbnail drawings and organizing your ideas. Once these ideas are clear and organized, creating finished storyboard panels is a smoother and quicker process.

FIGURE 9.3

Keep the drawings simple. Use pencil and paper only. Use arrows to show the direction of movements (arrows can be used here as a shortcut even if the finished drawings are continuity boards). Avoid color or shading. The drawings should only take a few seconds to produce. Most of the time should be spent thinking about what is important in your story. Here are a few elements important to get across in your thumbnails:

- Interesting composition
- Unique camera angles and a variety in your shot choice
- Interesting staging
- Resolve the screen direction
- Communicate the story point

Starting Your Rough

If you get stuck starting your rough, one good way to get the engine running is by drawing a vanishing point (Figure 9.4). It can be inside the image area or outside of it. Then draw some radiating lines from the vanishing point into the image area. Notice that even at this level, compositions have certain psychological effects. Some seem dynamic, others more serene, others may feel erratic, and still others may feel formal. Use this to your advantage as you start designing your shot.

Your roughs should be quick, simple, and unlabored. This is not to be confused with doing rushed, sloppy, careless roughs. The distinction between simple roughs and sloppy roughs is very clear. Often, beginners will rush through their roughs working extremely loosely and sloppily, expecting that their finished drawings will firm up and tighten any sloppiness in their rough. This is the opposite of what you should be doing. If you take the time to nail the roughs, and make them as clear and accurate as possible, you will build a strong foundation on which it will be easier to get away with doing loose, quick finishes.

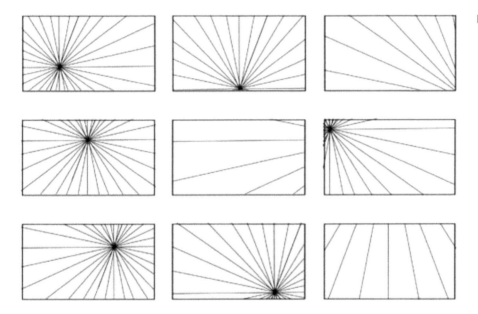

FIGURE 9.4

Double Check Your Work

Once you have roughed out a full scene in thumbnails, read over your boards a few times to be sure you've gotten all the important information onto the boards clearly and that you're getting the maximum punch out of the scene. Make sure the entire scene flows together well. If you had never read the script before and were viewing these boards for the first time would you get a good sense of the story and the feel of the finished movie? Double check your compositions to see if you can fix any problems. At this point, you can look over the boards with the director. You might get a few notes back from the director but after making thumbnails it's time to move on to finished boards.

FINISHED STORYBOARDS

Since you've now worked out all the major story problems, this is an easier step since you only need to focus on drawing and execution. Even though this is the opportunity to make the drawing as beautiful as possible, don't lose sight of clarity and simplicity. A finished storyboard panel should be clear and understandable. Again, the main purpose is to describe the story point and emotional beat of the story, not to be a finished work of art. Each storyboard type requires a different finish but here are some general guidelines:

- Give the figures solid poses with a clear silhouette.
- You can add simple tones, 2–3 grey tones is plenty.
- Limit the use of color. Save yourself time by only using color when necessary.
- Limit the use of arrows. Adding more panels with more character poses will help the action flow.
- Use clean "on-model" drawings for traditional TV boards.
- Add a perspective grid for maximum clarity to each panel.

(Figures 9.5–9.7)

FIGURE 9.5

FIGURE 9.6

FIGURE 9.7

Digital Storyboards

In discussing finished boards we have to talk about the digital revolution in production art. Before, storyboards were drawn on paper and scanned in to the computer to create an animatic. People still draw on paper to produce storyboards, but for professional production work it's now rare. The process for drawing panels on paper would be to use a storyboard template with the aspect ratio of the project and create drawings with pens or markers. You might start with a non-photo blue pencil then fill in the details with a dark pencil or ink pen. Some artists would create the line work in pencil then scan in the images to add tones. There are also tricks to creating pans and complex camera moves on paper by making a larger background image and drawing the characters on a separate layer as they walk across the shot. As any digital artist can tell you, creating digital storyboards is infinitely faster than drawing on paper. As a stubborn traditionalist myself, I thought I would never stop drawing on paper until the day I was forced to draw digitally at Pixar. As soon as I saw the speed and incredible amount of drawings I was able to produce I knew there was no going back to the days of paper and the photocopy machine. Digital storyboards are here to stay and anyone entering the field must learn to create storyboards on the computer.

Making thumbnails doesn't necessarily require using a computer. Sometimes doing thumbnails on paper can be a welcome change from the digital work to follow. Finished boards though should be created digitally to take advantage of modern tools and create complex and well drawn images. The most common way of creating digital boards is using a tablet or digital monitor made for drawing. Cintiq monitors made by Wacom have become the industry standard for digital art and especially storyboards. The monitor has a digitizer pen that you can use to draw directly on the monitor as if it were a sheet of paper. In conjunction with different art software you can create complex storyboards that would be extremely difficult to create on paper. To a lesser extent you can also use a digitizer tablet with a pen to create the digital drawings but this is less intuitive since you are looking at the monitor while drawing on the tablet. The Cintiq monitors are expensive, ranging from $1000–2500 depending on the size, but they need to be thought of as a necessary piece of equipment that will pay for themselves with the greater productivity. Cheaper tablet PCs and second hand equipment can also be used with equally good results.

Knowing how to use a computer, both Mac and Windows based, is a necessity. Another prerequisite to digital boards is learning to use the industry standard program, Photoshop. We will not go into the details of the software here, but any method of creating digital boards will use tools based on a Photoshop work flow. There are many great software packages that will also create awesome images, but a layer based drawing program is necessary.

In terms of finished digital storyboards, it is important to work in layers for maximum flexibility and changes. A typical image would have a background layer, perspective grid layer, character layer, and foreground layer among others. Tones can also be on separate layers to allow for changes and adjustments. We will discuss creating complex digital boards in Chapter 10.

CHECKLIST FOR IDENTIFYING COMMON MISTAKES

One of the most important skills for a storyboard artist is self editing. The ability to look at your scene and determine whether it's working or not and why is a key part of training your storyboard skills. With this goal in mind, here are some key questions to ask yourself as you stage and draw your storyboards:

☐ Does the shot fulfill the story point?

☐ Is this the *BEST* camera angle for my story point?

☐ Does the shot have depth? Is there a foreground, middle ground, and background?

☐ Am I using a profile shot? Is my composition too flat?

☐ Is there good silhouette?

☐ Are there too many horizontal and vertical lines in my shot? *Avoid symmetry!*

☐ Are subjects coming at the camera or going away from camera? *Maximize the illusion of depth.*

☐ Do I cut from a low angle to high angle? *Use variety in your shot choice.*

☐ Are the shapes in my composition interesting?

☐ Am I reusing this composition? *Avoid reusing shots. Keep the audience interested by creative shot choice.*

Here are a few questions you can ask yourself while going over a script. The answers to these questions, combined with some of the information in the shot selection section, can aid you making decisions about your boards:

- *About scenes:*
  - How many are in the scene?
  - What is the situation at the beginning of the scene and how is it different at the end?
  - Who is affected by this change?
  - How does this person feel about it?
  - How does this scene affect the scene after it?
  - How does it affect the one before it?
  - How has this scene been affected by the one before it?

- *Within a scene, these questions might help you find your shots:*
  - Who or what are we most interested in at this moment? What's the main focus?
  - Who is in control of the situation?
  - Where are we? Have the characters moved? If so, where?
  - What's the subtext? What is being said or done and what does it really mean?
  - What nonverbal cues might illustrate what's really going on?
  - Who is being affected by what is being said, done, or implied at this moment? In what way?
  - What are some of the consequences of the action taking place in the moment?
  - What do you want the audience to feel? Speed? Calmness? Chaos?
  - What's the overall mood?

NOTES

1   Robert Henri (1923), *The Art Spirit*, New York: Harper & Row, p.80.

2   See Chapter 5 on Story Structure, and Subtext in this chapter.

CHAPTER 10

Advanced Storyboard Techniques

The real fun begins when you can take a regular sequence and amplify the storyboards with some advanced techniques creating efficient and exciting scenes. The techniques that follow can help turn a flat boring scene into a thrilling visual experience.

CREATING EFFICIENCY

Use fewer cuts. Plan your staging so that you get the most efficient set-ups and can combine story points into single shots. This is the reason staging is so important and often overlooked by young story artists. Of course, this is easier said than done, but looking for opportunities to make the actions and cuts flow with staging will make better visual stories. Keep the staging alive. Make the characters move in their world to add to the visual appeal.

Imagine a scene with three characters as shown below and you want to use a tracking shot. (Figure 10.1)

FIGURE 10.1

The camera tracks right. (Figure 10.2)

FIGURE 10.2

This is what it looks like with a camera guide. (Figure 10.3)

Camera track right

FIGURE 10.3

The following images show what the track would look like as you separate the camera move into beats for an animatic. (Figure 10.7)

FIGURE 10.4

FIGURE 10.5

FIGURE 10.6

FIGURE 10.7

Complex Camera Moves

Start on one subject, end on another. Move the camera through the scene to reveal new information. If you start on a wide shot, try to move the camera and end on a close up. You should always chase more depth and create a dynamic space when the scene demands it. *A handoff shot* is a technique where you track with one subject then move to another subject as they pass in front of camera. The camera "hands off" the focal point to a new focal point and creates visual interest in the process. This can be used as a visual transition or as a mood setting opening shot.

Start on one subject and end on another to create a complex camera move. (Figures 10.8–10.18)

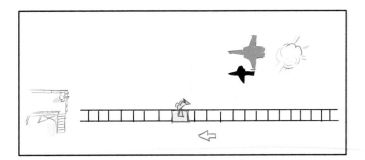

FIGURE 10.8

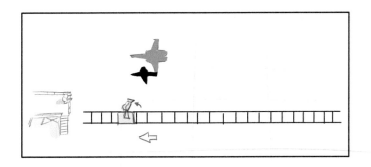

FIGURE 10.9

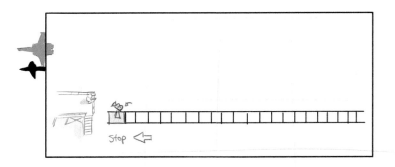

FIGURE 10.10

FIGURE 10.11

FIGURE 10.12

FIGURE 10.13

FIGURE 10.14

FIGURE 10.15

FIGURE 10.16

FIGURE 10.17

FIGURE 10.18

The above images show how you would board out the camera move. (Figure 10.18)

In opening shots the speed of the camera move and camera height can be used to great effect to show the mood of the scene. *Show* not tell with the camera. This will also limit the need for unnecessary dialogue. Conceptualizing a moving steadycam shot can create a dynamic scene where characters move and interact with the set thereby pulling the audience into the story.

TRANSITIONS

Transitions are the bread and butter of the story artist. How you carry the action from one scene to another in a smooth and unique way is the art of transitions. Some projects allow for more exaggerated transitions, but each transition should carry the audience smoothly from one story point to the next. Utilizing this tool will create efficient sequences and can make the difference between a mediocre project and a visually exciting thrill ride.

Visual Transitions

In a visual transition you use the camera to lead the audience from one subject to another. You could simply pan from the end of one conversation to an open window where another conversation takes place. Another technique is to cut to a similar composition or end on a similar shape as the preceding shot. The shapes in the composition can be similar from scene to scene creating a smooth visual effect. For example, you can end on a setting sun as the round sun shape cross dissolves to a grandfather clock. Using a handoff shot or other complex camera moves can also do the trick. Be creative using visual transitions. There are many examples throughout film history of good visual transitions. Watch movies, take note of how filmmakers, visually transition from one scene to another.

Story Point Transitions

A story point transition happens when cutting to a similar subject matter in the next scene. Most often you would cut to the action mentioned in the last line of dialogue. A group of warriors can be talking about the upcoming battle as we simply cut to the battle in the next scene. This can be as subtle or as shocking as we want it to be but the point is that we set up the audience for an expectation of the upcoming scene.

Audio Transitions

Carry the music from one scene to another. As storyboard artists, we don't often get to influence the audio or music, but in this case we can make notes and written suggestions, along with the panels to indicate an audio transition. Sometimes this can overlap with a visual transition as well. We can cut to a radio playing the same song in two different scenes. Or a character can sing a song that becomes part of the background score in the next scene.

Effects Transitions

Fades, wipes, dissolves, and special effects are used to blend from one scene to the next. This is almost like a visual transition only in a more exaggerated way. Montage sequences and musical numbers can use effects transitions where objects within the composition transform into objects in the next scene. If the project allows for it, effects transitions can be as creative as you want them to be.

CUTTING STYLES

Varying your cutting style throughout the project will also give your story more visual appeal. You can play more with long shots, or quick cuts. Whichever style you choose should reflect the content of the story. Whenever possible try to make seamless cuts by cutting on action and creating solid hook-ups. Have one action continue through to the next shot. Lead the eye through to the next shot, by way of character movement or camera movement. If a character exits the scene from left to right, try cutting to an object in the next scene also traveling from left to right.

CREATIVE DIALOGUE

Properly staging dialogue is a difficult task. Be creative when revealing characters' dialogue through shots. Try using longer shots, in conjunction with interesting staging, to take care of blocks of dialogue. Less cutting helps give better flow for dialogue and gives opportunity for more character interaction. How about using less dialogue? Tell the story visually, and you might be able to cut lines of dialogue.

Design your dialog so you make every word count. The words spoken and the actions of the characters can reveal story information that might be used in future scenes. You might be able to tie dialogue throughout your story. You can set up a line of dialogue in one scene and pay off the result of the dialogue in another scene. A character might say the wildest prediction as a joke, but in later scenes the prediction comes true. Think hard about secondary action and what a character might be doing as they say their lines. The secondary action during the scene can add needed character beats that emphasize the dialogue and create movement. A veterinarian in his office may need to go from paperwork, to looking at animals, and then washing his hands. This business can be staged and shot as he delivers his lines creating camera movement, fewer cuts, and interesting staging.

CREATIVE SCREEN DIRECTION

As a storyboard artist, a lot is said about proper screen direction, and the 180° rule. Often there is a rigid formality of screen direction in all of the scenes. But you can also use screen direction to emphasize the story point. By flopping the screen direction and crossing the 180° line, you can create a jarring effect to make the audience uneasy. You can do this from one cut to the next, or change screen direction by using a clean character exit, followed by a clean character entry in the next scene. This may confuse the audience on purpose which can be part of your story design. Something as simple as the camera orbiting around a character as the character reveals important story information will reestablish the screen direction and at the same time visually emphasize the story point by now showing the character on the opposite side of the screen. Showing the camera cross the 180° line in the same shot is less jarring to the audience and may have a subtle story effect that emphasizes the dialogue being spoken. In heavy action scenes, the screen direction can be arbitrary to give a cluttered and disorienting feeling to the scene. As with any of these techniques, it's important to be appropriate to the scene and add to the visual appeal. Flopping the screen direction, to emphasize a story point should be a conscious choice by the storyboard artists and not be seen as an arbitrary mistake.

AWESOME ACTION SCENES

Action scenes require a particular method to make them exciting. Remember though that action is pointless if there is no emotional weight. Let's assume for the purposes of this section you have already worked out the significant emotional beats necessary for the action scene. Everybody loves a cool car chase or exciting kung fu duel especially storyboard artists. Above all, it's important to remember to make the action scenes as a cinematic as possible. Dull staging or uncreative compositions can ruin an otherwise good action scene.

Start off by building the anticipation for the upcoming fight or action sequence. Increase the speed of the cuts. Move the camera in closer with each cut. Increase the levels of danger for greater intensity. It's absolutely key to make objects coming and going away from the camera to maximize depth. Try tilting and lowering the camera. Keep the action moving through the scene as well. Don't stage the fight or action in one place, have it travel along the set and track the camera with the action. Camera movement, along with the moving action adds a greater dynamic effect. It's even more important during action sequences to have shot variety with strong compositions.

When posing for a kung fu fight or hand to hand combat keep in mind these basic poses for your characters:

- *Guard pose* (power centering)—protect oneself
- *Anticipation* (powering up)—power in the shoulders
- *Set-up shot* (power conditioning)—glancing blows
- *The strike* (power unload)—impact

The choreography should reflect the skills of each character. Do your research, and get inspired with "good" kung fu movies. The more authentic you can make your fight scenes, the more realistic they will seem. Navy SEALs have a much different fighting style than a ninja. Make each movement as authentic as possible. Use cool fluid motion with dynamic powerful posing using strikes, blocks, evasive moves, and ducking.

Use these staging guidelines for awesome kung fu action:

- Establishing shot (either a down shot or upshot).
- Build anticipation by cutting closer from one fighter to the other in multiple shots until the fight begins.
- Medium shot on initial exchange to establish skills of both fighters (usually upshots).
- Intensify with a lead in close shot on one fighter in anticipation pose.
- OTS shot, of said fighter striking, on the other fighter parrying, blocking, or evading.
- Close up on a significant anticipation. Wide shot on amazing displays of acrobatics or skillful exchanges.
- Wide down shot on fighters to display danger in fighting near a ledge, platform, or any setting that has potential danger of falling to death, with occasional upshots for dynamics.
- Close ups on impacts.

Keep the camera moving along with the action, but the camera always follows the action, never leading it. Have your occasional action swinging towards the camera, and away for dynamic effect.

When pacing kung fu action or a fight scene try these rhythms:

- Strike, strike, strike, block
- Block, block, strike
- Block, block, strike, strike
- Strike, block, block, strike

Get the idea? Vary the beats, and have a good rhythm. Let the fights begin![1]

WINNING ANIMATICS

The purpose of many storyboards nowadays is to create an animatic. While overall solid drawing will do the trick, there are some techniques that make storyboards for an animatic much more fluid. Comic "swoosh" lines or action lines seem unnecessary and ridiculous in a still image, but when cut together in an animatic make a huge difference in the way the action flows. Don't forget to add the "swoosh" lines even if you feel they're unnecessary.

FIGURE 10.19

Always add motion or "swoosh" lines. (Figures 10.19–10.23)

FIGURE 10.20

FIGURE 10.21

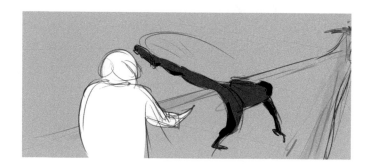

FIGURE 10.22

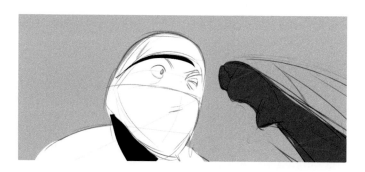

FIGURE 10.23

Storyboard images with good hook-ups will also add to the flow of the animatic. Look at the sequence of images below and notice how the action continues from one shot to the next for a good hook-up.

Creating the Illusion of Parallax

When creating digital storyboards you should create compositional elements on different layers. A foreground, middle ground, and background layer will move at different speeds when panning or tracking through the shot. The way to show this in your storyboards is to have a greater change with the elements that are closer to the camera than those in the background. The background layer will move relatively less than the foreground layer. Even in still panels, when cut together in an animatic the changing shapes in each panel will give the illusion of parallax. It may require 5 to 10 panels for one camera move to accomplish the effect. Using digital tools can make things much easier although proper planning and some elbow grease are also necessary. A zoom is easily accomplished by successively scaling up the image in different panels. A more complex camera move will take much more planning as the images below indicate. Think of creating a complex camera move the same way you would create a traditional 2D animation layout. You might create a larger background image over which you place a camera guide to use as reference. The size of the camera guide can change but the aspect ratio will be the same. Next, you could add more layers such as foreground layers or character layers as they move throughout the shot. Finally, you would digitally cut out the different camera positions in the shot and use those as the storyboard frames. The final effect is an effective and convincing camera move through the scene. These can either be composited with an image editing program such as After Effects or the storyboard artist themselves can create the images of the shots by overlapping the foreground and background elements in the still images. If you are working with an editorial department they will sometimes take your larger background file with the various layers and construct the camera move in After Effects. These still images when cut together will create the effect of parallax in a richly detailed scene. Instead of using arrows, add more poses. More character poses create almost an animation like effect when cut together in an animatic. Undoubtedly, you should have solid drawings with no sloppy perspective. Don't leave any shots up to interpretation because of overly rough drawings. The character placement, camera height, and staging should be clear. Don't rely on any other departments to plus up your work. It is up to you, the story artist, to make the important staging and compositional decisions that the project will follow.

FIGURE 10.24
Background layer.

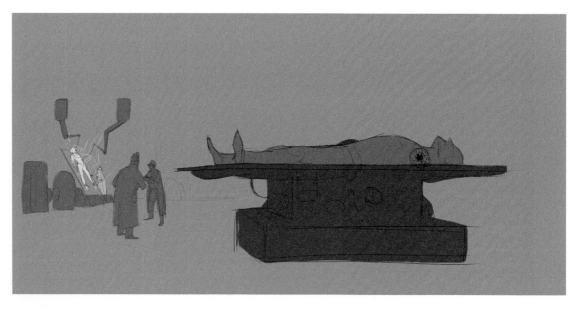

FIGURE 10.25
Additional foreground layer.

FIGURE 10.26
Add more foreground elements on separate layers.

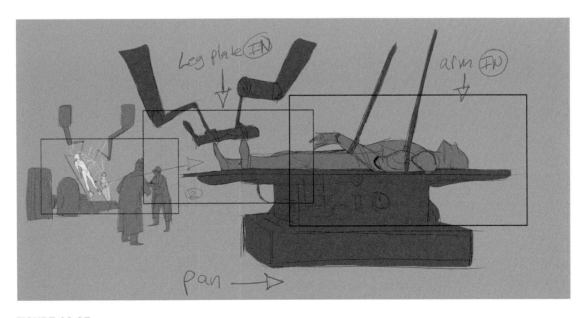

FIGURE 10.27
A final camera guide helps keep things organized. In the final animatic each camera position will be cut out as a separate panel and the resulting look is a camera move with parallax as we pan to the right.

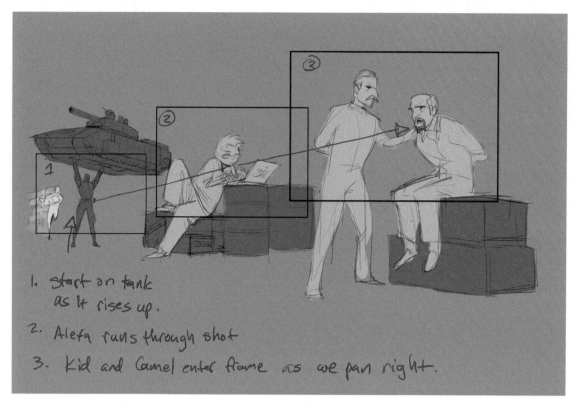

FIGURE 10.28
Another example of a complex camera move.

NOTE

1 Many of these techniques were referenced from master story artist and animation director Steward Lee.

CHAPTER 11
Portfolios and Promotion

After the difficult training, you still need to put these skills to work for you. The goal, after all, should be to have a career and get paid for doing the job you love. So it's time for a reality check—*Do you have the skills?* You need to master the basic storyboard principles in order to market yourself as a capable production artist. Be confident in your tools and your craft so that you can walk into any job and understand what is required of you. Remember, the only way to achieving these goals is to practice, practice, practice!

First of all, you need to *know what you want.* Are you looking for a job in video games? Or is your dream to work in feature films? Do you want to be a director someday and storyboarding is just a stepping stone along that path? Figure it out. Don't waste another second of your life without a plan of what you want. Before you know it you have wasted decades on meaningless jobs and assignments that get you nowhere in your career.

In order to find work you will need a professional portfolio and a way to promote yourself in the industry. First, you need to find out what jobs are available and what companies are looking for. Do your research. Not every storyboard job is the same. Each assignment will have different requirements and may even require a different portfolio to show to each client or studio. It's now easier than ever with the Internet to find out which companies are hiring and what exactly they are looking for. Most major studios will publish their portfolio requirements and job openings on their websites. Other animation and job boards also offer good resources to finding out what companies are looking for.

PORTFOLIO DESIGN
When dealing with portfolio design be professional as presentation is crucial. Every storyboard type may require a different portfolio. What we will describe here is a standard storyboard portfolio that you can use for many different jobs

and storyboard types. Most companies and studios still want to see a printed hard copy book. This can be an inexpensive art portfolio with plastic sleeves where you slip in printouts of your artwork. For most companies an 8.5 × 11 inch size book is fine. Make sure your printouts are in full color or are otherwise high quality prints. Keep in mind that you will physically mail these portfolios to companies as samples so do not expect them to be returned. *Never send originals.* Any company or studio asking for original artwork should be passed on. Losing originals is too risky and a high quality print is just as good. A typical art portfolio can be purchased at an art store or online through art retailers. Keep 5 to 10 copies of your portfolio on hand as you never know when the job will come up and you need to mail them asap. Along with a printed portfolio you will also need to create a PDF version for sending by email.

The majority of your portfolio book should relate to the job focus, in this case storyboarding. Don't put examples of your graphic design, fashion illustration, sculpture, or anything else unrelated to storyboards. Character designs and sequential art, however, can be included, although this should be placed in the back as a supplemental material. Remember, this is a storyboard portfolio so you will need lots of storyboards! Here's what you can include:

- A résumé.
- Around 10–15 total pages of your absolute best work.
- 8–10 pages of storyboards with a variety of samples:
  - Dramatic scene
  - Comedic scene
  - Cartoony
  - TV/feature boards
  - Realistic boards
- 3–5 pages of relevant supplemental materials:
  - Thumbnail pages
  - Storytelling single panel images
  - Character designs
  - Illustrations
  - Comic work
  - Layouts

Play to your strengths in your portfolio. If you are better at comedic scenes show more comedic storyboards. If your specialty is action and strong dramatic compositions, show that off instead. The main point is that whoever opens your book should understand exactly how your work can apply to the job they need. The first few pages should be your strongest work. You can open with a winning storyboard sequence, or even strong compositions that tell a story about the character or the situation. When showing your storyboards, limit the number of panels on the page to 4 to 6 per page. Any more panels on a single page will get too small and are hard to read. Include any necessary description or dialogue, but don't go overboard with text. It's the images the company wants to see not your written dialogue.

What to Avoid

Don't fall into the pitfalls of bad portfolio design. Here are a couple things to avoid in a portfolio:

- Sloppy presentation.
- Mediocre work. Only your absolute best even if that makes for fewer pages.
- Figure drawings—that's for students. Show them storyboards not figure drawings. If you have to add characters, make them relevant character designs that show story and good posing.
- Unrelated art—graphic design, portraits, etc. It's a storyboard portfolio, right?
- Animation samples. Relevant stuff only.

RÉSUMÉ BASICS

It seems odd to talk about résumés here, but so many young artists make cluttered and unhelpful résumés. For the most part it's the experience a company wants to see in your résumé. Start with an objective line. Tell the company immediately what position you are applying for. Keep your résumé to 1 page only. Two pages will do, but only if you're a rockstar artist, in which case you probably wouldn't need our advice anyway. Most guys feel like they need to fill up their résumé with tidbits about their Boy Scout service and magazines subscriptions. If you don't have enough experience that's fine, but don't double space your résumé and fill up two pages unnecessarily if there's no juicy information there. Above all, make your résumé clean and easy to read. Follow some of these guidelines:

- No picture or age. In the US, no one cares about that stuff.
- No personal unrelated nonsense.
- Add a cover letter if you are sending the portfolio by mail.
- Highlight experience.
- State the job objective.

CHAPTER 12
Finding Work

FIGURE 12.1

Now that you have an awesome portfolio and résumé, you can venture out to find work. This actually might be one of the hardest parts of being a storyboard artist. Finding work is a difficult job in itself not to mention all the preparation it takes to become a storyboard artist. Do not fear competition. Just as writers are unique in their style and approach, so too are storyboard artists. Every artist has a unique approach to solving a visual problem. This is precisely what makes them valuable. The more well-trained story artists there are the better our lives will be from the rich stories they create. Learn from each other and be inspired not by your "competition," but by your fellow brother in this artistic journey you've chosen to take. You may compete for the same jobs with other artists, but that's no reason to be jealous or bitter. The goal of a "true" artist is *growth*. A job may offer this, but it's up to us as individuals to continue our learning. A job may satisfy your bank account, but I have never had a job that satisfies my artistic soul. This is the reason why the brotherhood of artists should be one of support and nurturing. There is plenty of opportunity for us all if we continue to make the best stories possible.

ONLINE PRESENCE

There are a few preparatory things you can do before you begin your search for jobs. Your online presence is as important as your off-line presence. Make sure your social networking accounts are clean and clear of any random details that would discourage a potential employer. Employers do look and search for you online. Keep your online presence as professional and pristine as possible. Clean up those drunken pictures of yourself on Facebook and erase any flame wars you had on blogs and forums.

One thing you need to do, if you haven't done so already, is to create a website. This should be an online version of your portfolio, with perhaps some expanded pages of other artwork you wouldn't necessarily put in a storyboard portfolio. There are many low-cost and free alternatives to creating an art portfolio site. In this day and age, no storyboard artist should be without a website. In addition to your website you can create a Facebook page and a LinkedIn profile to make connections. Having a website will be the basis of making connections to companies where you can easily email your website URL to potential employers. Be sure to print your email and website URL on your business cards as well. Here are some online resources to create a webpage:

- http://mosaicglobe.com—free artist websites.
- www.foliolink.com—low-cost artist websites.
- www.wordpress.org—free blogging platform.

STARTING THE SEARCH

Begin your search online, and research any animation company or film company you can think of who would use storyboard artists. Craigslist.org is a start, then dig deeper with any contacts you may have and start researching film and animation articles about upcoming projects. Research the companies and find a contact or email for the recruiter or art department. Once you have a contact start by sending an introductory email and ask about upcoming job openings. The next step would be to prepare your portfolio materials and mail a physical package to the company. Check out some of these websites as good resources for storyboard work:

- www.StoryboardArt.org—an online community with a storyboard and educational focus.
- www.Conceptart.org—a concept art website with a decent job board.
- www.Cghub.com—an online community for digital artists.

■   www.AWN.com—the Animation World Network has great articles and a decent job board.

NETWORKING

The single most important thing you can do when looking for storyboard work is *networking*. The majority of any seasoned artist's jobs comes from word-of-mouth and past clients. Even if you're just starting out it's crucial to reach out and meet the artists and recruiters in the industry and show them your work in person. Start by sending them introductory emails and invite them for a coffee and a chat.

If that doesn't work, go to the industry events where you know artists and other professionals will be around to ask questions. You may not live near any of the industry events, but if work is important to you save your travel money and plan to be at some of the major events throughout the year to network and meet people. Find a contact on the inside of the company where you want to work and keep in touch with them throughout the year. A word of warning—be cool. There is a fine line between contacting a recruiter and harassing the recruiter over a particular job. Make sure all of your contacts and emails are professional, and you come across as a person who would be a pleasure to work with and not a menace. Here are some common industry events in the United States:

■   Comiccon—July in San Diego, California
■   Wondercon—March in San Francisco, California or Anaheim, California
■   Alternative Press Expo(APE)—October in San Francisco, California
■   Creative Talent Expo (CTN)—November in Burbank, California

Also check out these industry groups for networking and industry events:

■   ASIFA—the International Animated Film Association
■   Directors Guild of America (DGA)
■   Producers Guild of America (PGA)
■   Visual Effects Society

UNION VS NON-UNION

Unions still exist in the animation film industry even for storyboard artists. The usefulness and need for unions is debatable, since more often than not unions become an exclusionary force and drive up wage rates unnecessarily causing industry unemployment. The perpetual Catch-22 still exists. In order to enter the union, you must first be on a union job, and to be on a union job, of course, you must first be in the union. The collective bargaining power of unions sometimes gives wage and benefits to the preferred group within the unions but often comes at a cost to those artists looking to break into the industry since they are excluded from consideration for the same work.[1] There are benefits to union members in bargaining and employment conditions. Through union dues, the union can have the power to hire lawyers that can go head to head with those of the employers. Also, by virtue of having large memberships, unions can offer health insurance to their members at lower group rates.

There are currently two unions in the Los Angeles area that serve the interests of storyboard artists. Both are part of IATSE, the International Alliance of Theatrical Stage Employees. They are IATSE Local 800 and IATSE Local 839.

IATSE Local 800 (www.adg.org)

IATSE Local 800 is also known as the Art Directors Guild. Local 800 currently serves the interests of art directors, scenic title and graphic artists, illustrators and matte artists, and set designers and model makers. Storyboard artists and illustrators used to have their own guild, known as IATSE Local 790 until 2008, when Local 790 was absorbed into the Art Directors Guild. Local 800 currently has about 2000 members.

Most major live action films and TV shows produced today in the US are union signatories. When a film becomes a union signatory it means the film producers have an agreement with the union to follow certain standards in terms of wages, working conditions, etc. IATSE 800 members are all on what is known as the Industry Experience Roster. This is a list of artists who have accumulated what the union considers to be a high level of professional experience. Producers who are signatories to the local are encouraged to hire from this list before considering hiring anyone else.

Here are some ways of getting work on a live action production and/or getting into Local 800:

- When all the storyboard artists of the Local 800 are working on a film or are otherwise unavailable, producers are free to hire outside of the union. So if you hear through the grapevine that all the artists in the Guild are currently working, it's a great time to start looking for work! Additionally, if you do get hired and work for 30 days or more on a film, you can get that experience onto the roster and join the union.
- Sometimes, a film starts as a non-union film and at some point signs on to become a union signatory. Not all films are union signatories. Often, these are small budget indie films, but not always. If this happens, and you have been working on the film for over a month within a 365 day period of the show going union, you may have the opportunity to be grandfathered into the union.
- Another way of getting into the union is by accumulating experience in commercials and reporting it to the Contract Services Administration Trust Fund.[2] The CSATF administers and maintains the Television Commercial Roster and the Industry Experience Roster. To get on the Television Commercial Roster, you have to work at least 30 days in a job classification covered by the agreement within a 365 day period immediately preceding the date of application. Once you have done that you may qualify to work on union commercials. Having done that, once you have accrued an additional 60 days of commercial work, you are eligible to upgrade to the Industry Experience Roster. Once on the Industry Experience Roster, you will be on the producers' radar and the Local will solicit a membership from you.

If you have some skills or talent that are so unique that the production will only hire you and not some other member of the Guild, someone on the production could vouch on your behalf and make a case to have you hired onto the show. It should also be noted that union freelancers can work on both union and non-union shows, but non-union artists can only work on non-union shows. This obviously makes it hard for the non-union artist, since union artists can compete with any non-union artist for a job but not the other way around.

IATSE 839 aka the Animation Guild, serves the interests of people working in the animation industry. Since most animation work is staff, rather than freelance, getting into the Animation Guild is generally simpler than getting into IATSE 800. If you are hired at a union company and work for 30 days, you will simply be asked if you want to join the union. IATSE 839 offers a 401K plan, pension and health plans, plus other benefits.[3]

WHAT'S YOUR RATE?

Know what you're worth as an industry artist. You should understand the market and adjust your rate accordingly. Don't know how much you should charge? Here we will give you some guidelines, but rates will vary depending on your experience and geographic area.[4] A good basis for industry rates is to look up the union rates published at the union website or through their publications.

A decent board artist can make anywhere from $150–350/day as a mid-level artist to $450–700/day as a high-level artist. Weekly rates go from $1000–1500 to $2000–3000 for a high-level artist. On an hourly basis rates can range from $30–50 per hour mid-level to $60–85 high-level. An entry-level salary on a staff position can be $40,000–50,000. Senior artists and supervisors can make six figure salaries but, of course, their responsibilities and production quotas will be greater. The truth is you can make a decent living as a storyboard artist. The last time I checked, a storyboard artist can make more money than those more conventional jobs such as an architect or insurance agent. With any job, if you have no experience you have to start at the bottom and work your way up. If you are a freelancer, you should charge more for contract work. If someone asks you what your rate is, you need to have an answer. You should tell them a weekly rate or an hourly rate that closely matches your experience. You can be willing to negotiate the rate based on how badly you want the job, but be confident your skills are in the rate that you can command.

INTERVIEWS

It almost goes without saying that you need to be professional and presentable for an interview. As a filmmaker and an animation artist, you do not need to wear a tie, but you should look like a professional and dress like a professional in an interview. A button-down shirt with snazzy slacks and matching shoes should do the trick. Be humble and be cool, but be yourself. You need to show people in an interview that you are a person who they will enjoy working with.

Always bring a copy of your printed portfolio with you, even if you know the company has one of their own. Before the interview learn as much about the company or job as possible. Do your research. Under no circumstances, *ever* criticize the project you're interviewing for. The people working on the project are always right. Even if you feel like a project is not going in the direction you want, *the people working on the project are always right.* Check your ego at the door and be pleasant and supportive to the efforts of your fellow artists. Before you leave, make sure you get the contact information of those who interviewed you and follow up with them after a few weeks if you have not heard anything.

FREELANCE WORK

We have already mentioned many of the trials of a freelance storyboard artist. Much of what it takes to make it as a freelancer is a great deal of hustle and maintaining good networking relationships. Keep in mind that you need to provide good value for your services. If clients feel as if they get more in return than they pay out by hiring you they will hire you again, and they will refer you to their friends. Keep in contact with your clients with mailers or email updates every quarter. Be sure to build a personal network and use it. You might even have to advertise through industry publications on websites like craigslist. Again, a personal website is indispensable when it comes to working as a freelance artist. As a good friend of mine always says, "quality is the best business model."

GOT THE JOB—NOW WHAT?

The first thing you'll need is a contract in writing. Even a signed quote you provide the client can serve as a contract. Be wary of "spec" work. Jobs on "spec" are no pay gigs that trade present work for the promise of a future payout. More often than not, you will never see any money from these types of jobs. Even a little bit of money is better than working for free since you know the client is serious by paying something out. Don't begin any work based on a phone call or even a face-to-face meeting. Get every detail in writing and ask the client to sign and confirm a printed document or a PDF document before you begin any work.

Ask for a deposit or retainer up front, which can be 30–50% of the total job. Do not begin any work without having first received the deposit. In your written quote or contract, be specific about the services you provide, including the number of drawings you will create or the number of hours you promise to work. You can charge more for weekend work and overtime hours. Anything not specified in the quote or contract should be an overage charge, and authorized in writing by both parties before any work begins. At the end of the job immediately send an invoice to the client. It is standard practice for clients to pay within 30 days of the finished job called *net 30*. Keep this in mind and have money reserves on hand, knowing it could take a month before you see the payment arrive. Be professional with your billing and invoicing as it will reflect on your work and the overall customer experience you give the client.

If you do find yourself in a situation where the client owes you money or you somehow feel shortchanged, keep your emotions in check. This is business and emotions are useless in the business world. You gain nothing but damage to your reputation by getting into shouting matches with your client or employer. Maintain your composure at all times and simply state your desires over the phone or by email without the use of threats or harsh words. Contract disputes are what lawyers are for, and they are well worth their money. If the amount of the job is significant you can hire a lawyer and have them contact the company. If the contract amount is not significant, assuming you have all the paperwork and you did everything right, you can open the claim in small claims court. Sometimes though, being burned along the way is a learning experience that will teach you to do things correctly the next time with contracts and lawyers.

For any job over $10,000 (including staff positions), I recommend you hire a lawyer who specializes in contracts and entertainment law to look over the paperwork for you. A qualified lawyer may cost $300–400 an hour, but can usually look over contracts within a few hours and spare you much heartache down the road should you end up in a dispute. Lawyers working on your side are well worth the money and, in fact, they might even be able to negotiate higher rates for a particular job.

NOTES

1   For an enlightening talk about unions see Murray Rothbard (2004), *Man Economy State*, The Scholars Edition, Auburn, Alabama: Ludwig Von Mises Institute, pp.704–19.

2   For more information visit www.csatf.org

3   IATSE Local 839 (http://animationguild.org)

4   This is a good benchmark to use based on the date of this publication. Rates will change so do your research before applying to jobs.

CHAPTER 13

Spotlight

The Professional Storyboard Artist

Entering the world of storyboards, unlocks a close knit community of artists and professionals. We all learn from those who come before us and those artists who continue to innovate. In this sense, the brotherhood of professional storyboard artist can be thought of as a resource and inspiration. Each artist's individual approach to story is unique to their experience and skill set. Here we highlight some working professionals whose work and journey can serve as an inspiration to us all.

INTERVIEW WITH BENTON JEW

Give us your résumé. Tell us what you do and what things you've done in the past.

Currently I'm a storyboard/concept artist in Los Angeles and I work freelance doing motion pictures. I started working in the film industry as a storyboard/concept artist at Industrial Light and Magic (ILM) while I was still in school and also worked as a visual effects art director over there. I worked at ILM for 13 years, and then I moved on and moved to LA and worked freelance. I do storyboards and I also do comics, illustration, and occasional video games, things like that.

Can you tell us what some of your credits are?

Well I worked on *The Mask* as a visual effects art director while I was at ILM. I was a storyboard artist on *The Phantom Menace*. I did creature design on the first two *Mummy* movies, the first two *Men in Black* movies, *Ghostbusters 2*, storyboard artist on *Terminator 3*. I did costume illustrations on *GI Joe*, *Thor*, and also did storyboards on just a lot of different things.

Let's talk about how you broke in. You know, going to school, starting up. How did you get from being a student to where you are right now?

Well, as a high school and junior college student, I had already done a little bit of freelancing here and there for small things. I did some comic books while I was in college—going to art school. I would always show my artwork to different artists and get their advice and while I was studying at the Academy of Art University, I showed my work to Stan Fleming, who was a storyboard artist on films like the second *Indiana Jones* movie and some other films. And he shared my interest in comic strips and comic books and I showed him some comic book work that I did while he was giving a lecture at The Academy of Art. So he remembered me and recommended me for a job that he couldn't do or didn't have time to do while at ILM and so I was at my last semester at The Academy of Art. They hired me to work on a job. It was a simulator ride called Body Wars as a freelancer. So that's how I got my start working at ILM and then they decided to build a bigger art department, so I was a part of that art department for 13 years.

Now, when you showed them your portfolio, what did you show them?

The thing he remembered was kind of a comic book style thing I did for the Oakland A's. I had done two five-page comic book inserts inside an Oakland A's Magazine and I showed him some of the original artwork and he liked my style. I just grabbed him after he gave his talk and a lot of people were showing their portfolios to him and he remembered my stuff because it was kind of an old style comic strip style. He was a big fan of Stan Drake and I was a big fan of Stan Drake so he apparently remembered me. After that, we became friends later, and that's how I got the job.

Now, you're talking about Stan Fleming. But when you went to ILM what did you show? Did they ask to look at your work or was it purely Stan's recommendation?

Well, it was my last semester in art school, so I had basically shown them what I had done in art school and a few of my freelance jobs. Some of the comic book style samples that I did and some of my school work. Not a whole lot. We didn't really go through my portfolio that heavily. They could sense that I could draw and do the job.

So this was a freelance job? And how long did it last?

It lasted a couple of months.

And they required you to work onsite?

I had one class on Fridays at the Art Academy and then Monday through Thursday, I worked at ILM.

So they were accommodating your schedule.

Yeah.

So after that they were hiring to fill out their art department . . .?

Yeah, generally, they didn't have a centralized art department so they decided to have one and were sort of looking around at the freelancers they had used before and bringing them on staff. At the time there wasn't a whole lot of people who did storyboards that can be used for visual effects style films, and so they were having a hard time finding people. A lot of people are in L.A. and they actually pulled a lot of people from L.A. but they also wanted to find local people. But it was also hard to get people to come from L.A. and come up and work in the Bay Area, I guess, initially.

So eventually they built a staff of other freelance artists. How big was the staff?

I was there at the beginning, so it started with Steve Beck, who was the head of the art department and it grew from around 10 people and then by the time I left, it was close to 50 people in the art department.

So going in, this was about what year?

It was 1988.

And you left when?

I left about 2000.

What changed in the industry at the time you were at ILM?

Well, the whole digital thing changed everything. When I first started at ILM, the digital age hadn't really started yet. We still made stuff with models. There was some CG stuff but it was all very rudimentary at that point. And I just kind of started when that whole digital thing was just in the very early stages. So that was the main difference. Also in terms of what we do, in terms of storyboards, there was no Photoshop at that time. Everything was hand drawn, with pencils and markers and stuff like that. So it was a lot of penciling and xeroxing. You couldn't comp things together in Photoshop or anything like that. We just had to hand draw it.

So when digital came along, not only was the work a little more out there, but in terms of what the artists themselves were doing they were also going digital, doing things in Photoshop. Talk about how that changed for you. Not just for the industry, but for you. How did Photoshop, the digital aspect change?

It made things a lot easier. I never used Photoshop for storyboards in the beginning. Mostly it was used for concept art. In the early days of Photoshop, it was a little bit cruder but it was still a pretty good tool to do things that were quite difficult to do, unless you did it as a straight illustration. But it just made things easier to be able to cut and paste things together and smear things or whatever it was in those early days of Photoshop. But as Photoshop got more sophisticated, the things you could do with it became more sophisticated and it pretty much opened up to near limitless things that you could do with it in terms of creating an image.

And things still continue changing . . .

Yeah. New tools are being invented all the time.

So after you did your time at ILM you went freelance. Talk about what that process was; that must have been a scary leap.

Yeah, I had met some people who had worked in L.A. I knew there wasn't a lot of work in the Bay Area, so I decided to make the move to L.A. I had known some people from L.A. who had worked freelance up at ILM so I hooked with a lot of those people and asked them a lot of questions and things so I could find out more about more about what it's like to work in Los Angeles. And eventually, I was able to work on *Terminator 3* because some people had recommended me and liked my work but they had seen what I'd done on *Phantom Menace* and some other stuff and so I was able to get on *Terminator 3* right before it went union. That's how I was able to get into the union.

Now you had done a few jobs before you were able to get into the union, right? You had done some freelance jobs before.

I did some ad agency stuff and I did some commercial stuff and some stuff for some toy companies and things like that and video game stuff just to keep my head above water. I was fortunate enough to get into the union fairly quickly after moving to L.A.

Talk about the storyboard position in general. When you get on a job what are you contributing to the job? What value are you adding?

Really, when I'm doing storyboards, I'm there at the director's disposal, so he's basically writing down notes, visual notes. I am creating a tool for him so he can communicate with people on the crew, so he doesn't have to explain things over and over again and help him visualize things and sort things together in his own mind and have a better idea of what he wants the film to look like. And it can be a slow process—a lot of stuff you do and then you do it over, until you get something that kind of resembles what he sees in his head. So it's a lot of trying to communicate with the director and pulling out of him what he's seeing in his mind's eye. A lot of times he doesn't know how to explain it so you're working with him until he gets what he wants. And if you're doing concept art it's a similar process. You're working with a production designer or an art director.

Do you find yourself contributing in terms of story?

Yeah. Mostly when I'm storyboarding something. The director sometimes wants a lot of creative input with ideas so they can bounce those ideas around and others can know exactly what they want. Other times they will describe exactly what they want you to draw. But it really depends. Sometimes they want a lot of creative input, sometimes not. Being successful in this industry means you've got to be flexible in what you do, so sometimes you're going to be more creative, sometimes you're going to be less creative so you have to adapt to every situation.

What skills do you think are important to have going in to working on films?

I think you should have a good eye for film and how to tell a story dramatically. But I think you have to have a really good ear. You have to be able to listen to what a director says and what he means by it. And what questions to ask to draw what he wants out of him and be able to translate it on paper. A good grasp of drawing—you should be able to draw anything and draw in perspective. You should be able to draw clearly and cleanly. Be able to see things from any angle that they might ask you to do and have an idea of what that actually looks like without a lot of trouble. It just means you have to know how to visualize things very quickly and confidently.

Once you get the job—once you've been looked at for the job—who hires you? Who are you talking to—who are you trying to impress before you get the job?

Usually I'll get a call from somebody on the crew, be it the director's assistant or the P.A. (production assistant) or whatever. They'll initially contact me and ask for a sample. Often I'll just email a sample or they'll ask me for a website or something like that. Or sometimes they'll want to meet me in person. I have a physical portfolio that I bring to meetings when I meet them in person, because sometimes they want to meet you in person and find out what kind of person you're like in addition to whether you can draw, and they want to talk to you and see if you're thinking on the same wave length as the director. Any way I can get the work in front of them I do it. It helps when I can find out about the project I'm working on, so I can gear my portfolio to them. If it's a movie with a lot of wildlife, I'll show them boards I've done before with a lot wildlife. Other jobs, I might have to look for myself, so it's good to know what jobs are going on in town. What films are starting to gear up and have a sense of what's in production and what's going into production. Sometimes you can find that out by reading the trades like the *Hollywood Reporter* or whatever online, talking about the new films that are coming out. Usually I will check IMDB, find out who might be working on those films and usually from that I can talk to people who have worked with those people who are on the crew and from there I can gather more information. Like if I know somebody on the crew, I usually contact that person and see what they know about the film—if they're hiring and things like that. So that's one way. So that's why it's good to know a lot of people in the industry because they might be working on a film or they might know somebody who is working on a film or worked with somebody before. So it's good to gather as much information about what you want to work on or what you're planning on working on before you're working on it as possible.

It's going to be hard for a lot of people just starting out trying to get into film. A lot of films are going to be union and its going to be hard for somebody just coming out of school to get into the union. Do you have any advice if they eventually want to get into doing film?

First, they should be able to honestly evaluate their own work and say "Are you as good as the people who are currently doing the job?" Have an idea about what's out there. Try to meet some storyboard artists or whatever and look at their work and look at your work and honestly be able to say "I'm as good as this person or better". If you can't say that, then there's really no point in you looking for work until you can develop those skills and be good enough to compete with them. Once you've done that, then it's a matter of working your way up the ladder. It might start out with small jobs, commercials, things like that. So that you learn about what your role is in the making of a film or a commercial and where you fit in. And once you've done that and proven that and have sort of a book of stuff that you've done, you can be able to move into bigger things or bigger movies. But generally, you're not going to get on the big pictures immediately, unless you're really, really, really good. But even then, there's no guarantee. But it starts by knowing what your job is, and probably having to start on small things or things that are only somewhat related. You might start on doing music videos, you might start on commercials or whatever just to have a sense of what it's like to work with a director and what they expect from you.

If you're going to be working on films do you need to be in L.A.?

It's probably the best way to go. I know other people who live outside of L.A., but generally you kind of have to establish yourself in L.A. first. Unless you're working through a visual effects firm like ILM or something and they've already got a system where they're getting the work already. Generally, most of the films are made in L.A. There are other cities that have some film work, but L.A. is one of the few places that's going to have a lot of it year round. But other places like North Carolina has a little bit of a film community and like Vancouver and Toronto up in Canada, they have a little bit of a film community, New York has a little bit of a film community, but if it's big Hollywood motion pictures, you have to be in Hollywood.

So until then, you should try to look for other kinds of illustration work or storyboarding work.

Or sometimes there might even be indie films. Small indie films. There's always a film school or something like that, they might need something. If you're just beginning to get your feet wet, and you've never done anything before, that's as good a place to start as any. That, and you might want to do video games, you might do commercials, comic books or whatever just to at least have an idea of how to work when it's a film.

Let's talk about process a bit. Once you've gotten an assignment and you meet up with the director, what usually happens?

Usually, once I meet the director, they'll give me a script to read and I'll read the script. And usually the director will show me all the materials that they have—all the artwork that's been done, if any. They might have boards that have already been done. They might have photoscrap that the production designer has pulled that looks like sets that you might be working on. Or photos of what the look of the movie is supposed to be. Mostly the storyboards are just going to be working with the script. Sometimes they give you a script breakdown of the scenes they want you to work on, but generally it starts with reading the script and then having a meeting with the director. And usually the director will tell you what he wants you to board, what he wants it to look like. Sometimes he might just say, "start with page 1 and go forward". So it really depends on the director.

In most situations, what are you doing? Are you doing assignments a scene at a time?

It really depends on the director. Sometimes they might just let you go. Usually what happens is they say "go from page 5 to page 7" or something like that— they'll want a short chunk. Usually, the storyboards will be something that involves some type of action or visual effect—less talking heads. But they'll usually have something that's hard to visualize. Sometimes they'll help you thumbnail something out. But usually, I'll have a meeting with the director, find out what he wants. I'll take notes and quick thumbnails that are just stick figures. I'll approve those with the director and I'll work to finish the sequence and then come back a couple of days later and then refine it as we keep on going.

And are you usually working at home or are you on the premises? Are there other artists there?

Again, it really depends. A lot of times, I'll work at home and a lot of times, I work in a studio situation. I kind of prefer working in a studio situation because usually you can work with the other storyboard artists and you also have all the material there in front of you and easy access to the director for questions or whoever else might be on the staff for questions. And you have a better sense of where the movie is going in front of you when you have the rest of the crew there.

What are some of the typical problems that come up and how have you dealt with them?

You just have to be adaptable and clear. I've been in situations where the script doesn't make any sense or the director isn't sure what he wants. Or things that they want are contradictory. I've been in situations where I'd be asked to do something where the guy is driving, at the same time he's punching somebody and talking on a cell phone —and you can't do that because you don't have three arms. You have to point out little logistical things that don't make any sense and work your way around them. Oftentimes you're put in a situation where they want a lot of work in a short amount of time or they haven't prepared the materials for you. You don't have enough time to get stuff done in the time that they want.

What do you find is generally the norm for how much work they expect, how much time and how detailed?

That again really depends on the director. Some want really detailed boards. Others just want the barest of indications, just so they get the idea out. So you've got to be prepared to be able to work both ways.

How do you find out what they want?

You just ask them straight up, "Do you want more boards with less detail or do you want fewer boards with more detail?" is generally how it works.

What's the toughest part of your job?

Each job is individual, a lot of times it's just the logistics of things in the first place. Some things are difficult logistically, so you have to be able to visualize all that stuff in your head. Probably the most difficult part is making deadlines. You want to get as much done as quickly as you can. You're always up against the clock and as the show goes on you fatigue and just the volume of work involved in doing storyboards, it gets to you after a while.

What do you think is the most important thing that they're looking for?

They want speed, accuracy. They want as much stuff as they can in the shortest amount of time possible. That only makes sense.

What's the one best piece of advice you would give to students just starting out?

Work at your craft. Be as good as you can, but be as flexible as you can. Enjoy what you do. Learn to draw. Learn to draw really well and learn how to tell a story.

Telling a story—where do learn that kind of stuff?

By watching movies, reading books on filmmaking, or just being interested in film in general. Look at movies . . . sometimes you can look at comic books— you know, the really good guys who could really tell a story.

How about some names? Movies or comics. . . .

Well in terms of movies, obviously the classics like *Citizen Kane*. I can't think of one particular movie. You can find something in almost any movie, but it depends on what you're looking for. Some films are good for looking at lighting, other films are good for looking at a chase, other films are good on how to build tension and suspense. Look at them on DVD. Look at them over and over and ask "What is it that they're doing that's creating that effect?" I would say just look at the movies that you like and go from that. There's so many, I couldn't really choose just one."

I'm asking all my interviewees to give two tips. First, one that's more a techie tip—a technical trick that you've learned that's helpful.

One of the things that I like to do that makes things easier is to—, if I'm assigned a sequence, lightly thumbnail the whole sequence out from start to finish as quickly as you can and make sure that it works right. Make sure that's done before you start any of your drawings. Make sure that it's designed correctly first as opposed to doing it one storyboard at a time. Because if you just inch along like that, you'll never get it done. I find that if you just do quick hen scratchings that just gives you the basic idea—the design of each frame—and that will give you a guideline. So the rest of the boards you can just *do*. Just turn off your brain and just draw. Just draw, but make sure you have all your duckies in a row first.

Any tips that are more general, business related, or philosophical?

It's good to have good artist hands, it's good to have good artist eyes, but it's especially good to have really good artist ears and listen to what is being asked of you and execute it.

FIGURE 13.1
Storyboard by Benton Jew from *The Collector*, a short film written and directed by the artist.

FIGURE 13.2

4. M.C.U. Dion looks in anger and disbelief at Pau
Paul merely looks down and without a single
word, begins to walk around Dion. Paul is oddly
unemotional about the situation. Dion
stops Paul in his tracks with a hard shove.
Dion stares down Paul, but he merely continues
forward past Dion without looking at him(their
shoulders bump slightly)

5. L.S. (Paul still displays no outward
emotion whatsoever. Somehow this seems to enrage
Dion all the more.) Dion turns as Paul walks
past him, but restrains himself from escalating
the situation further.

FIGURE 13.3

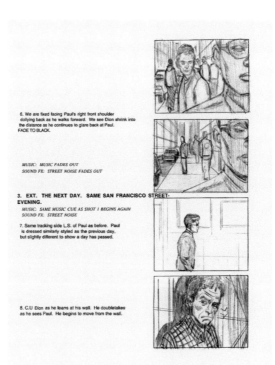

6. We are fixed facing Paul's right front shoulder
dollying back as he walks forward. We see Dion shrink into
the distance as he continues to glare back at Paul.
FADE TO BLACK.

MUSIC: MUSIC FADES OUT
SOUND FX: STREET NOISE FADES OUT

3. EXT. THE NEXT DAY. SAME SAN FRANCISCO STREET-
EVENING.
   MUSIC: SAME MUSIC CUE AS SHOT 1 BEGINS AGAIN
   SOUND FX: STREET NOISE

7. Same tracking side L.S. of Paul as before. Paul
is dressed similarly styled as the previous day,
but slightly different to show a day has passed.

8. C.U Dion as he leans at his wall. He doubletakes
as he sees Paul. He begins to move from the wall.

FIGURE 13.4

9. PAUL'S P.O.V. as he maneuvers through the crowd. We see Dion in the distance. He walks forward in front our path.

10. M.S. of Dions's back as he stands defiantly in Paul's path. Paul steps to his righ, but Dion blocks his path. Paul steps to his left, but Dion again blocks his path.

FIGURE 13.5

11. C.U. Dion (over Paul's Shoulder) with a slight smile, confident and defiant.

12. C.U.(over Dion's shoulder), Paul stands staring forward into Dion's chest, angry, but not sure what to do. Dion grabs Paul by the lapels, his hands over Paul's chest. Paul looks down and stares at Dion's hands, then he slowly looks up and stares Dion in the face.

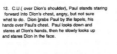

13. M.S. as two passersby suddenly break the two up. Paul slips away in the crowd, vanishing.

FIGURE 13.6

14. L.S. Dion breaks away from the samaritans

15. C.U. Low angle on Dion as he steps into frame.
He's angry, staring in the direction Paul disappeared into.
FADE TO BLACK.

MUSIC: MUSIC FADES OUT
SOUND FX: STREET NOISE FADES OUT

4. EXT. THE NEXT DAY. SAME SAN FRANCISCO STREET-
LATE EVENING.
MUSIC: SAME MUSIC CUE
SOUND FX: MINIMAL STREET NOISE

16. Same tracking side L.S. of Paul as before. Paul
is dressed similarly styled as the previous days,
but slightly different to show another day has passed.
It is slightly later in the evening than before, and the
streets are empty.

17. We move through the street from PAUL'S P.O.V. as he
walks through the street. The streets are
EMPTY. Suddenly, Dion enters frame in M.C.U.
stopping us in our tracks.

FIGURE 13.7

18. C.U. (hand held) The two begin to scuffle a bit.

SOUND FX: SOUND OF FEET SCUFFLING

19. C.U. Dion's back as he falls forward wiping frame revealing
C.U. of Paul's hand with a stun gun sparking.
FADE TO AND HOLD ON BLACK.
MUSIC: MUSIC FADES OUT
SOUND FX: STREET NOISE FADES OUT

FIGURE 13.8

5.   INT. PAUL'S ROOM
      MONTAGE:

20. FADE IN. E.C.U. of Dion's right eyeball. It looks around.
SOUND FX: SOME MOANING. BREATHING

21.   We see the ceiling an upper areas of a small room.

22. E.C.U. Dion's eyeball looking around.

23. C.U. Dion's right hand. It is chained to the gurney.

   SOUND FX: SOUND OF HANDCUFFS CLINKING

FIGURE 13.9

24. E.C.U. Dion's eyeball wincing.

25. C.U. of Dion strapped down chest

26. E.C.U. Dion's eyeball.

27. C.U. Dion's feet. They are also chained to the gurney.

   SOUND FX: SOUND OF HANDCUFFS CLINKING

FIGURE 13.10

28. E.C.U. Dion's eyes. Camera slowly pulls back revealing a C.U. Dion. His mouth is gagged shut with a plastic spit-ball that is strapped to his face. He looks around, bewildered. He tries to rise, but can't get up as he is strapped down. He violently struggles and thrashes in extreme frustration and finally surrenders to his situation for the time being. He pauses to catch his breath. He hears something and looks up.

SOUND FX: SOUND OF DION STRUGGLING, MOANING. HIS BREATHING IS MORE LABORED

29. Dion's P.O.V. past his feet to the door. The door opens. Paul walks in and stares at Dion, silently and without emotion. Dion struggles violently at the sight of Paul. Paul, without a word, calmly leaves the room.

FIGURE 13.11

30. E.C.U. Dion's face as he angrily struggles in response to Paul's ignoring him.

SOUND FX: SOUND OF DION TRYING TO YELL THROUGH THE GAG. MOANING, BREATHING HEAVILY

31. Dion's P.O.V. past his feet to the open door. We wait a few seconds and Paul finally returns. This time he has a light on a stand. He sets it up in front of Dion.

SOUND FX: RATTLE OF THE LIGHT STAND

32. E.C.U. Dion

33. E.C.U of Paul's hands as he slowly and carefully unrolls the neatly rolled cord and plugs it into the wall.

SOUND FX: SOUND OF CORD BEING UNROLLED

FIGURE 13.12

34. E.C.U. Dion's face. He is completely puzzled by this. He squints as Paul clicks the light on.

SOUND FX: CLICK OF THE LIGHT SWITCH

35. Dion's P.O.V. past his feet. Paul once again exits the room. He finally returns with a video camera on a tripod. He aims it at Dion. Paul once again exits the room.

SOUND FX: SOUND OF TRIPOD HITTING THE FLOOR

36. E.C.U. Dion's face. He has no idea what's going on and shakes his head in disbelief.

FIGURE 13.13

37. Dion's P.O.V. past his feet. Paul stoops down and looks for something on a shelving unit.

38. C.U. over Paul's shoulder at Paul's hands moving through a shelf. On the shelf we a see neatly lined-up row of brand new wrapped video cassettes. Below it, another neatly lined-up row of video cassettes that have been opened and labeled, apparently by date, the most recent at the near, open side. He removes one of the wrapped video cassettes and begins to open it.

SOUND FX: SOUND OF CASSETTES, CELLOPHANE WRAP BEING OPENED

39. E.C.U. Cassette label as Paul writes the date with a felt-tipped pen

40. C.U. Video tape camera as Paul pops the tape in.

SOUND FX: SOUND OF TAPE SLIDING AND CLICKING INTO VIDEO CAMERA. WIRES BEING JIGGLED

FIGURE 13.14

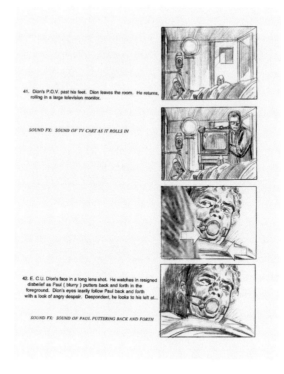

41. Dion's P.O.V. past his feet. Dion leaves the room. He returns, rolling in a large television monitor.

SOUND FX: SOUND OF TV CART AS IT ROLLS IN

42. E. C.U. Dion's face in a long lens shot. He watches in resigned disbelief as Paul (blurry) putters back and forth in the foreground. Dion's eyes learily follow Paul back and forth with a look of angry despair. Despondent, he looks to his left at...

SOUND FX: SOUND OF PAUL PUTTERING BACK AND FORTH

FIGURE 13.15

THE BOOKSHELVES
43.MONTAGE of shots of strange collected things on the shelves, bugs, butterflies, cufflinks.

44. E.C.U. Dion as he turns to look forward again

45. Dion's P.O.V. past his feet. We see that Paul has set the monitor up to the video camera, as Dion's face is caught live in close-up on the screen.

FIGURE 13.16

46. E.C.U. Dion turns his head in disgust and once again looks at the shelves to his left.

THE BOOKSHELVES.
47. MONTAGE of more objects. We see more butterflies. Trinkets. We see something we hadn't noticed before. Jars WITH AMPUTATED HUMAN FINGERS IN THEM.

48. E.C.U. Dion's face as his eyes widen in disbelief.

FIGURE 13.17

49. Closer shot of jars of fingers.

50. E.C.U. Paul's hand as he writes down the date on the jar. we tilt up to an C.U. of Paul. He turns to look at Dion.

SOUND FX: SOUND OF PEN SCRIBBLING

TILT UP

51. E.C.U. Dion's strained face as he looks down towards his hand

FIGURE 13.18

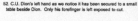

52. C.U. Dion's left hand as we notice it has been secured to a small table beside Dion. Only his forefinger is left exposed to cut.

53. E.C.U. Dion. Dremel tool with electric saw blurry in foreground. We rack focus.

SOUND FX: ELECTRIC CUTTING INSTRUMENT WHIRRING.

54. C.U. Dion's P.O.V. We see Paul moving forward with the cutting instrument. We move past Paul and push into the C.U. of Dion on the video monitor that eventually fills frame. The sound of the electric blade grows louder as we cut away to black. Simple white titles appear over the black reading " The Collector". Credits roll.

SOUND FX: SOUND OF DION'S WHIMPERING, HIS BREATHING BECOMING MORE LABORED.
THE SOUND OF THE ELECTRIC CUTTING INSTRUMENT WHIRRING.

FIGURE 13.19

THE COLLECTOR

INTERVIEW WITH JEFF ZUGALE

First talk about your background and how you got into the industry.

I got into it the hard way. I came in kind of backwards. I did not go to art school, but I've been drawing since I was a little kid. I first started out in the music business and that didn't wind up working out so I had to get a real job. And I wound up working at a print place. So I worked in print and reprographics and color xerox and then large format digital printing and poster stuff. And I started doing graphic design along with that because here I am sitting at a computer with Illustrator and Photoshop and QuarkXPress on it so I learned all those things. I did graphic design at the print place and then at another print place and then I got hired out of there to work as the in-house designer at a construction company.

And this was about when?

This was about 1995. So really the professional artist career starts about where I started at the construction company. And I was just there doing in-house presentation and we were doing three or four presentations a week. It was a very busy construction company. From there I started doing some comics. I was working on a self-published title with my friend Chris. In 1998, I moved out here to California and I was working as a freelancer basically just doing comics and some graphic design and stuff while trying to get myself set up.

And where were you, New Jersey, right?

Yeah, New Jersey. Not a great place necessarily to make a living as an artist, whereas Los Angeles is a great place to live and work as an artist because there's a lot of art being made here. Then I freelanced, and I ran out of money. I had to get a day job. I went to work at a dot com as a web designer, but I went into book design and illustration there. It was Edmunds.com, the car site. At the time they were still publishing books so I had experience with that, so they put me in charge of that. And then from Edmunds I had been working on concept design and illustration and stuff like that on my own time; taking some classes at various places. And I got hired out of Edmunds to a video game company. So I went from being a web designer, graphic designer, a book producer, to concept artist in the space of a week.

And this was done on your own time . . .

Yeah, I did all my training on my own time. And some of it was on-the-job training because obviously there's down time at work. So if you have all that software to play with . . .

But you were doing graphic design at Edmunds. . . .

Mostly. I was doing web design, graphic design . . .

Not producing any art at this point . . .?

Well I wound up actually illustrating a book. I wound up producing the book as the book designer/production guy, just did the whole thing in InDesign, pretty much did it on my own. But it wound up being a book that had some cartoons–illustrated. So I did get to do some of that along with the graphic design. Web advertisements; we did a lot of that. The site needed to be redesigned a bit so . . . I really did it backwards. I've kind of been doing concept design and comics or board-like work since I was five or six, you know since I could pick up a pen. But I was doing that anyway, and it kind of went around the back way. It's good to go to art school. It's a quicker way to do it. I approve of that path rather than the one that I took. But it was fun.

So you got hired at a game company. How did you find out about that?

I had been starting to send out résumés and books to people and getting various responses back. But a really good friend of mine who was working there as a writer said, "Hey, they really need a concept artist and not only can you do the job technically, but they need a guy who can work on *The Sopranos*, and you're from New Jersey, and you're Italian and so is the art director. So you should come in and talk to this guy, I think you could do real well on our team." And it turned out it worked really well. I'm from north New Jersey. That's where I grew up. So if you ever watch *The Sopranos*, and you look at the background, that's where I grew up pretty much. So it was really easy to just slip right into just drawing where I grew up when I was a kid.

And your friend knew that you were familiar with working in . . .

Oh yeah. I had done some storyboards and concept design for him. He makes his own films. He's a screenwriter when he can. I'd done a bunch of stuff for him on that. He'd seen all my comics. So it just turned out to be kind of a magic mix where it was like "Hey, that's pretty nice, here's this kid from New Jersey who knows Jersey, he knows *The Sopranos* really well, he knows the whole thing, so . . ."

So do you want to say the name of the company?

It was 7 Studios. Actually Damon Conn, he was my boss. He hired me.

So you were working over there on *The Sopranos* doing concept art . . .

Concept and storyboards. It was one of those games with a lot of cinematic stuff in it. It's based on a television show, so every five minutes or so, there's some kind of interaction where either you're watching a conversation between other players or you're part of the conversation. And you're . . . kind of like the Bioware system—Knights of the Republic, or any of those Bioware role playing games, you have choices of things you can say or you have a chance to interact with people. So all those things need to be boarded out to a certain extent. And there are cinematics on top of that. There are in-game cinematics and then rendered cinematics. They all needed storyboards. So I wound up doing a lot of that along with all the concept and character design. There were a lot of characters.

What kind of things did you show them in your portfolio?

I showed them my all comic book work. I showed them a lot of—let's see most of what I had done up to that point besides comics was sort of sci-fi design, but a lot of it had architecture in it, and they were going to be doing a lot of environment design at that place. I basically wound up sketching some stuff right there with the art director when I went in for the interview. He was like, "How would you do this?" And I whipped out a pen and started sketching and was like, "This is just like West Orange where I used to ride my bike down in this place, and you can do this and can do this and this." So I didn't necessarily have so much stuff that was perfectly applicable to the job, but because of my background and my enthusiasm for the project—I love *The Sopranos* . . . great show . . . I think that's kind of what worked. I had to step up my game real quick with the character stuff because all my character designs at that point had been comic book type stuff so my art had been ink and pencil and stuff like that, and I had to do photorealistic characters for this thing. And I had to do it starting on the second day I was there. So I wound up doing about 70 photo-rendered painted characters. So the reason we needed to do that was because HBO had to sign off on all the characters, and they're not used to working with pencil drawings or ink drawings or anything like that or even 3D models. They're used to working with people. We needed to show them art that looked reasonably . . . like actual photographic people. As if it were an audition.

What was the day to day like working at a video game company? What was the pace like, who do you answer to?

Well I worked for the art director, and through the art director, for the producer. Basically, I got handed a list of stuff to do and they said, "Hey, we need all these by the end of the week," or by the end of the day or whatever. Sometimes I would finish something and say, "Hey, I'm done with that," and they'd say, "Okay, here's the next thing, just do this. . . ." It was pretty fast paced, because there was a lot of stuff that needed to be done. The character paintings wound up—I wasn't really allowed more than a couple of days, so I had to learn how to . . .

How many were you expected to do in a day?

Like a half of one. By the end of the thing—by number 40 or so—I was able to do one in about a day. The later characters seemed to need not necessarily as much detail. Sometimes they would ask for more.

These are like full turnarounds[1] or . . .

No it's just a single painting. It's a single painting, but of a full-length character in costume, with some kind of indication of their attitude, along with the way their face looks and their hairstyle and their clothing. So if they say, "Hey, we need 'young, mob thug from Philly—a Philadelphia mob thug,'" he's got to have a certain kind of attitude, and I had to find a pose that gave off the attitude, and I had to find the clothes that give the attitude, and the facial expression and stuff like that. And I had a couple of days to do each one.

So you did character design, but I understand that you also did concept.

A lot of environmental design. I didn't have to design cars or anything like that because we just used real old stuff. But there were neighborhoods and there were buildings, there were interior locations. I designed a casino, a whole dock complex, a couple of warehouses—you do a lot of warehouses in video games, There was a law office that we did, there was a converted Victorian house—there's a lot of those in New Jersey. And I wound up doing floor plans for everything as well as just drawings. So that was running concurrently with the character stuff. They'd say, "Okay, we need this character by the end of the day tomorrow, but here are some environments you can put him in." And I'd sort of run my own show as that would go. And it changes because the producer will realize, "Oh we need this and we need it very quickly, so you have drop everything and whip that thing out and turn it in to the producer so we can send it to the client."

So you did environmental art, you did characters, and you also did storyboards?

Right, the storyboard stuff—a few things were done pretty early because they needed to be worked into game mechanics—but for the cinematic stuff we had to be more conversational than scenario based stuff, it was all done later in the game. The action stuff was all basically things like, "Okay, here's the lead character, and you're going to take this guy's head and slam it against a wall or against a curb," and I had to show how the control would be moved and then show a drawing of what the guy was doing as the control was run. So that was the action related stuff. We did a lot of stuff where I was doing camera spec when we were trying to figure out, "Where's the camera going to be?" "How's it going to interact with the environment?" There's a lot of things that go on in video games, sort of in the background that you don't really think about, but a lot of that stuff needs to be enumerated, like the camera's got to be 10 feet behind the guy or five feet behind the guy, and when he goes around the corner, is it going to rotate around with him? Is the architecture going to go transparent and the camera's going to fly through it? And we draw through a bunch of scenarios.

And these are for the interactive parts. You wouldn't normally expect that to be something that would be storyboarded.

It was more like a set of sequence drawings, but it was very much like a storyboard. So here's the guy, and he comes into this part of the garage. And there are columns that hold up the ceiling and then there are cars. How is the camera going to react to the columns or the cars if he does this? How's the camera going to react to the ceiling or the walls if he does that? And there's a lot of scenario based stuff like that.

You had to think a lot about cinematic stuff even for gameplay stuff.

In either a first person game or a third person game where you're either looking over your shoulder or you're looking through the character's eyes, there's always a consideration of "What's that frame going to look like? What's the character going to see?" There's always a lot of rendering stuff for video games. The Turok game from a couple years ago comes to mind, where they did a whole lot of paintings of "Here's what this should look like from the character's eyes as a first-person shooter." And even further along in that process they got actual frame renders from the game and painted over them to say, "Okay, it should be improved this much, and the lighting should be like this." So yeah, there's a lot of cinematic stuff that goes into any video game that has that kind of play in them.

Are you doing stuff like some of the action movement for some of these kinds of boards, maybe to help direct the animators at all? Posing stuff out?

A few things I have posed out, and some fight choreography. At the very beginning, I did probably eight different fight scenes, like interactive, just showing the things that would happen during the fight scene, blocking out where and when these things would happen. Like the dialogue thing where you get to choose things you say? Well sometimes when you choose one thing to say, it just enrages the guy who you're talking to and he stands up and takes whack at you. And then during the fight, you have choices of things to do during a fight. You're sitting there, and you'll throw a few punches, and then some kind of grapple takes place. And there in the grapple, either you have to move the controls or you've got to hit a button or something like that. Then that branches. If you win the struggle, you whack the guy's head into a filing cabinet; if you lose the struggle, he shoves you back in the window, so you're out the window.

I would imagine with this branching thing, it could translate into a lot of boards because there are so many different things that could happen.

Right. And then you have to bring it back around. There's only two endings to this, so we can't branch it too far and all the branches have to come back in. But the actual actions, where I would show, "Okay, you're going to grab the guy here, and you're going to run over to the window, and then you're going to slam him against the wall." That kind of stuff. So there was comic book style fight images put in there. They could have been done in animatics, but we didn't actually do that.

And later on you ended up doing the non-gameplay cinematics?

Right. The more conversational stuff.

And this, I imagine, took place pretty close to the end of the production?

In this particular instance it took place very close to the end, probably too close to the end of the production. And what actually wound up happening was they realized with about six weeks to go, that the design team—who were supposed to be the ones who were going to set up these cinematic things in the game—were not going to be able to do that because they had too much work to do. And myself and the other concept artists and a couple of the other game artists didn't really have a lot to do, so the programming team whipped up a tool in a couple of days to allow us to place camera, and block characters out through a scene. And myself, the other concept artists, and two other guys wound up doing actually all of the in-game cinematic using that tool in four weeks, four and a half weeks.

So the other guys on the team didn't really have so much to do with this?

Well, the design team was supposed to do it, and they had done a lot of the blocking, but the actual execution of going into the game engine and setting the characters where they were going to go and putting the camera where it was going to be on each line of dialogue—the tool was locked to the character who was speaking. So when a character was speaking, it would switch to a camera that was attached to that line of dialogue. You could put that camera anywhere.

Were you doing drawn animation for anything?

No, this was actually done in the engine. The characters had their own speech animations and some canned walking or waving or animations like that already created. The animators had actually already done all that. And we had to take each line of dialogue and put the character where we wanted them to be—give them that behavior.

So you were really doing . . .?

Working in the game engine.

So you were not so much doing storyboards but you were doing previs?

No, it wasn't even previs, it was as if we were shooting the scene for real. And we had to do some boarding for that, especially for the other guys who were not concept artists or storyboard artists or designers or . . . who didn't have any experience doing that. Myself and the other concept artists, we went in and set up a whole bunch of generic cameras. So one would be over the shoulder, a close shot, over the shoulder for the back, you could do a left side two-shot, a right side two-shot. And we'd have to coach these guys through all those rules of don't break the 180, flip the thing back and forth when these people are talking, how to block out a change so that we're going to move this guy over here, how to make that happen so the eyes aren't jarring. We had to do a bunch of boards for that to show the other guys who were working . . .

These are all drawn boards?

Yes, these were drawn boards. So we could say, "Here's a situation that we're going to have and this is how you block it out. If you have any questions, refer to this visual guide, it will be easier than asking us questions, because we're just as busy as you are." So for four and a half weeks of twelve hour days, we banged out all our cinematics. And they worked pretty well. At that point, one of the things about being at a video game company if you're a 2D artist, is you may wind up being asked to do a lot of other things besides the 2D art. Concept artists tend to work pretty heavily at the beginning of a project, and if you've only got one or two games in the house, when you're done with the concept art, they're going to say, "We need you to do this." They may set you up with a completely different skill, maybe you'll be asked to start building object models—really simple 3D stuff—and they'll show you how to do that or some other kind of actual production work.

What percentage of your time would you say is devoted to storyboards versus concept work?

At the video game company, I would say about 30 percent. I did a lot of boards for *Sopranos*, I did a lot of boards for *Pirates*, because those cinematics for *Pirates [of the Caribbean]*, they were all outsourced. So we had to do boards for all of those. They weren't particularly complex boards, they were pretty quickly drawn out, but they were at least sequence boards and some shot layouts. About 30 percent.

So you worked on *Sopranos* then you worked on *Pirates* . . . ?

Pirates of the Caribbean: The Legend of Jack Sparrow. Yeah, and that was concurrent with the last part of *The Sopranos* game.

So generally, there's more than one game going and they're staggered.

Yeah, most studios, they keep you busy, and when you're not busy, they'll find something else for you to do, because it costs too much to have you just sitting around.

When I worked in the game industry, there are rare times that you'll be sitting idle, which is a very different thing from any film—they have you on for when you're needed and you're gone when you're not. . . .

Right, and that's something that doesn't happen so much at video game companies. Video game companies tend to want to hire people and have them in there as part of the family. It really is kind of a family mentality. It's like "we want everybody on the team to be on the team all the time and in here." So that's why, in a lot of cases, if you want to work at a video game company, it's helpful to have other skills besides the one thing that you love to do. So if you're a concept artist, it's helpful if you can do storyboards. It's helpful if you know something about 3D, and can do a little bit of 3D modeling. Or if you can do

Photoshop texture, so you can help do faces and clothes and so forth. So the game business is very often a business where your specialty is going to be needed, but it's going to be really helpful to be able to do two or three other things fairly well. You don't have to be a great 3D modeler, but if you can bang together a potted plant in less than a day, then you'll probably be okay.

So how did you move into freelancing?

Oh, I got laid off.

That happens, too. That's another reality.

I was freelancing before that. I've had my own little freelance business since I moved to California, so I've been around 13 or 14 years now. But it was much harder to do at the beginning. Once I had gotten a lot more experience, it was easier for me to get work. So I got laid off in October of 2008. We were in the middle of working on—I don't know if you remember the film *Nine*? The one with the little rag doll critters? Pretty cool movie—we were working on the video game for that, and then the publisher went under. And we didn't have any money to keep the concept people on. So the concept guys got laid off, a bunch of designers and a whole bunch of people got laid off at that point. Subsequently the company has been shut down, unfortunately—just last month. But in October of 2008, I got laid off, and I got a decent severance for it, and I got unemployment. But then I said, this is a good opportunity to try and go freelance. I asked around some friends, and our mutual friend Trevor Goring suggested I go to this agency Famous Frames and see if they could get me some work and they did in fact get me work, and then I went out and got some work doing some other stuff on my own.

Was it your board work from the game company that got you into Famous Frames?[2]

Boards and illustrations, because I did a lot of illustration work and concept design. And a lot of that was painting, so I went in with everything I had and showed them all my boards and we went from there. It took them a while to get me the kind of commercial board work that is now the main thing I do. Once they got me one or two jobs doing that, it was real easy to start getting more. It wasn't hard for me to get in at Famous Frames because I had such a pile of work to show, and some of it was really intricate painting and stuff. You know, it was visually impressive. Not necessarily the kind of thing you do in storyboards, but it was like, "Yeah, okay, clearly you're an artist and you can handle this."

Did you find yourself getting a lot of game related work or things like that from Famous Frames?

They haven't gotten me any game concept or storyboard work, because again, that's something the game companies try to keep in house. But I wound up doing actually a bunch of cover art for games, for UbiSoft. I've done like five different ones, but only one of them was actually used. But they paid me for it, obviously; it was great. But yeah, not so much game work, most of the stuff that Famous gives me is advertising storyboards. And it's not usually shooting boards, it's pitch boards. Which is kind of a different world; it's not the same as doing shooting boards. But it's good work and it pays well, and it's fun. . . .

And pitch boards can be prettier. . . .

Yeah, the pitch boards—you don't have to do as many of them in a day, but they're all color and you can do a pretty nice rendering job on them. I stick with kind of an old school marker style that's been digitized.

And you work in Photoshop, right?

For those boards, I mostly work in Painter. Painter allows me to do the kind of stuff that I want to do for those boards much faster than Photoshop does. That may be changing with the latest version of Photoshop where the brushes are much more programmable. But I've got some marker brushes and kind of an oil brush that mixes colors for me in Painter that I've used for years and I'm really, really quick with those.

Can you compare and contrast working freelance with working in house doing storyboards?

Well, your hourly rate's a lot higher. But you never know when you're going to have work. If you're with an agency that's great, because they do the leg work for you. They take a percentage, but it's worth it. They call you up and say, "Hey, I've got a job for you at such-and-so," and you go and you do the job and there it is and you get a paycheck. So that's nice. But working as a freelancer without an agent, that's much harder. It takes a lot of networking and it takes a lot of calling people up and sending out postcards . . . So yeah, there's a lot of self-promotion, a lot more research you have to do to find out who's doing what and where it's being done and who you should talk to about finding out who the art director is or the production designer is or just who's doing what and sending them the right stuff.

What are some examples of things you can use to promote yourself a bit to get work?

I have actually found that the most effective thing to do is to find out who's doing stuff and actually physically go there and bring your book or your iPad or whatever you have and talk to people. There is no substitute for networking or even just showing up and saying, "Hey, I'm an artist, here's my book." They might not look at it right away, but if you will leave something for them to look at, they will eventually look at it. I've done a lot of work for a company called Zoic Studio. They're a visual effects house. They work mostly on television shows and commercials. They do Fringe, they do Game, they do CSI. I got work with them because I went to one of the Gnomon School events where they had all the artists there, and they usually have a little career day. And there were a couple of people from Zoic there and I had really enjoyed what they did on Battlestar Galactica and Firefly and I just went over there and I told them that. I said, "Hey, I really like what you guys do—Firefly looked fantastic, Battlestar looks great. I love drawing spaceships and working in sci-fi and if you guys are doing a lot of that, I would love to draw spaceships for you sometime." And I showed them my work, and they liked it, and I gave them my information, and six months later they called me up and asked me to design spaceships for them.

That's awesome. I think one message that's coming out is that even though there's a lot of internet stuff—though a lot of people like to do email blasts and stuff like that—face-to-face is . . .

It makes a big difference to actually talk to the people who you want to work for or somebody who works at the place where you want to work for. I think it was the L.A. Siggraph show in 2003 or something like that—I wound up talking to the recruiter from Bioware for like an hour. She went through every piece in my book and she was like, "Whoa, this is really good!" and she gave me lots of advice, and she was like, "This isn't the kind of stuff that I hire for, but here is the kind of stuff I hire for." And I just sat there and wrote down notes furiously. And I've kept in contact with her and they've pretty much got moved to wherever they are. It's a video game company, that's kind of the way it is. But I've kept in contact with that person. She's no longer at Bioware, she's at like an independent recruiting agency. She was at Bioware, and then she was at a similar game company, and now she's working on her own. Because everybody's feeling the pinch with the financial dust up. So there's no substitute for talking to people. Introduce yourself. Give them your card. Have your stuff to show them. iPhones are good for showing stuff, iPads are better because they're so large. I got to show Stephan Martiniere my entire portfolio at Comic-Con this past year just because he was there, and I had talked to him. He did a thing at CBA and I had talked to him there, and he remembered me so I showed him all my stuff. And he's the art director at Id and he was working on Rage, that's his thing. So it's good to be able to do that. Postcards can help, as long as they get to the right people and they look really good. I can only say that you're work's got to be good. It's got to look good. You've got to look at the people who are at the top of your game of what you want to do, if you want to be a storyboard artist or concept artist or whatever. Look at the people who are doing the top end stuff and try to make your stuff look as much like that as possible. And if you don't have that skill, go to school and learn it. Find resources. The quality of the work is what's going to catch their eye and your enthusiasm and personality is what's going to help sell you.

For those in school or just starting out and wanting to be a storyboard artist, what kind of advice would you give?

Knowing what I know now . . . First of all, decide what kind of storyboards you really have the most fun working on and try to do a book full of those. So if you think you want to work for Pixar some day as a storyboard artist, watch every single Pixar movie and freeze frame them, and sketch what's going on. Do an entire sequence where you stop the thing every two or three seconds and sketch that. And look and see what those look like as storyboards, because that's basically what you'll be doing.

That's great for looking at poses and composition and . . .

And flow . . . Being able to stop a DVD, and look what's going on and just look at that scene in its own point. You'll get a feel for taking that thing and seeing where the beats are. Like, here's where this character enters the frame; that's really important. What's the next thing that happens? Something happens that the character reacts to. Make sure you sketch that. Go through the sequence and find all those little important things. And find out, especially with Pixar movies—I mean I can go on all day about *The Incredibles*. There's so much fabulous, just so eye-moving . . . eye-control, that's really what it is—eye control. There are so many subtle little things, with hands moving, and eyes moving, even hair moving stuff in *The Incredibles*, where your eye is being bounced around that scene exactly where it needs to be every single time. That's the kind of thing that you want to learn, because you're doing it in a storyboard. Every frame that you do has to control the viewer's eye. You've got to have the 1-2-3 read: the first thing you see, the second thing you see . . . So study that and try to do a bunch of boards in front of your own stuff. If you can get your hands on film scripts—any kind of scripts—grab those, download them, read them, board them through in your head. A fun one to try to play with is if you can get the original version of the script to *Star Wars* which is nothing like anything that was actually made, the very first original version of the script . . . that's a fun one. Storm off and just say, "Okay, George Lucas never did this film, because it was so different from the one they made." And board that out and do some sequences from it. There are so many different kinds of storyboarding, really cinematic stuff. There's examples of it you can see. So with films, that would be my suggestion: take those DVDs and do that and just dig into it. There's some comic book artists who you should probably be studying because they're masters of moving your eye around the frame—Will Eisner is probably one of the best ones. One of my personal favorites who a lot of people don't know about is Adam Warren. He's one of the most brilliant. One of the books that he did, the Dirty Pair book called Sim Hell—he wound up coloring it, and I have the original black and white version—I used to open that thing up to get reference for stuff—everytime I would open that book, I would wind up reading it to the end. And I didn't know why. And I noticed that after the fifth time I did this—every time I pick up this book, I can't put it down, I have to read to the end. The reason why, I found, I looked at the pages and Adam has everything set up so that your eye is just literally, the book just reaches out and grabs your eyes and pulls you through. You literally cannot resist the power of this force. There's a lot of comic book artists, the old school guys who are really, really good at it. Not so many of the new guys, I think. Because they're making . . . every frame is like a splash page almost. But the older guys were really sensitive to story. Kirby is a good example, he does great work. Wally Wood. You know who 's actually pretty good at it? Michael Golden, a more of a modern kind of artist, he does that too. Hergé—Tintin. Moebius, any of Moebius' stuff if you can get your hands on that, because he does fantastic storyboards too. So eye-direction—really, really important. Cinematography—really important. *Butch Cassidy and the Sundance Kid.* There are so many fabulous shots in that film. That is one of the very best films to study if you want to learn about cinematography, shot composition, shot sequence. That thing alone is a course. You could teach that for a whole year. Just go frame by frame. There's one sequence at the beginning where it's all in sepia tone, where there's a guy standing in the corner, and because of the black/white, you don't see him at first, because he doesn't move. Because of the way the black and white is dancing across that shot. And then he moves from the corner where he was standing. I was like, "Oh my God! Where did that guy come from?!" And he was just so perfectly worked into the scene, and when he starts moving, it's exactly at the point where someone needs to move to increase the menace. Because Sundance is standing there and this guy's behind him. And you don't see this guy behind him. And he don't know he's there either. And then you see this guy move to a position where he can shoot him in the back. So very subtle, but really, really, really powerful kind of thing. And it's just a very simple blocking move, but in composition, it's a brilliant piece.

INTERVIEW WITH JOSH SHEPPARD (www.thestoryboardartist.com)

My name is Josh Sheppard. I work as a live action storyboard artist in Los Angeles, and for the past few years I work pretty much only on films, but I did do shooting boards for TV commercials and music videos before that for eight or nine years running around Los Angeles.

FIGURE 13.20
Josh Sheppard.

Why are storyboards important?

Why are storyboards important? Storyboards are important because it's the quickest and cheapest way to make sure that the story gets told in an effective and efficient way. Especially with the way films are so complex these days, there are so many people involved. I've seen it happen many times and every live action board artist has seen this—where the storytelling, the core story of either the whole movie or a sequence or even a scene gets lost. And what it gets lost in is usually the chaos of production, sometimes it's just the action, the complicated action that is happening on screen, sometimes it's visual effects, sometimes it's all of the above. People that don't work in the film business and even some that do, I think, are always surprised to hear that very often there is no one, or there's almost no one, that is just looking out for the story. The writer is doing their job, the director of photography is doing their job, the director has many jobs to do, so they're hopefully looking out for just the story, but it does happen very often that it comes down, at least from my perspective, to only one person—that's the storyboard artist. Visual effects is doing their thing, everybody's doing their job and basically the storyboard artist is in the difficult position of saying, "Wait, this isn't what this scene is supposed to be about. The director, when we discussed it—the director is not here right now—but the director when we discussed it said this scene is supposed to be about how she loses her boyfriend when the monster tears a building down and it collapses on him or whatever. That to me means that the scene is about her. It's not about all this crazy visual effects. We can have that stuff but the camerawork and shots and where we shoot it from and how we shoot it needs to be all about that actress in that moment. The director is going to want, when the camera is there and the actress is there, that's what they're going to try to be focusing on, and so that's why I think we should basically stage the shots in this way."

That little speech would be a speech I'd be giving to the previs team I'm working with or the previs supervisor, or very often these days, the previs supervisor is really working for the visual effects department head. They are doing a great job but very often they have their own agenda which is making awesome shots. Yes we need awesome shots in movies, but awesome shots don't make movies. It's the movie moments that really get you. I remember watching ET with my kids. First time they'd ever seen it, and when *ET* is sick and looks like he's dying, both of them are there with tears in their eyes saying, "Is ET going to die?" Well, that's a movie moment and even though they didn't have a CG version of ET—they just had this puppet—the director really figured out how to milk that scene for all that it was worth.

That's the kind of thing that we are always trying to do, even in the midst of all the millions of other things that are going on. The different things that the different department heads want to happen while we're planning it or while we're there.

I wanted to talk a little bit about, in my experience, how storyboards are used these days and how sometimes they are misused or not used all. The first example that comes to mind is I've done storyboards for re-shoots on a few films where it's a film that I didn't work on, they've already filmed it, everybody has gone home. They're in the process of editing it and the producers and the director come to the conclusion that this film unfortunately needs re-shoots. There's all kinds of different reasons. Sometimes it just needs to be rewritten, sometimes some performances weren't as good, etc. In these two examples the producers told me that they basically didn't get all the coverage to tell their story. And I said, "Well did you work with a storyboard artist?" And they said, "No." Now, maybe I'm just advocating for my own craft, but I feel pretty strongly that if they had somebody storyboard the scenes with the director, that would have given the director an opportunity to preplan it and to look at it and say, "I think here we're going to want this type of coverage. We're going to need a moment where we see the two of them holding hands looking over the Grand Canyon or whatever." That's what storyboarding is all about. It's a way to preplan your shoot so that you get all the shots that you need to tell a story.

Some directors are experienced enough, they're going to think of it right there on the day, and other members of the team too. I've worked with first assistant directors who are so experienced that they may know the type of shots that they are going to need. I've seen them actually put these things in their schedule.

They're very experienced people. But, I think that the most effective way to plan something like this out is just to have a storyboard of it. If there's a storyboard, then that drawing, even if it's the quickest little drawing, is going to go in the schedule.

There is going to be, if you look on the schedule later, that shot will be in there. It will have a shot number and it's planned, and so despite any chaos that happens when it comes, at night after the busy day of shooting, the AD [assistant director] will look at that with the director, they'll look at the schedule, and they'll say, "Oh, tomorrow we'll be doing this shot, that shot, and that shot." They get up in the morning, they get there, there is all kinds of things going on. People make mistakes, they forget to get shots, but if it's all planned out ahead of time then you don't have to go through that.

In this particular case I sat down with the editor and looked at the scene and you could tell, now that they shot the stuff and had the stuff edited together, it was very obvious what shots were missing. Unfortunately the whole crew had gone home months ago, they don't have the equipment, don't have the actors, don't have the location. They had to get a mini production set up again at great expense and go and shoot the re-shoots. I don't know how much money it cost them, but it was a ton of money just to get these shots that, again, it's just my perspective, but they could have saved thousands of dollars if they would have just had a storyboard artist sit there and make the director kick the story shots around with the artist or even just tell the artist what to do, "Draw this." But in this case, instead, I got the edit, took screenshots of it, dropped the screenshots into my storyboard template, and then drew the shots that we needed where they were supposed to be. Then I also wrote in the dialogue that was existing from the edit so that it was very clear where this would fit. Then I gave those boards to the editor and the editor cut the storyboards into the edit, so it was basically a movie with a few of my crappy drawings in there. But as they cut it together they could see, "Yes, this is gonna work." So then they made a whole new schedule for, whatever, a two or three day re-shoot schedule or something and they flew thousands of miles away to do this.

I think that there is a little bit of a misconception sometimes about storyboards and what they are and how to use them. I've seen storyboards from, say, a game company where they had artists working on a storyboarding cinematic for this game and then they'll send it to a previs company. But they don't actually send a storyboard, which would be shots with descriptions and maybe dialogue in sequence with an indication of whether these three drawings in a row indicate a shot and a cut and a shot and a cut, or if it's shot frame A and then frame B and then a cut. What they do is they send basically some JPEGs, and I've seen the previs supervisor, previs artists sit there and toggle through by hitting the arrow key, looking at these things, you can't tell anything. Sometimes it's obvious, but often you look at it and you can't tell if this is a single shot and then you're supposed to cut and go to the next shot or if it's a sequence. What that means is the animator will end up sitting there making their best guess. Like if there's an arrow moving through the frame, does that mean that the character is walking and the camera is still, or does it mean the camera is walking with the character, or does it mean that the camera is moving past the character? Because the storyboard artist isn't there, it's up to somebody to interpret that. Sometimes the previs animator can do a fine job of interpreting it. Sometimes their previs supervisor can do a fine job of interpreting it, and sometimes there's a storyboard artist there who may not have even done the drawings who can look at it and take a best guess. But I think a good storyboard has to be done completely, meaning full descriptions and an indication of whether to cut or continue and any notes or overheads of diagrams that show different department heads what and where you think this should be staged and all the other information.

In my work working at the Third Floor previs company, I've been pleasantly surprised that they were smart enough at what they do to know that they need somebody full time to—more than one person actually—to make storyboards for projects they're working on or to interpret existing storyboards that come in to make sure that the story is told in the most effective way. I was working on a project where we had three different previs teams and two supervisors or something. So I just made an overhead of this 80-page storyboard for the whole team so that they could look at this and they'll know exactly where the camera is supposed to be. This is an example of—it's almost like doing re-shoots. This was another artist's drawing and here I indicated that it's a cut. The next frame isn't even a drawing, it's a screen capture from the previs, and I revised it by putting up an arrow over there that says "pan down" and indicated that it is A and B. Then the next thing is a drawing, so it's sort of a hybrid storyboard from what we used to do. Here this is one of those cases where we got in doing multiple passes at this very difficult sequence, and at one point, between the director and the studio, they wanted to see two different versions of this huge sequence. To make sense of it all between us three storyboard artists, the two previs supervisors, the two or three previs teams, and the visual effects people, and the studio people, I went and screen captured from the existing previs and made a storyboard out of it again so that everybody could tell what this was, and in some cases, what particular take it was. I would put in the actual shot number of the shot from the previs sequence. So it's just one of those ways that helps everybody stay organized and helps a complicated process stay focused on story.

This was an example of the opening of a movie. They had already shot the movie and hired animators and a title company to come through and animate the opening, but the studio said it wasn't working, so it was kind of like re-shoots. I got this QuickTime movie of it and I screen captured it and went through and just redrew parts of it. And that got it approved and they then went and hired another animator and did more visual effects work on it, but it was something that just helped to keep everything organized. I've also done that with visual effects where they've shot the film and they've got previs in there to indicate what the visual effect is supposed to be, but maybe they have made a last minute tweak and they need a visual effect to work story wise. So I'll get the edit or one of the dailies from the film, plus I'll get the previs that was cooked up long before they filmed it, and I'll kind of cobble the two together and make a new storyboard showing the visual effect working story wise. Because the visual effect pipeline works with individual shots. Basically they break them down, they give them a shot number and they hand them off to individual artists. I'm generalizing, but in my experience that's what I've seen.

And of course, what can get lost in there is story. You can have one artist working on one shot, another artist working on another shot, and those two shots are going to be edited together and they're supposed to work together. But those two artists may not talk to each other. In fact sometimes they're actually at different companies on different continents. There are people that are supposed to make sure that doesn't happen, but they often have much bigger fish to fry, basically, and especially in visual effects and postproduction when it's getting closer and they're chasing a release date for the film, it can get pretty hairy trying to get their job done, let alone making sure the story works.

I've had jobs where I didn't really draw very much but I went in and I basically screen captured the stuff, did a little bit of Photoshopping on it, put it together in a storyboard and gave it back to them showing how these visual effects shots that are in progress should be done just slightly different, just so they all will cut together. A job like that sometimes doesn't last very long, it might only be a day's work or it might end up being a week's worth of work—it depends. It can be done at a visual effects house or sometimes it's the previs company that's doing it. What else do I have to show you here? Well, these little thumbnails. Sometimes doing work like this, when they need so much work done so quickly, I just will do stuff really just very quickly, because I know that this isn't a drawing that's going to be published and distributed to all the department heads and we're going to have big meetings on it. Sometimes this drawing may only live for 20 minutes while the previs artist is cooking it up. Let's see if there is anything else, any other thoughts I had.

I think that's the reason why storyboarding is so important, is to plan and save money and make sure the story gets told. You know, we've all heard examples of movies that everybody is waiting to come out and then it doesn't come out for an extra eight months. Very often that's just marketing and visual effects postproduction issues, but also sometimes it's story issues. Sometimes there's— I've worked on comedies where they're almost done shooting the film and they basically want more funny scenes. And so the writers are scrambling to cook up funny gags and then the director will hire a storyboard artist to come and draw those gags and drop them into the edit, the rough edit as it's being built, and see if, just from a storyboard, if they can see if this is going to work. Is it going to be funny? And the star who is the comedian will look at it and say, "I think that's gonna work, so let's shoot it tomorrow." So then they go and do, or they may say, "This isn't reading funny, it's taking too long."

Another thing with complicated films, an example from *Where the Wild Things Are*, some of the filmmaking processes are getting so complicated now that you need somebody to try and pull all the pieces together. In the case of *Where the Wild Things Are*, it was a unique situation because the characters were going to be in real suits, but the faces were going to be CG face replacement. The blocking of the characters was going to be dictated by a video shoot on a soundstage with the actors who are the voices. So this is very much like when you see the making of *Kung Fu Panda* and the actors are in a recording booth, doing the dialogue and also maybe making funny faces, and the animators will look at that funny face they made and put that into the animation. But in this case it was also the specific blocking when Gandall Feeney shoves some character and walks over there and lays down, that stuff had to go—I had to look at the videos and it went in the storyboard. Then his facial performance would later, maybe a year later or months and months later, inform what a CG animator would do to replace the plastic face. Then months later down the line when they were in the forest filming the thing, they'd have the storyboards and they could see the storyboard artist's drawing of the blocking that the actors had cooked up on that soundstage. Then they would recreate it in the forest there, and I'm sure change it there too, and try and get these big guys in these big suits to copy that blocking and that body language. And so it was the storyboards that were sort of pulling all that stuff together. Then we took that and we were sending it out to the writer and also Spike's editor, because he was also finding through his editorial process stuff that he felt just didn't work and he was sending that back to the director saying, "This whole thing that you guys did, this bit of business, it's just not working," or, "This feels slow," or whatever. So we all tried to work together, but in that case, it was one of those jobs where it was so complicated. I remember thinking, "How on earth would they do this without storyboards?" It could quickly spin into chaos and then you'd just have, you'd get there and nobody would know what to do and try to remember what they had planned. You can make notes until you're blue in the face but a picture is worth 1000 words.

What are some of your movie credits?

Um, movie credits. I worked recently on a movie that's coming out Christmas 2011 called *War Horse* for Steven Spielberg. It's based on a book about a horse in World War I. Before that, what have I worked on? There is a Bryan Singer film coming out, *Jack the Giant Killer*. I worked on *Where the Wild Things Are*. I was the lead storyboard artist on that, working with a bunch of really talented guys. I worked on *Hellboy II*, just off the top of my head. A lot of bad comedies. I worked on *Ladder 49*, a firefighting movie. I think that's all I can think of right now.

FIGURE 13.21
Storyboards by
Josh Sheppard.

FIGURE 13.22

FIGURE 13.23

FIGURE 13.24

FIGURE 13.25

FIGURE 13.26

FIGURE 13.27

FIGURE 13.28

FIGURE 13.29

FIGURE 13.30

FIGURE 13.31

FIGURE 13.32

FIGURE 13.33

FIGURE 13.34

FIGURE 13.35

FIGURE 13.36

FIGURE 13.37

FIGURE 13.38

FIGURE 13.39

FIGURE 13.40

FIGURE 13.41

FIGURE 13.42

FIGURE 13.43

FIGURE 13.44

Alright, let's start with your background—how did you get started in the industry? What is your, you know, educational or artistic background?

I got started in the industry—I moved to Los Angeles to get into film with, really, no plan or anything. I really had no idea what I was doing and I thought,"Well, I better go to film school." I applied to USC and I just talked to them and the program sounded like I just wasn't ready for it. It just sounded like the people who were in there were really super serious about film and I realized I'm a film fan, but I wouldn't say I'm really excited about being the director or writing scripts and all that kind of stuff. But I went and got work as a production assistant. I think I got a flyer off of a car and I ended up working for free on a student film. And from there, I kept, I just jumped to the next one, and within what feels like two weeks I actually had a paying job working at an office in a little tiny production company, basically just the producer and me. He was trying to get some film made and the director who was going to direct that film actually worked as a concept artist and storyboard artist. He was doing some storyboards for this film and that was the first time I had ever seen them. I just, somehow, you know I don't remember ever seeing a making-of book or documentary back in those days. It was, I wanna say, 1992 or so.

So that was the first time you had seen storyboards.

That was it. I know it's funny because everybody that I work with, seems to be that they saw *Star Wars* when they were a kid and then they found out everything they could about it and then hitchhiked to ILM and knocked on the door, or whatever. Well, for me, when *Star Wars* came out, I remember seeing on television—this would be in 1977 or something—just one brief shot of a sketch. It was a Ralph McQuarrie sketch I now know, a sketch of Darth Vader's helmet, and it was a different shape. At that age, say I was eight years old or something, I remember thinking, "Wow, that's cool! Somebody drew that!" And that was it. I never thought about it again until I saw this guy's storyboards in 1991, or whatever, '92. Mauro Borrelli, talented—do you know Mauro? Really talented

FIGURE 13.45
A page from
Josh Sheppard's
sketchbook.

concept artist, Mauro Borrelli. Trained at, I think at Cinecitta, the studios in Rome. Anyway, there he was drawing these storyboards, and me with no hope of . . . I didn't know what kind of job I was gonna get once I left that company. Well I saw these storyboards and I thought, "That I can do!" because I had always drawn, I was a big comic geek, like a lot of storyboard artists. But, I lost interest in the superheroes around age sixteen–seventeen. I continued drawing, but I just had no idea where I could ever make a living drawing. I didn't want to do, you know, superheroes in tights, so I didn't pursue that. I thought for a while about being a tattoo artist and I used to—I had a friend who was a tattoo artist—and I used to go to the tattoo studios with him and different friends and I noticed in those days, there wasn't a lot of drawing ability, you could say, back in the eighties, that I saw and so I thought I could draw and I could be a pretty good tattoo artist. But, I thought, "Well, I don't want to get a bunch of tattoos and you can't be a tattoo artist if you don't have any tattoos." I sold some drawings— they call it flash—at a tattoo studio once but it was like ten dollars, five dollars, you know, and I remember drawing at parties. Like, there would be—once in a while there would be—this is kind of in the punk scene back in the eighties— like, some guy traveling around, he had his own tattoo gun and people would be at the party, they'd be getting drunk, whatever, and they'd want a tattoo. A friend of mine would say, "Hey you draw it!" Then I would say, "Well I'll split the fee with the guy." That was one of my first—I mean, again, it was like ten bucks, fifteen bucks, whatever.

But anyway, so, I saw these storyboards and I even, I think, I had to deliver some papers to him working in some art department somewhere; I can't remember what it was. And so I got to walk through an art department. I saw the concept artists. I saw the storyboards. And I just thought, "Man, I could do this. There's nothing else in the world I could do but I could do this." So I asked him what to do and he said, "You gotta make a portfolio. If you don't have a good portfolio, you'll never make it." So I made a portfolio and I got some business cards made at one of those little machines in the grocery store. And my brother lived in Hollywood at the time so I gave him some of the business cards and he passed

FIGURE 13.46

them out at parties—you know, we were in our twenties or whatever. He said he passed them out to everyone wearing black, he figured they were in the film business! True story! And a guy called me, and his friend was an agent for storyboard artists. So I dropped off some stuff in an envelope—this was before email, and everything—and eventually it got to the agent and the agent called me. I went down there and then he had all these binders in the office of different board artists' stuff. And they said, "Look at this, you need to get to this level." And I looked very closely at the stuff, I think I even xeroxed some stuff and took it home and I started rebuilding my portfolio. I was real serious about it. I completely rebuilt my portfolio, submitted to them again, took all their advice, followed it. I didn't argue with them and I didn't realize it at the time but that was one of the keys to getting me started was just that I worked with them because, years later, the agent would—I'd be in the office, dropping something off or something and the agent would say, "Hey, look at this, some guy came in with some samples." And this happened, you know, a couple dozen times over the years. And I'd look at the stuff and they'd say, "What do you think?" I'd say, "Well, boy he can really draw. He's great at this and that." And then inevitably they would say, "Well yeah, but, you know, we asked him to do a couple more samples and right away he starts saying 'I went to this school and I, you know, I worked seven years in animation, and blah blah blah,' and basically saying, 'I'm not gonna do this, I gave you good samples—get me work.'" And it was a good lesson for me, realizing that, here's somebody who can draw a lot better than me, has a better education than me, but they're dead in the water because they are not willing to work with the agent. And the agent, from their perspective, is thinking, "I can't send this person out on a difficult commercial assignment because this is all I know about them is that they can draw well and that they've got attitude." So I always, as I moved along I tried to learn from other people's mistakes and their strengths, you know. There were some really good artists at the agency and I looked closely at what they were doing. I had always been copying. My education was copying from my favorite comic book artists, Jack Kirby and John Buscema and later Alex Tothe, of course. But with storyboards it is a different style, obviously, because you've got to work so quickly, and I just tried to look at it, copy the style, do what I had always done, and look at the kind of samples that they had, listen to the agent when the agent would say, "Well yeah, that sample is well drawn but it's boring," stuff like that.

How long was the period between when you first made contact with them and the time when they finally took you on?

It was just, it feels like it was just a few weeks, and—

So you were building your portfolio in just a few weeks pretty much from the ground up?

No, I had spent a couple of months, probably, dragging my feet and at a certain point I got real serious about it when I realized, like, I need to make a living. I can't keep driving, you know, being a PA and a driver. I want to make money

FIGURE 13.47
Another page from
Josh Sheppard's
sketchbook.

doing what I love. But I was living really cheap at the time, you know, we paid like seven hundred bucks a month rent and I drove a four hundred dollar car so, you know, my bills are a lot more nowadays. So yeah, it seems like I submitted stuff and within, maybe, six weeks or—I can't even remember, it's a long time ago but, they said, "Okay, we'll take you on." And I rather naively signed an exclusive contract. I always tell artists don't sign an exclusive contract with an agent unless they are already getting you work, but anyway. I had no other avenues, so I signed a contract and the first job I got was like, a Rolaids commercial—just the guy standing against a white BG talking. And the director told me exactly what she wanted and I went home, drew it up, brought it back, and they were happy. I remember being pretty surprised, the money was so good for what I had drawn. It was just like this guy standing there holding up a Rolaids and a close up of the—or it was Alka-Seltzer—you know, like, a close up of the glass with a—and I thought, "That wasn't too painful." You know, I just drew this up and I got paid a week or two later or something.

But the first year, I just didn't get a lot of work. There were a lot of other artists. So I think I made like, eleven thousand dollars the first year. It was a struggle. But I did take the jobs that other people didn't want, like, you know, working on, whatever, Thanksgiving or Memorial Day; working nights, doing all that work. And I learned a lot real fast because working, as you know, freelancing, you know, in those days your pager would go off and you would just call this number and they'd just say, "Can you be here in twenty minutes?" And you rush over—you don't know what it is, you don't know who. Because these production companies, commercial production companies in Los Angeles for some reason are often very anonymous—there's no sign, there is just an address. So, it was just a challenge even finding where the place was, getting there on time, and then, they're always busy and they don't—they assume that you have all this information. I've done many jobs where nobody knew my name, they just knew there was an illustrator and I didn't know what the job was for—they just told me what to draw. And I'd have to ask them when it was due and if there was any more work to do.

You know, it's very—it's a chaotic business, as you know. And then, the next year I got a whole lot more work and it just kept going from there. I think before the interview we were talking about the dot com years before the bubble burst and there was tons of work. I mean, there was a point, I remember I didn't save my money very well and it slowed down for like seven weeks and I was really broke—I had to borrow money from my agent. That's a painful thing to do. But aside from that, generally, there was just tons of work. And then after the dot com bubble burst I was well established enough. I still had clients that were working and that's about it.

Let's talk about what's your typical week like as a freelance storyboard artist. What's your day like or even your week like? How much time are you spending, looking for work and how do you get work, and what's it like once you get on the job?

Well it depends, when I was doing commercials and music videos—you're waiting for the phone to ring, so, even when I was very busy I was working three or four days a week. But, the other day I was still working on one of those, so really you're working, if you're really busy, you're working five days a week, but you're not running around in the car and going to production companies all the time. You gotta be at home drawing or in that office drawing. I'd get a job, and it would be a day or two of intense work, and then like a half day of revisions and then I'd be off the next day. It was a pretty good schedule. Nowadays I work in film so, when I got on a film, I get there at nine, I leave at seven, and it's just five days a week. And the job, the one I'm on right now, looks like it will be a year, which is pretty long for a film. The one before that was about four months. But they usually are something like, anywhere from, a month to four months, something like that, of just full time work.

I know some people work at home, but I prefer to work at the office because films are just so complicated, there's so many pieces to put together that I like to be there with the art department seeing concept art, with the set designers, having access to that, access to the assistant directors for the schedule, you know, get a copy of the new script. And also, I don't know if this is true but it seems to me that if I'm in the office, they can see how valuable I am rather than if I just show up every three days and give them a stack of xeroxes and leave. Going back to the commercial business—I was doing shooting boards for TV commercials and so I would get a call, I would show up there and it kind of always seemed to go like this. The production company would get the go ahead from their producer, basically, so they would say, "Okay, we're going to try to get this job for this beer commercial." And that decision would then put in motion a whole bunch of things. The producer would get the production manager to get their coordinator in and start calling people and inevitably the storyboard artist gets the call at about two o'clock: "Be here at three o'clock." And then you get there at three and they make you wait forty five minutes and then the director comes in and is busy and doesn't really have it together until four thirty and then they finally give you a copy of the agency boards, if they have them. A script, if they have it. Thumbnails maybe—sometimes yes, sometimes no. They may have location photos or they might want you to come with them to locations on a scout, or they might be in casting, so you gotta sit there and wait for that, talk to them in between actors coming in. And basically, they give you pieces of the puzzle, and then you ask them when they need it, and they always need it, basically, now. So there's a problem already that they don't have the boards and they're paying you and they want them now. So then you try and get them done as fast as you can and that means a lot of night work. I always tried to avoid it but there's really no way to do it. If they call you in the afternoon and they need it the next day, they've already told people they're going to have it the next day so you just gotta do it. And the music videos were similar, a similar dynamic to that although the deadline to get the boards seemed to be, sometimes it was a long deadline, like—nobody is in a big hurry—or it's like, you're actually there while they're filming and you're trying to draw stuff on the floor of the stage or whatever, so, it's a pretty chaotic business.

For the people who are just coming out of school, I'm sure they'd be interested in hearing about how the entire process works. How are you working with the director? Do you have a lot of access to the director? Do you ever find yourself in situations where you're in a studio, you don't know who or where anybody is, and you have to hunt down the director if you have any questions?

Absolutely. One funny story is, I got a call for some job—I didn't even know what it was really—but I assumed it was a TV commercial—turns out it was a pilot for some celebrity news show or something—this was years ago. But, I got there and there was a room full of people. Everybody was just standing up from this conference table and there was chaos everywhere and everybody was rushing out. The director was on the phone with his wife and she's in labor in the hospital and he's telling her, "I'm getting in the car, I'll be there in just a minute, I've just got one thing to take care of," and I realized what was going on and I just said— he knew I was the artist because I had my bag with me, I guess—and I just said, "You should go." So he split. And then I was alone in the conference room and I thought, "Well this is typical, I don't know what the job is—the director is gone, I know I'm never going to see him again. I don't know what's happening." And then finally, I went and got someone and they said, "Oh, yeah, we're going to get someone." I didn't really know what that meant, and I waited, you know, an hour, and somebody came in and said, "Are you the director?" I said, "Well I was hoping you were," and they said, "Am I?"

That's a pretty, kind of an outrageous situation, but it underscores the chaos of some of these jobs. And so I said, "Well let's—I think they called you in, like, to fill in for this director because his wife went into labor," and he said, "Oh okay," and then we sat down and then he said, "Well, I want a shot like this," and then at that point I always have to say, "Well, what is the job?" And they'll go, "Oh! You don't know? It's . . . You know, we're gonna do, whatever, a commercial for this, or a teaser for a TV show or something." Then I start to get a better idea of it, and then—so, in a way, to get the information from the director, whoever I'm working with, a lot of times I have to remind them that I don't know what job they're on, even though this may have taken up their whole week. And then I start asking them what the storyboards are for, because storyboards is a catch—all term that means something different to everyone.

Sometimes, it turns out—I remember one student filmmaker hired me to do storyboards when I was first starting out. I went to his house and he pulls out the Ralph McQuarrie book with those famous paintings that he did for George Lucas to get *Star Wars* launched. And he said, "I want some storyboards like this," and I was like, "Well those are paintings that took weeks to produce, I'm sure. I thought you wanted, like, quick sketches or something." At which point he explained to me what a storyboard was, you know, some college kid.

So a lot of times it's a process of trying to get the information out of the director. Really what you're trying to get at are the shots out of their head. Some directors are great at it. I remember working with Scottie Bergstein—he's a commercial director—and he knew what he wanted, he had his shot list written out before I got there and we would thumbnail it together and then he would say, "Add in any extra coverage you think and then we'll look at it together," and that was great because, you know, that's a director that is organized, knows what he's doing, knows what he needs me to do, explained it clearly to me, he knows I'm busy, he's busy, so we both can get to work. But there are plenty of directors who'd come in and they'd say, "Listen to this song," you know, they'd put headphones on me and then they'd just start babbling about, how "Isn't it cool in this movie how they do that shot, that shot in *Top Gun* is awesome," you know, and you're like, you don't want to stop them because they're enthusiastic but basically they're not helping you at all. And, sometimes those meetings would end and they would think that they gave you shots, like somehow they have this impression that they've helped you, but then you realize, "Well, this is another job where I'm just going to have to make it all up." They're not telling me to make it up but they're gone, there is a deadline, I gotta get it done, so I do that. Then when I give the boards to the producer or the production manager, whoever, they're assuming that those are the director's shots but sometimes the director hasn't even seen them. Hopefully the director does get to see them before the storyboard gets published to the production team but sometimes it doesn't happen. In film, it's a little bit similar, although, because film, you know, is at least 90 minutes long, they may not storyboard at all, but it's quite expensive obviously to do all the stunt and visual effects work and the schedule is tight. The director is more involved, but there are some who basically don't have time.

You've probably experienced this where they meet you and they say, "We're gonna get together," and then they never do. I mean, I've done—every storyboard artist has done—a dozen films where the director, for our purposes, may as well not even be there, just because they're in New York casting or they're scouting or doing this and that. That's a pretty nerve wracking situation because if the storyboard artist doesn't have access to the director it means that a lot of other departments don't as well. And so they start coming to you—I mean every department comes if it's a situation like that. You get a second unit director coming in, you get transportation people, stunt people, even location people and they're asking questions and you can't really say, "Well, I don't know, I never talked to the director. I'm making this up as I go." So they come in and they look at your storyboards sitting on your desk and they start asking specific questions and you realize, "Well, I guess I have to just believe in this sequence that I'm drawing as I go along and nobody has looked at it and make sure I tell these different department heads that this is a work in progress, this may not be the shots." And then they say, "Can I get a xerox of it?" And then at that point, I always, I go usually to the line producer and explain the situation and say, "Can I publish this stuff?" And at some point they'll get the boards to the director, wherever they are, the director will usually say yes or, "Revise this, revise that."

So that is a situation where the director is not that involved. There are other situations on the other end of the spectrum where it's much closer to what most people would think a storyboard artist works like, working with somebody like Hitchcock, where he just knows every single shot. I worked with Guillermo del Toro on *Hellboy II* and he was like that. He knows every shot and he just wants you to bring in some blank storyboard templates and he sits there and he quickly thumbnails on the pages exactly the shots he wants and he explains it and hands it to you and says, "Go, do that, draw that as fast as you can." And he actually worked as a storyboard artist for three or four years, he told me. It was after a particularly long week—it was a Friday, he was leaving the office—and he told me he did that. And I looked at him and I said, "So you know?" and he goes, "I know man, you got a hard job!" He's a good guy. Most of the time it's a combination of the two where the director—in film again—where the director is giving you specific shots and then there is other stuff that they say, "Well, I haven't worked this out, why don't you take a shot at it and then I'll look at it." And that is very often the case, where they basically say, you know, especially if they're working with an experienced board artist that they can trust, they say, you know, "Take a shot at this and I'll revise it." And that revision may be that they look a bit and say, "No, this is completely wrong, the whole thing, throw it away." Or it might be, "Okay, this is good, but you're missing a beat here, where the hero and heroine are supposed to look at each other and this is a moment of faith and then they jump off the waterfall, or whatever." Or it may be that you've got all the beats of the sequence working fine but there are specific shots that they really want to do and they say, "I've always wanted to do a shot like this, where they're falling toward us and the camera—they're gaining past camera, so it starts out, you know, wide shot looking straight up, and then they pass us and we cut as they wipe past camera, or something." And so in that case I'd be sitting there with my drawing pad trying to sketch this stuff out as fast as I can, and these are just thumbnails, not proper storyboards. A lot of times, because you can't really draw that fast, a lot of times I'm drawing overheads, and an overhead is just a map of either the blocking, which would be: "This actor stands here facing that way, this one stands there facing this way, the waterfall is in the background behind them here," and then the director will say, "No, it should be over on this side."

For that, in a situation like that, that's a situation where we don't have a location but we have a gag or a sequence that is either in the script or it's going to be in the script, and so, we're just making it all up, it's not tied to some location. Other times there is a location and they have photos.

Nowadays with Google Earth it's a lot easier, it's great—but it used to be that they would be explaining the location because the photos hadn't come back from the lab yet, or whatever. Or sometimes there's a set that's going to be built, so before I talk to the director, a lot of times I'll go to the art department and really, you know, introduce myself to everybody there and, you know, meet the set designers, the assistant art director, art director, the production designer, and I'll go meet the location people and I'll just ask them. I'll go like, "What do you think is going to happen with, you know, the waterfall scene?" The location person will say, "Well, we've got three or four ideas and one of them is like this." And I'll say, "Well, would we really film right there or is it, like, something we're going to cheat?" And they'll understand what I'm saying and they'll say, "Well, there's a bunch of big rocks here blocking this part so, we'd have to film, whatever, up on the ridge," or something. So, armed with that information or similar information from the set designer when he says, "Well, it's going to be like this and the stairs are going to be here, there's a big window out there, and out that window we're supposed to see the barn," then when the director comes and gives me their five minutes of time, I can understand what they're saying. Because, a lot of times, they assume that everyone knows what they're talking about, and sometimes they just have so little time that they'll just kind of go, "Well, when she looks out the window, you know, in the background—" and I'll say, "Is it gonna be the barn?" and they'll go, "Yeah, that's what I meant. So that means back there you gotta have—" and I'll say, "her dad, you know, burying the mother." "Yeah, near the barn, burying the dog, rather—you know, Old Yeller or something."

That process of thumbnailing with the director sometimes, depending on the director, can be nerve wracking because sometimes they do want you to really draw it out, almost properly, so that they can clearly see it, and in that case, it's a little bit like they're just over your shoulder and you're sitting there sweating it out, trying to draw this stuff as they say it. But also, that's what they hire us for. That's why we're so valuable, you know, even though there is a lot of technology out there, much of the time, especially early on in a film when nothing is built or designed, somebody with a pencil and a sketchpad who can draw rapidly and realistically can really be valuable for discussion purposes. So, a lot of times, while I'm drawing something like that, the director will get someone to come over and he'll show this to the location person or the art director or a producer and say, "This is what I was thinking, something like this." I hope that answers the question.

FIGURE 13.48

FIGURE 13.49

FIGURE 13.50

FIGURE 13.51

FIGURE 13.52

FIGURE 13.53

FIGURE 13.54

FIGURE 13.55

FIGURE 13.56

FIGURE 13.57

FIGURE 13.58

FIGURE 13.59

FIGURE 13.60

FIGURE 13.61

I think one of the good things about storyboards is that it's like being able to watch the movie before anyone actually films it, so you really do get a sense of what the film will look like once it's—

Yeah, before you start spending real money and going to reallocations. Another thing in the case of *War Horse*, we—I was on that with Phil Keller storyboarding that with the Third Floor previs guys there. We were cooking up sequences together. The art department was all the way over in England and we were in a bungalow at Universal. They had this big complicated World War I battlefield where they were digging trenches, but instead of making an entire World War I battlefield they were—you know they didn't have a ton of money—they were trying to basically make, I think it was like one hero trench, and recycle it for all kinds of different shots. In that case we—I really stayed in close touch with Rick Carter, the production designer, and with the set designers and art directors so that I made sure that—there were instances where we'd say, "Well, there's a shot we've come up with, or a shot that Stephen Spielburg really wants, and we think we would film it here, but it looks like you guys are going to have this whole wooden structure there, but I think that's the best place for the shot." So they would end up revising the set, the quote-unquote set, if you will, to get a shot that the director wanted.

The way we were able to explain that was, I'd do a quick sketch and just send it off to them in England. In that case that meant also the day of, there's somebody in a backhoe who may or may not be digging huge amounts of dirt out of this field and so it even—it's one of the interesting things about storyboards is that they touch every department except craft services, I guess, the catering. What we do or don't put in the storyboards very often affects everyone, even the transportation. I've had a trans captain come up to me after looking at the storyboards and a diagram that I drew and say, "Where am I supposed to park all my trucks?" I'm like, "Hey man, I'm just trying to tell the story!" It's just a good fast and fairly inexpensive way to plan what is always a complicated, slow, and incredibly expensive collaboration between hundreds of people over great distances, sometimes, and a lot of time. So I think that's the best thing the storyboards can do is save you time, money, and heartache.

What do you think are some of the trends that are moving in? You mentioned that you worked with The Third Floor,[3] often doing animatics. Are your working on animatics or are you working on previews? Is that something that is relevant or a change? I notice that there are different changes that are happening in the industry. Another one is that certain animation companies, and a few individuals do everything digitally, rather than with paper and pencil. So can you talk about some of the changes that have been happening?

Well, the biggest change happening right now in storyboards is in the film business, and I'm sure it's happening in the commercial business too, but in the film business specifically, my experience, there now are, in L.A., five or six previs companies, and they do 3D pre-visualization animation, sometimes with sound, of these big sequences—the stunts and the heavy visual effects stuff. At first when they came into town, a lot of us live action storyboard artists were sweating it thinking, "Wow, they're really taking our jobs," and the truth is, they really are taking them, or making them shorter. But, as films—*this is the biggest surprise for me*—as films get more and more complex, especially with the heavy visual effects, CG animation, and now with 3D, the preparation for how to stage these sequences has also gotten more and more complex, and, surprisingly, more and more the previs companies need us storyboard artists to go in there and work out the story beats.

So, one thing that I have been doing the last few years is I'm not doing as many finished boards as I used to do. I got into this business really to make a living making pretty pictures but as a storyboard artist you can't always do that. What you need to do is get the shots right and get the job done on time. So I got used to doing quick sketches early in my career, so now, a lot of times we're doing what I call a rough storyboard, and really doing them—sometimes I'll draw the thing and just tear it out of my sketchbook and just hand it to the previs artist who already has a model of an environment open and has a rigged character there, and they just start animating the camera and the character. And so, that's a case where I'm not finishing the drawing, I'm not publishing it to a whole department. In fact, a lot of times now working with previs artists and teams, it's very different because I'm longer in production. There is no line producer, there's no locations, it's sort of like a writers room where we're all sitting around maybe another storyboard artist. I'm working with Mark Moretti right now—and a previs supervisor, a couple of previs artists, and maybe an editor, and we're just kicking ideas around, all of us, and as a storyboard artist your job is to, you know, really make sure that this works story wise and so, the previs artist may say, "Well, I got a great idea for this shot." Their sensibility is very different from, say, our sensibility or the editor's sensibility, and so I found it extremely valuable to have people like that to bounce ideas off of and to work with people who come from—like I never came from any video game background or anything but some of these people have worked in video games or played them for years or worked at visual effects houses or worked in CG animation and so they've got ideas that I would never come up with for these complicated sequences. You know nowadays we're making movies, of course, that are live action mixed with CG characters mixed with all kinds of crazy environments that we never had before. So I've found it works pretty well to work with a team like this. And it depends on the people. If you're working with people that are not good collaborators and they're sort of very immature and wanting to "own a sequence"—then there's nothing you can do. But most of the time in the last few years, I'll be doing quick sketches. I can hand them in if I'm drawing on paper or I draw directly in Photoshop. I get a bunch of jpegs, you know I'll screen capture them, put them in a folder, name them sequentially, and then I give them to the editor and the editor drops them into an edit. And so, some people would call it an animatic, some people in animation—I think they call it a story reel. But basically, it's—I would call it a boardamatic, because there is not actually any movement. It's just a lot of drawings and we're popping through them rapidly as you scrub through the edit. So the character moves or the camera moves and very often it's pretty rough.

And also it might be a real hybrid, like if it's a big complicated environment, which a previs modeler has already built, then I'll get the model from them and I've learned some Maya, so I'll open up Maya and move the camera around and screen capture, you know, twenty or thirty, forty shots rapidly of what I want this camera move to be. And then I'll go in Photoshop and just really crudely draw my character over those Maya screenshots and that might be the storyboard. Or, other times, I've drawn more carefully over that background screenshot and sort of blurred it out so that it's soft in the background and make a more finished storyboard. Especially if it's something like, once in a while we end up doing like, dialogue scenes, but with a big camera move, you know, some romantic moment or something, or a sad death moment. And so the story reels, at least, as I've done them, a lot of times are kind of uneven quality because some areas need more love than others. Some, it's just, you can pop through it really fast because it is explosions. And then, once we start cutting that together—and by the way, sometimes it's not with an editor, sometimes I just use—Apple has program called Keynote which you can make a slideshow out of, basically. And I just, by pressing the forward button I can pop through and just verbally talk the team through it. The previs supervisor will have thoughts about this moment and the editor will have ideas about this moment. So sometimes we don't even get to the point of actually editing, like making a QuickTime. It just ends up as verbal pitch and the previs team can get started. And as they're working, they'll do kind of a first pass on trying to basically make a version of what we're doing but it's much rougher.

So basically we're looking at you doing some kind of a rough pass of a storyboard, a shot by shot story reel, and then shot by shot, each shot is getting replaced by some kind of previs?

Exactly. And it's, a lot of times again because our sensibility as storyboard artists is different than what a previs artist might be doing at the time and anybody that has fooled around with any kind of CG animation or Maya knows that it's just an absolutely satanic program. It's so complicated and so it's easy to get— I think it's easy for the previs artists even if they're good at story or have a good eye for composition, I think it is very easy for them to get lost in what they're doing. Very often we're, as storyboard artists, we're the ones that are saying, "Well, look, in this moment this is when the guy dies and this moment is supposed to be a sad moment so we need him to die and then keep the camera rolling for basically the violin music which is going to be in there at some point but as you have the shot now he dies and then you cut instantly, which is not a good movie moment."

It sounds a lot like you're directing. Do you think storyboard artists need to be good directors? What skills do storyboard artists need?

It depends. My idea before I became a storyboard artist of what a director does is close to what I'm describing now, but now that I've worked with a lot of directors over the years in TV and film, I noticed the job of director is much bigger than just picking the shots and telling the story. They have to be very much a producer, a team leader. They have to know what they're doing on the set. They have to know, I mean, I have no opinions about movie posters or casting or—you know a million things that a director does that a lot of people don't know that have nothing to do with my skill set. So, yes, in a way it seems like we're directing the sequence but directing a film is a lot different than just directing an animatic, if you will. Very often we are in charge of cooking up— we're kind of co-supervisors with the previs supervisor and the editor of coming up with this animatic whether it's drawings strung together with no sound or it's a combination of drawings and some previs and some sound, or whatever.

The storytelling skill seems to be what is separating you from, say, the Maya artist who would, I'm presuming, be more inclined to have some fancy flying shots rather than, sticking on a dramatic moment. So, storytelling skills— can you talk about where that came from?

Well, yeah, the storytelling skills are the most [important]—that's why we're still there. Our skill set in some ways seems antiquated, but stories are never antiquated. If you look back—when I was trying to learn story, I remember somebody gave me a book, that book, what was it? Aristotle—*Poetics*. He talks about story and I think it's in there that he talks about how difficult writing is and how the audiences, even back then, were disappointed when a story didn't go well when they would bring the gods down on this pulley system, this machine, to basically wrap up the whole plot without really trying to do the

FIGURE 13.62
Another page from Josh Sheppard's sketchbook.

important story work. So I think it was difficult back then and story is still difficult—that's a big part of our skill set. The previs artists—it depends, some of them have story skills, some of them don't. But I think even if they have story skills, their job is so complex and specific that they're not really in a position—they're not often in a position—to oversee the sequence. I'm sitting there as a storyboard artist and it's a full time job, 10 hours a day, trying to solve this and figure it out and come up with some image. You know they're coming up with an image by doing previs. I'm doing it drawing or Photoshop or manipulating a photo or a screen capture from a CG set but basically my time is all used up trying to fix the story and meanwhile they, their time is all used up trying to animate this character, trying to animate this camera, trying to get this explosion to work, trying to build the set, and so even if they have a story sensibility, a lot of times they're busy doing that and my job happens to be story.

Now the storyboard supervisor kind of wears both hats. They, at least in my experience, if they're good at story then they'll weigh more. Sometimes they're more of a technical supervisor and there's, as I said, so many technical issues that come up doing previs, that they may just concentrate more on that and completely leave the story department alone. Not leave us alone. I mean, we're still talking with them and saying, "Well look, in this scene I really think we're not even going to see that whole section of the set so I wouldn't have your modeler waste time doing that because we've figured out—we think this would be a better area to stage this." So we're trying to work well with this new, complicated team that we have been thrown into. One of the funnest things is being able to use sound much more effectively than we used to doing just straight storyboards. We'd draw sound effects and stuff but it's great to sit there and look at the edit when it's, say, 90 percent of our drawings have been replaced. Now it's previs with full animation, lights and sound and then we'll look at it and we'll say, "I think you need some great musical sting right here. I don't know what it is but something that . . ." and then before you can finish the sentence, the editor probably has a great idea, or one of the previs team will go, "Oh, in *Harry Potter* there's that moment when blah blah blah." And that's a lot of what we do when we cook up these sequences—we're always referencing other movie scenes and trying to—we have a lot of DVDs sitting there. We'll put it on and we'll look at the scene and we'll go, "Oh, well that's—our idea is too close to that. We don't want to copy it." Or we'll say, "Wow, that worked perfectly. The only thing is, it's like too scary when that certain thing happens and we're working on a kids' movie here, so let's do it like that, but not as scary," something like that. Because everybody is all film fans, we speak the same language, which, in my experience, it starts with *Star Wars* and it goes out from there.

I imagine that's probably a big thing—language of film—where a lot of that comes from. Let's jump ahead and go into advice for beginners. What skills do you think are really important to being successful at this job?

Well obviously, drawing is the number one skill. I'd say if somebody wants to become a storyboard artist, the first thing I think they have to do is just be responsible about teaching yourself the basics, the important elements of drawing. If you're talking about live action storyboarding, I would say that basically means figure drawing, specifically the clothed figure, and perspective, and then also story. You know, you've got to learn story and that is something that comes with experience, with analyzing films and even TV commercials.

You've got to be a movie geek?

You've got to be a movie geek, yeah. Also I think you actually have to move beyond being just a fan. That's one thing that I think is important to underscore. Yes, someone that wants to be a storyboard artist may have seen, what's an example, I don't know, may have seen every *Harry Potter* film, but have you sat there and watched any of the scenes, say with the sound off, and just sat there and tried to analyze what it is they're trying to do? Like what's the point of this scene and how did they achieve that? If the point of the scene is that Harry is—this is such a scary school that Harry might not have any friends here or if you're trying to get the audience excited for an action sequence that's coming, look at the scene and figure out, well did they set that up well and how did they do it? Where was the camera? Try and guess why did they film it this way?

I've worked a little bit in games doing storyboards for cinematics and what they said, you know the first thing I would tell them, I'd say, "Well, I don't know if I'm the right person because I don't play video games. I've never played any of these like World of Warcraft, Halo, any of this stuff," and I've heard the same answer over and over. They'd say, "Well, that's fine. We can find people that are game geeks. We need film people because we're trying to make a cinematic that is cinematic." So sometimes they'll show me storyboards they want me to redraw or they'll show me their old cinematic or a new cinematic in progress and they'll say, you know—I've heard this twice—someone would say, "Well, my supervisor at the game company says something's wrong with this and he doesn't know what it is but he wants a film person to figure it out." So I would look at it and I would say, "Well, right away I think one problem is the camera is just flying around like a mosquito and it's completely distracting for this moment which is supposed to be sad, because in the cinematic this character is now getting killed and it's like oh my God now the character is alone for the rest of the game, or something. And so, I don't know if that's a good point to just start flying around like a mosquito. Why don't you just stay for a moment and pull back with the character as they are looking at something off-camera and they're devastated? And then as the camera pulls back the dead body comes into the shot or something. You know, something that feels a little more emotional. Or do a POV, something that's subjective or something like that." Also, they may just be filming it in a way that just feels odd. It's hard to say but it's like, if you watch a foreign film—like I remember watching a movie from Hong Kong and it had some really cool stuff in it but right in the middle of the movie was a music video, and it was so jarring to my sensibility, coming from Hollywood, that it made me realize, "Oh, that's just a different sensibility it's not mine." But sometimes in the game stuff I think they're trying to make a film, except they are not using film camera techniques or movie moments. They're using stuff that is kind of from the video game world, if that makes sense. And I think the question was what skill-sets . . .

. . . are important in storyboarding?

Well, figure drawing, perspective, storytelling, and specifically shot picking. And also communication skills—it's vital, I think, that anybody that's going to go into any kind of business, especially as a freelancer, has to be able to communicate well. It's one of the things that I say when I go and talk to that story—I talk at this class that's like storyboarding for directors up at Art Center. My friend Aaron Saud teaches and one of the things I always say to the college kids is, "I hope when you get out of this expensive school, that one of the skills you get is the ability to communicate well. Like, to clearly and succinctly communicate to whoever you're working with what you want them to do or what you're trying to do." Because I tell them stories about working with directors who just, they don't have that skill. Especially younger inexperienced directors. I've worked with a lot of first-time directors in both film and TV and it's always so frustrating when they can't explain what it is they want. So a lot of times I've found myself—like, they'll say what they mean. Like, they'll go, "There's this great shot in *Blade Runner* that's like, I mean it just feels like," and they're just not able to say it. And I'll say, "You mean you want to do that scary moment when they're coming up in the elevator and Tyrell—is trying to prevent them from coming up and there's this shot past Rutger Hauer onto the guy, Sebastian, where he's very nervous. He's nervous because he's with with the replicant but he's outsmarting the guy at chess." And they'll say, "Yeah, that's it!" And I'll say, "Well, I think one of the reasons it's so effective is that there is, if I remember right, I think there's no camera movement. It's just sitting there with Rutger Hauer's totally creepy face right in the foreground." In that case, I've now translated for the director what they were trying to say.

I think a director needs to be able to communicate well. I think a storyboard artist need to be able to communicate well. Also I really think a storyboard artist needs business skills. Just the ability to show up, meet deadlines, follow through on what they're expecting you to do, anticipate questions, and ask them, go and work with the team rather than just hunkering down and doing a bunch of work and then finding out, "Oh, God, I should have gone down the hall and talked to the locations, because it turns out this is all wrong." Common sense, I think, is a good skill set. I get asked—students email me sometimes saying, "Should I go to art school?" I had a really bad experience in art school 25 years ago but back then it was bad. They were trying to teach us Abstract Expressionism and they were not doing the fundamentals. I had drawing one which was drawing the soup cans and shoes they put on the ground, and drawing two was drawing the figure, and that was it. I remember when I brought in my drawings midway through the term to show to the teacher of the figure drawing class. He went on and on criticizing how I had drawn the figure in the middle of the newsprint, how it was a bad composition. Looking back 25 years later, I realized he didn't give me the right feedback. He should have been talking about proportion, which was my problem at the time, not about the composition of this sketch on newsprint. So I think nowadays art schools seem to be more focused on realism. I think if you can afford it, go to art school, but you don't need it to be a storyboard artist. What you need is a portfolio, really. The Catch-22 is you also need experience. You have to do some small jobs and build up your résumé, as well.

So if you're a student trying to do a portfolio, what would you put in it? What would you suggest?

I think that what needs to be in a portfolio for a storyboard artist is exactly the type of work that they want to do and only that. I would never put in comic book pages, figure drawings, you know, any of the stuff that you see in a lot of students' portfolios. You usually see a mishmash of stuff that if you or I looked at it you can say, "Oh yeah, this person can draw to a certain level." But if you show it to, you know, the line producer's assistant on some Disney movie, they may or may not have any idea and so they'll just look at it and think, "I'm not going to show a bunch of comic book pages to my boss. He's going to get mad." So that's one thing. And basically, I think you need to have a variety, you know, five or six or 10 good samples of the type of stuff we board like heavy visual effects scenes, stunt scenes, moody scenes, and they should show storytelling skills, not just a whole bunch of random action stuff. I think that's one thing that beginners and even some pros make the mistake of, just having a bunch of really kinetic drawings but there's actually not a beginning, middle, and an end. There's no real story or point to these scenes, which is kind of an unfair criticism because there's dozens of movies coming out of Hollywood every year that are like that too, that don't have any point to them.

For TV commercials and music videos, same thing, you know, have samples of commercials that show, you know, something happening that is not just, I wouldn't just do mundane kitchen scenes. I mean do a Nike tennis shoe commercial or something that's exciting and definitely show the product at the end. A lot of times I've seen samples that students do that, they forget that the whole point of this thing is to sell tennis shoes and so they don't actually show the tennis shoe very well in the spot, if that makes sense. Nowadays all of that has to be, in my opinion, has to be on a good, a decent website so that you can email it out electronically. I hope that answers the questions.

Well, so now I've taken my class, I've learned how to do my perspective and figure drawing, I've got my portfolio. Now, I'm a student, how do I go out there and get some work?

Well, the first thing, as I said, I think the best thing you can do is make a good portfolio, put it on a decent website, and then once you have it you can start

FIGURE 13.63

FIGURE 13.64

FIGURE 13.65

FIGURE 13.66

emailing it around. You could email it to the various agents that handle storyboard artists. That's a good place to start because they have clients coming to them. They have established clients and you might get a chance to work on something. That was how I did it, but it was before email and Internet and everything, so I just had a physical portfolio which I gave to my agent. In my opinion that's probably the best way to do it but you can also network with other artists and they may be able to recommend you. I think the best thing you can do is be prepared. Being prepared means having enough samples and a variety of samples that someone who would probably hire a better artist, a more experienced artist, but they don't have much money, they can look at your portfolio and say yeah, it looks like they could probably do it. I think a lot of students make the mistake of having good drawing skills but not having them in their portfolio. You see this, that's why they put figure drawings in because figure drawing looks really good, and it says I can draw the figure really well, but really what you should have is a storyboard sample with a bunch of well drawn figures. Whatever jobs you do get, do your best and then give a copy of it to your agent or put in your portfolio, put it on your website, and keep updating it.

Basically networking is my best advice to students. I think the number one thing that kills beginners in their chances of success is not updating the portfolio, not working on their portfolio. That's the number one thing. I think the number two thing is themselves. It's their attitude about their perception of what is or isn't going on. I can remember emailing back and forth a few years ago with a guy that showed a lot of promise and he was a little bit dragging his feet with his samples, but basically he talked himself out of going into film because of this whole sticky situation of how hard it is to get into the union and I tried to tell him, "You know, there are people who have whole careers, 30-year careers, they were never in a union and it hasn't stopped them, so why are you, where you've never even gotten your foot in the door, talking yourself out of it already?" Another thing that stops people, I think, is this whole situation—there's always been this tension between artists and agents and I think you could talk to any artist, they'll tell you how evil agents are and how they take advantage of you. Much of it's true, but it's also an agent, if you look at it another way, is an opportunity to have someone who is experienced help you get into the business and stay there. But I know for a fact, I've seen it many times, where up-and-coming artists get off on a bad foot with their agent and so they just are like, "Forget agents. I'm never going to have an agent." Then they're stuck out there trying to build a career by themselves just from scratch just because they vow, they make this blood oath: "I will never work with an agent again ever, no matter what, even if nuclear winter comes." I think that kills a lot of people's prospects. It's a very difficult business to get in to and I think you need people. In Hollywood that means there's a lot of strong personalities, a lot of people who got where they're at because they're talkers and they're extroverts and basically not the kind of people you would want to spend a lot of time with. But, sometimes in business it's uncomfortable and you have to make some compromises, I would say.

I've been asking everybody for two pieces of advice. One—something technical like, a favorite tool that you use, and two might be a broader question on some idea or attitude that you should know to move forward. So can you give me one for each?

Technical tip—I think the best I can think of to improve your, the realism of your drawings, we're talking about a live action storyboarding now, is to improve the head and hand drawings. Most of the time, if I look at a student's portfolio, it's the first thing I say when we're talking about the subject of improving your drawing, not necessarily improving shot picking or storytelling. But if you can just take the same exact samples that you have and just redraw the heads and hands, instantly it looks like a better drawing. Sometimes the figure is so bad that it just looks terrible, but that is probably my best piece of advice drawing wise. Philosophically, I would say anybody that wants to go in to storyboarding, be aware that this is not the best time in history to become a storyboard artist. The future is pretty bumpy because of all the previs that is taking so much of our work away. I believe we'll always be here, but who knows? Things change rapidly. But that said, if somebody wants to do it, nothing I say will stop them and they should go for it. But I really think if somebody is going to be a storyboard artist, they have got to realize that drawing is only 50 percent of the job and what I've seen in my experience with so many talented people struggling and not finding work, there are external forces that keep artists from being successful. In my opinion, so often artists shoot themselves in the foot with having a bad attitude, just not networking, not talking to the people that they're working with, and as I've said before, not improving their portfolio. Basically just basic common sense, realizing that there's a whole other side, half of the job is not just drawing. It's solving problems, taking care of business, networking with people, looking honestly at your own work. There are some people who, some artists who just refuse to see that they need to improve on a certain aspect of their drawing and they just will not do it, they won't go there. In fact that's one thing that I've heard someone say that art school does, is it doesn't necessarily teach you to draw but it teaches you to watch yourself drawing and to then, hopefully, be objective enough to say, "Oh, wow I'm no good at drawing the figure or cars," or whatever, "I've got to work on that!" So, if that makes sense, that's my best philosophical advice. Be friendly to the people you work with. Be responsible.

Alright, so, is there anything else about storyboarding that you would like to talk about, or that you've been thinking about that you want to get off your chest? Go ahead and freestyle it.

Freestyle it! Let me think. Well, I think I speak for every storyboard artist out there that, of course we all wish that we could somehow get more recognition for what we do. You know, so often you see a making-of documentary on a film or the making-of book of a film that comes out, and what you see art wise is all of the beautiful, amazing concept art, and rightly so because that sells books and that's what people want to see. But I wish there was some way that the fans of these movies and even the other directors and filmmakers that hire us, I wish there was some way they could know what a difficult and important job this is. Where, you know, all of us live action board artists have all worked on films where there was no director even hired yet, there was no crew. I've worked on films where it was just me and the producer and there's no script and we make part of a movie just like that, just us sitting alone in a room. And then people start getting hired. I found this very intimidating when I was first starting in film, sitting at a table with a dozen other people who have all kinds of experience and skills going back to when I was in second grade, even, and they're sitting there and they're scrutinizing shot by shot, drawing by drawing, this storyboard. And you think, "Wow, I was in that building there when—they'd rented the building but there was no one there but me and the janitor, that was it. And I cooked this thing up out of thin air and now they're questioning me." I can't really say anything, but I sort of wish somebody would sort of say, "Oh gee, you made this all up? That's great! You deserve a prize," or something. The prize is they pay us, but I wish there was some way that storyboard artists' contribution to films could get acknowledged more. We're not even guaranteed credit on union films. I've worked for months and months on films where a first-time director was hired for political reasons or whatever and I made up whole sections of the movie, including adding placeholder dialog, and it got in the movie, and by the way this is just me—I think any live action artist you talk to will tell you the same story. And then the film comes out and my name's not even in the credits just because of whatever reason. They didn't wanna spend the money for the prints or whatever. I've had arguments with producers—I try not to argue on the job, but I had a producer call me on a movie that I worked on for nearly a year and said, "Look," he was apologizing because I knew him well, he said, "I just want you to know, we're not going to be able to put the storyboard artist's credits in there." I just said, "I gotta tell you, we made up this much of that film, and I think it would be really uncool to do that. Just plain old uncool." And, amazingly in that case, he capitulated. But it was—I could hear it in his voice— It was a money thing. I think that it—I literally think it has to do with how many feet of film or something. I don't get it all. It's the most ridiculous thing. That's the one thing—I wish that we could somehow get more acknowledgment for our contributions but it's not that type of job. It's the type of job where you go down in the mine and come back with gold and you hand it to whoever paid you to go down in the mine. Hope that helps!

INTERVIEW WITH SHERM COHEN STORYBOARD SUPERVISOR AT DISNEY TELEVISION ANIMATION (www.StoryboardSecrets.com)

Sherm Cohen's first professional job was doing a California Raisins comic book. He spent a lot of his early years freelancing: inking on comics, doing gag cartoons for men's magazines, and spot illustrations for local magazines. His creation of an independent comic book lead to him working on the *Ren and Stimpy Show* as a trainee. Then he went on to Nickelodeon for *Hey Arnold* starting as a revisionist, then as a board artist, then later as a storyboard director. Between1998 and 2005 he worked on *SpongeBob SquarePants* for both the series and the movie as a board artist and board supervisor. He later went on to Cartoon Network for *My Gym Partner is a Monkey*, then to Disney for *Phineas and Ferb*. After returning to Nickelodeon for the first season of *The Mighty B!* he returned to Disney for *Phineas and Ferb* and *Kick Butowski* as a director and is currently (as of this writing) on *Fish Hooks*. Sherm also runs an online storyboarding class at www.storyboardsecrets.com.

Let's talk about how you started. Your education, what skills you had going in before you started doing any kind of storyboarding at all.

It's interesting because I never had any intention of becoming a storyboard artist. I was always interested in being a comic book artist, and way back when out of high school I went to college, for a year, majoring in art and then right away I realized that wasn't for me at all because I didn't understand the distinction between a commercial artist and a fine artist. And I was really fuzzy on the whole notion. So once I could tell that I wasn't interested in being with the fine arts crowd, I decided to enroll in the Joe Kubert School, and this was back in the mid-eighties, and I wanted to learn to be a comic book artist; I was really into superhero comics and other things, and I went there for two years—learned an awful lot of stuff. It was a really great education, because those guys are really focused on deadlines. They're old pros and they were teaching those old school sort of ethics. And they were teaching us really rock solid basics especially about storytelling and visual storytelling. So that was a really great background to have. And coming out of that school, and again I was interested in finding work as a comic book artist but I found that there was very, very little market for doing funny type cartoons or funny type of comics and it just happened that during that time that I was at Kubert I realized that my work was gravitating more towards the humorous side, but then I found that there was no market for it. And I kind of dropped out of looking for work, because I was really discouraged for quite a long time and that's something that I want to get back to. Eventually, after about five years of going back to college, trying different jobs, going into retail, going into working in a psychiatric hospital, all kinds of weird things, I finally decided that I was so miserable not doing cartooning that I was going to have to figure out what to do. So I just started making my own comics, just independent comics and I went to sell them at the San Diego Comic Convention. This was back in 1994 then.

So were these just mini-comics or were they published by somebody?

No these were full-sized comics, but it was self-published in a sense. It was myself and one partner where I did all the artwork and story and he took care of the printing and distribution with Diamond and all that. So that's where things started to happen for me. I had these comics and I was selling them at the San

Diego Con and one of the directors from *The Ren and Stimpy Show*, was at the con and looked at my stuff, he was probably looking at all kinds of things as a fan, and this was Bill Wray and he looked at the comics, he could see we probably had a lot of the same influences, mostly Harvey Kurtzman, and he said, "Hey, have you ever thought about doing storyboarding?" and I was like, "Well, uh, gee, that sounds great, but I don't know anything about it!" And so he was very nice to say, "Oh, when you come back in LA, give me a call and we can have lunch, and I'll tell you about it." So he did, and that's sort of cracked open the door. But the next section that I want to tell you about is probably the most interesting for students. The really important thing is to get your work out there where people can see it, because if I hadn't done that, I would never have caught that opportunity. So that's a big thing I always try to tell people is that whether you get your work on the web or whether you xerox it and go to shows, you need to get your work out there, otherwise nobody's going to know what it is you can do. But the second thing is he gave me an opportunity to show my work to him, and I did and he critiqued it, and he said, "Well, this is good, but this isn't anything like what we need for storyboarding." The thing is that the difference between comics and storyboards, one of the big differences, is that when we draw comics we learn to compress time. We try to fit as much into one panel as you can for economy's sake. And in storyboarding it's the opposite, you really have to pose things out and you can't have two actions happening in the same panel, let alone the many, many dialogs and things you have in a comic. So I was learning how to do that. He didn't like what I had very much and I told him, "Ah, let me work up another batch of samples." And so I went back and like for three weeks, just worked like crazy trying to create some new samples based on what he told me.

Now were you making up stories on your own, or were there some old scripts you were working from . . . ?

That's a good question. At the time I was just drawing poses. I was just trying to draw dynamic poses or . . . it's a little hard to recall . . . or to recreate scenes from the *Ren and Stimpy Show* at the time. But the second time I showed him my work, he was like, "Well, I could see that it's getting better." He said, "It's better," but he's like, "It's still not good enough to show the people back at *Ren and Stimpy*." And I was at that point like—"Wow." Knocked the wind out of my sails, but just for about 10 seconds, whereas I just sucked it up and it was like, "You know what, let me see another few weeks. Let me give it another shot." And at that point, that's when I pulled out the stops. I wrote a little scene. Wrote my own storyboard, basically, it was about 15 pages long. And I just wanted them to see—yeah, I could write, yeah I can come up with this stuff, and I had examples of storyboards, which at the time were very hard to come by. Nowadays, with the internet you can just do a little bit of searching and you can find some fantastic samples so you can get the format right. And I brought in that third set of samples, and he was like, "You know, let me bring it in and show Bob Camp." And Bob was the supervising director at that time. And they gave me the opportunity to work there as a trainee. This was a non-union shop at the time. And so it was basically a foot in the door position. I think I was making about a quarter of what the starting rate would be for storyboard artists. But I was very happy to get it.

And this was for *Ren and Stimpy* or . . .

Yes, that was for *Ren and Stimpy*, it was for Games Animation. And at that time . . .

Did you say Games Animation?

Games Animation was the production company. Nickelodeon Animation Studios didn't really exist quite yet. Games Animation was a little entity that they created after they took the show away from Spumco. That was their production company. So I started there as a trainee. And I had an opportunity, even though it only lasted six months before the show was cancelled, to learn as much as possible. So that would be the third phase. The first one is getting your work out there; do as much as you can to let people see your work. The second one being if you have an opportunity, you got to work like crazy to grab on to that opportunity and not let it go. And the third thing is when I got in there I just asked as many questions as I could as I was doing the work; being helpful whenever I could. If that meant making xeroxes, I would make xeroxes. If it meant getting somebody lunch, I would get somebody lunch. But ultimately it just meant that any time I did something, especially if they didn't like it, I would ask them, "Gee what's wrong with it, how can I make it better?" So I think I learned about two years of experience in that six months. The next part about that—it is fascinating for me to trace in back in my own mind—is that one of the directors was Craig Bartlett, who went on to create *Hey Arnold!* for Nickelodeon. And Craig started on *Ren and Stimpy* around the same time I did—near the end of the run. And we were both the new kids. And even though he had lots and lots of experience behind him, he was new there. And we got to know each other pretty well, and by the time that *Hey Arnold!* launched at Nickelodeon, we already had a relationship, he already knew my work. I wasn't given a job, but I was given an opportunity to take a test for the job. And I got the job on *Hey Arnold!*. And I had that job for about the next four years. And it was during that longer stretch of time that I really had the opportunity, starting as a storyboard revisionist, to learn, become a storyboard artist next and then about a year later, become a director, and so I really took that opportunity again by asking questions all the time, and seeking to find wherever possible to gain those skills from the environment that I was in, to really get a firm foothold in the industry.

You said you did a little bit of revision work. Can you talk about that?

Absolutely. Storyboard artists, that position is an incredibly demanding position. In TV animation that probably means churning out about 12 pages a day. Sometimes 15 pages a day of storyboards for a total of storyboards that are going to be 200 or 300 pages long in just a matter of a few weeks. And considering that a lot of comic artists are interested in doing storyboards, but there are very few cartoonists who are doing comic books that would be able to churn out a 200 page comic book in five weeks. That's just like, "It's berserk, that's insane!" So to hit the ground running as a storyboard artist with no previous experience is very, very difficult. And the people I've seen try it, really, really struggle with it, and end up either quitting or getting fired, or just struggling with it quite a bit. So I had the opportunity to start as a storyboard revisionist, which meant that I was just basically helping the storyboard artists by cleaning up scenes that they didn't have time to clean up. Taking their rough drawings and making them clean. Or drawing crowds in the background of a scene. Or more frequently, it had to do with the director of the show, after the storyboard's been finished and that storyboard artist has moved on to another episode, because they keep coming one after another, if they have to make fixes to that board, or re-write any sections, well that storyboard artist is, like I said he's already working on something else. It can't stop. It's like a freight train and if you try to stop it, you get a big crash. So the director will then say, "Hmm, you know what, we re-wrote this scene," and he might describe me the scene or he might give me a page of script, and instead of having to deal with a 20-page script for a 200-page board, a storyboard revisionist might get a half a page of script, or a description of a scene and then they'll have the opportunity to have a few days to do that one scene. And it helps you really get your feet wet and build up to speed and build confidence.

For being a revisionist, a lot of our readers might want to know how quickly they're going to have to work, how many boards they're going to be coming up with a day or a week . . .

It's a very, very fast paced job, but it can also have fits and starts, because there may be days when there's nothing going on, and you're waiting around for work. And in a poorly organized studio that would happen. In a more well-organized studio . . . they'd still be making fixes to storyboards . . . at the rate of about 10 pages per day to start out with.

10 pages meaning how many panels?

Oh that's a good question. It's based on a 3-panel storyboard. But the key to note is that the storyboards don't have to be really cleaned up. There's a degree of finish that happens in animation storyboard that is quite a bit different than feature storyboards where a lot of the drawings look like illustrations. But in TV storyboards, because we're churning them out so quickly, oftentimes the level of finish can be quite rough, like it is on shows that I'm working on currently like *Fish Hooks*—the drawings are relatively rough compared to other shows I've worked on. Like *Phineas and Ferb*, which I worked on for a couple of years has a much tighter rendering style, so it also depends on the show. Another key, and this is hopefully a helpful tip, is that in TV animation, if you have one scene that goes across a number of panels, let's say 3 panels or 5 panels or 10 panels, the most important thing is to clean up that very first panel very clearly so that you can see all the characters and their costumes and the backgrounds, everything very clearly—and then it allows you in subsequent panels to draw it a little bit more loosely, concentrating on the gesture and on the expression, because you set the basic scene and all the details in the first panel. And that's a way that artists, if they really have to go quicker, then it's like make sure the first panel is really, really clean and then you can go a little bit rougher on the rest.

Now a lot of these boards are sent overseas. So as long as you get the first panel right, after that you're mostly dealing with acting, right?

Yeah, primarily you're dealing with acting unless there happens to be a camera move of some sort, you know you want to address the shifted background drawing. And that's a good point about shipping the show overseas, is that you're not going to have any communication generally between the storyboard artist, and the overseas studio, so it's important that you draw things in such a way that someone can look at it and understand it very clearly without having to ask questions, or even frankly read the scene description underneath. It's very common for TV storyboards at any rate to have descriptions of the act underneath the drawing just to cover up any ambiguity, but what happens is the scene descriptions are translated into the target language, which might be Korean, it might be Chinese, it might be Indian and you can't really rely on what they're going to say, so it's really important to make your drawings as clear as possible.

So we'll get into how you first broke in—you were working as a revisionist, and how long were you doing that before . . .?

I was doing that for roughly a year. And what happens is, even though it's difficult to find work as a storyboard artist, meaning it's not the kind of job anyone can just walk in off the street and get, it takes a bit of perseverance, and quite a bit of hard work and a good portfolio, good ability at drawing and storytelling . . . What I want to say about that is, as hard as it is, as difficult as it is to break into a storyboarding position, there's always a demand for good storyboard artists. It's hard to get a job in the first place, you just need to realize that the studios are chewing up and spitting out artists very quickly, and because of the demanding schedule, there's always a need for good storyboard artists. So if you can prove yourself—that you can do the job and you can do it on time—then as soon as possible, the people that you work with are going to just scoop you up and put you into that position, because people quit, people move on, people get fired, who knows what. That's what happened with me, I was gradually over that period of time showing myself to be able to do more work without so much individual attention from the director. At one point, I got a whole show that the director didn't like, and he said, "Just fix this." And I said, "What do you want me to do with it?" And he said, "Ah, do it over!". You know, he really didn't like it, and so it gave me the opportunity to—I wasn't working from scratch, but I could see what was done there and any of the scenes I thought might be pumped up better, I would re-draw.

By this time maybe you'd shown yourself to have some kind of writing talent?

No, not at this point. At this point everything I was doing was not related to writing. It's a very good question that you have, because the writing aspect comes in a couple years later. But during the *Hey Arnold!* show, that was a scripted show. So mostly it had to do with the way I was able to interpret a script and put it into visual terms. And have the characters acting and also the filmmaking use that I was doing. Rather than hooting, or drawing everything as though it was on a flat stage, I was able to internalize the story enough to know when are the moments when you're going to want a close up, when are you going to need an upshot or a down shot, and that comes from something else I was doing during those years which was studying films like crazy, trying to learn consciously the film language that we all take for granted. And it's a thing that a lot of people will do instinctively . . . knowing when to draw a frame a certain way or when to tilt the camera a certain way. It's something that all of us as visual people, sort of internalized from watching a lot of TV and a lot of movies and a lot of cartoons, but at some point if the artist can study and consciously try to figure out what they're doing, then all of a sudden it will take your work to a huge new level, because as a storyboard artist, you're really the first line of being the director of sorts before it even gets to the director especially in the animation field. So you need to bring a personal vision to it to make it something that's actually going to stand out and be worth noticing. It's fairly easy to be average, but to stick out among the crowd, it requires you to always be trying to better yourself. And learning something about film—I was literally watching a feature film every day for a couple of years. It was like, I'd go home, I'd watch a film. At first, the question was, there are so many millions of movies out there how do I know which ones to study—the good ones, and which are the bad ones? So I figured I'd just look at the ones that were time tested. I'd start watching the classics from the forties and fifties or more modern classics that have stood the test of time. I would also follow other people's recommendations. People were recommending things to me that I would never have sought out like silent movies, which turned out to be one of the great joys of my life, learning about Chaplin and Keaton and Harold Lloyd and early Laurel and Hardy because they're all just pure storytelling. For comedy purposes if you're doing funny stuff that's a great thing to look at. So the writing part didn't actually come in until after my experience on *Hey Arnold!* But there is one more thing on *Hey Arnold!* that I want to mention is that during the course of this time, I went from a board revisionist to a full storyboard artist then to a director on that show, and the way that happened was pretty strange and very fortunate for me. Our executive producer on the show was just interviewing people, I don't know what possessed her to do this, and she was like, "Well, what are your goals? What would you like to do?" And I said, "Well, like a year from now, I'd like to be a director." And so they partnered me with Dan Povenmire, he's the creator of *Phineas and Ferb* right now, so I've known Dan for quite a long time, and we worked together as a storyboard team where he was a director and I was the storyboard artist, even though the director does tons of storyboarding as well. And we worked together very closely and we learned a lot of things. And at one point, our producer called me into her office like a year later and said, "Okay, we're ready to make you a director." And it shocked me that she had taken what I had told her was my goal and apparently, she was sort of saying, "Okay, that's what we're going to do with you." So it's also really, really, important once you have a job, if you have ambitions to do something else, or to do more, to let your co-workers, your bosses know what that is, because when there's an opportunity, then they may come to you for that opportunity. I was frankly quite shocked by it. It's not like I wasn't prepared to take it on, because I was, but I was just so happy that someone was not only listening to me, but taking an interest in my own goals and in my own career. Of course, it's a two-way street because it works out better. It's not like producers are Santa Claus and their whole goal in life is to help me, but it works out good for them, it works out good for me because like I said, they always need people that can do this kind of work and I had been trained with Dan Povenmire for a year who is really an accomplished director, and so then I was ready to take on directing on my own shows.

Let's talk about the job itself. Your relationship with the director, what the job entails.

In general, most shows start with a script; unfortunately, there are a handful of shows that are written and drawn by the cartoonists purely in visual form, but let me address the scripted show first. Scripted shows, again, that's 90 percent of the shows that are made, in a TV show for a typical 11-minute show you'll get a script that is between 18 and 22 pages long. A script shouldn't be more than 15 pages long, but they always make them much longer than they need to be. That's a whole different topic, but you'll get the script and typically, you'll either work with two people where one is like the director and one is like the storyboard artist, or for someone who is more experienced they may have just one person working all by themselves. So it seems like there's twice as much work if there's only one person, that is true, but it just depends on the budget of the show. At Cartoon Network, it was the first time I ever had to do a show all by myself, and then later on when I went back to Nickelodeon for *The Mighty B!* I was also working on a show for five weeks by myself, but typically five weeks and a script. And what usually happens in the first week of your five weeks is you try to do thumbnail drawings of the entire storyboard that you can really map out in a really loose format, where you're going. And those thumbnail drawings, can literally be an inch and a half by an inch in the margins of the storyboard. They could be on post-it notes, they could be on big sheets of blank paper. The important thing is that you just have a clear idea of where you're going.

Are you thumbnailing the entire show before you're doing any final boards or are you just doing a section at a time?

Usually you would thumbnail out the entire thing. I will say that, partly because you need to show it to the director frequently, after that week, you kind of need to pitch it to the director by sitting down with them and showing them the work that you have . . . where you're planning on going because it's very risky to turn a storyboard artist loose for five weeks, not seeing anything at all, and then all of a sudden at the end of five weeks you get something that maybe doesn't work. It's very typical, that a storyboard artist, after thumbnailing will need to show the board to somebody—whether it's the director of the show, it might be the storyboard supervisor. At any rate on every show, there's going to be that person that you need to report to.

Are you going to be reporting to them every day, or . . .?

It's typically once after about a week, with your thumbnails. And they will give you notes, typically. If they like everything that you've done, they'll just say, "Okay." But usually, they'll find a certain section, where they may look at your thumbnails and . . . it may be that it's a spooky, scary sequence, and the director might look at it and say, "You know, I think you need to make this a little scarier, try to show some more things in shadows, or show tighter angles that you can't see around the characters." There could be a number of things depending on the situation. Or let's say it's an action sequence. The director might ask you to draw it more broadly, to make sure that there's more action. One of the keys in working through a show is to make sure there's a lot of highs and a lot of lows so that the show has a certain amount of a ride, like a rollercoaster, where it starts out in one place, the tension picks up, and then it goes faster or then it goes slower and maybe it's very exciting at some points and maybe it's very quiet . . . that's a part of the pacing that you need to learn only through experience and observation about story. But that's basically your first week. Typically then, out of your five weeks you'll have another two weeks in which you can rough out the storyboard on full-size paper, or digitally now. So storyboard on paper is frequently three panels per page, but it's sometimes two panels per page lately, because the screen ratios have changed in the last few years. Because more work is produced in widescreen format, it's frankly harder to fit three panels onto a page, so the two panel storyboard page has become more common. Much more common has become the digital storyboard which doesn't work in pages at all, it just works in individual panels. So all of this talk about pages may be outdated in a few years, but you could just multiply the number of pages by two or three to figure out how many panels you would need to produce.

So the idea of drawing in the rough form—on the actual paper or on the screen—is to make sure you've integrated all the director's suggestions and notes, and also you're going to come across things you hadn't thought of at the thumbnail stage because you're really working everything out. One of these is posing and acting. Usually in a thumbnail, there's really no point in acting out all of the scenes in detail. You're just trying to draw some of the key poses in the scene, so the rough form becomes where you really let everything play out in detail. It's just that the drawings are very scribbly. You're just trying to get them down as quickly as you can. And it is always better to have a completed board that's rough than to have an incomplete board that's clean. It's one of the key things. Because if the production ends up with a completed board that's rough, they can still either get a revisionist to fix it, or they could ship it with some additional clarifications. But a board that's incomplete is completely useless. And in television, just like many other businesses where they use storyboards, the deadlines are not just for the individual, but the whole production is set up like a production line, meaning that every week something is expected to ship because somebody is waiting in China for the next board that you're going to send them. And if you're late that means that your studio overseas has downtime and they're not doing anything, but you're still paying them, etc.

So there's really huge stakes. Each of these episodes costs, I don't even know how much, it's clearly a few hundred thousand dollars per episode. And when the schedule gets knocked off kilter, it's a disaster. So that's one thing about the rough stage is that if you know the whole thing is done in rough form and it works, then you're cool. At that point you have a meeting. This is the end of the third week typically, it does vary from studio to studio, where you will now pitch that rough board to the director, give them one more chance to see it, to find out what's working, what's not. Sometimes things seem to be reading well on paper but you may want to pitch the board by pinning it up to the wall, this is something that's fairly common with cartoon storyboards, you pin the thing up on the wall and literally go through it and read it and act it out either in front of a small crew of directors and writers, or it may be the entire crew. The point of that is to find any of those sections that are just dropping dead. If you get laughs, laughs, laughs, then you know you're doing well, but if you get laughs, no laughs, no laughs, and then more laughs then you know that somewhere in the middle, gee this section isn't really working. One of the things, typically we would do, is usually you'll want to cut those things. Shows tend to run longer all the time, than you want them to. So that's what happens after the rough, is you're really getting closer to boiling it down.

Are you finding yourself working a lot from prerecorded soundtracks? Is the soundtrack being done at this time?

That's an excellent question. Ideally on the script of for the show, you would be given a tape or an MP3 file which they call a track, some people might call it an EMR even though that's a completely outdated term that stood for Electro-Magnetic Recording. And it would be like an inch wide tape. Some of the people who have been in the business a really long time might say, "Oh, make sure you get the EMR," even though there is no such thing. So you're working from a recording. Unfortunately, in the real world, about half of the time that you're doing a storyboard there will be no recording because the production has gotten behind. I don't know how many times this has happened where you're starting a board with no recording to work from. And in that case, you're just working from the script imagining what the acting would be. And maybe later on, after the show has been recorded, a storyboard revisionist might have to go back in and change the expressions where there may be a big difference in expressions.

Shows like *The Mighty B!* were really extraordinary in that (Amy Poehler) . . . she's on that show *Parks and Recreation*, *Saturday Night Live* . . . Anyway, the star of *The Mighty B!* who co-created the show, she's a fantastic comic actress— absolutely great—and when she would record, those were the best tracks I ever worked off of, because I could listen to her voice, I could listen to the way she was acting, and I could totally see the character doing all of this stuff in my mind. And it made it very easy for me to draw funny drawings because she was acting really funny. So if you have a recording available to you—first of all, you have to listen to it a few times, you just have to or else you're going to get everything wrong, but the other thing is that it's a really huge benefit if you do have one, so thanks for reminding me about that. After that rough, and after you get approvals or corrections, the final two weeks are typically the time to do clean up, and that's where you're literally at this point just focusing on drawing. Most artists find that this is the easiest part of the job. That's where you get to sit down, typically, you can put your headphones on, you could listen to music, you could listen to audio books—some artists watch TV shows on their computer while they're doing this. Because it's the part where you don't have to worry about storytelling. You've already taken care of that stuff, and you're just trying to make pretty drawings out of it. I mean it still requires some degree of concentration, but an artist can't be on fire all the time, and so that clean up stage, even though it's a lot of work, is sort of the mental down time for the artist. And you do need to churn out tons of pages at this time. Remember 200 pages of clean up drawings is 400 panels over the course of let's say 10 days. So that's 40 panels per day . . . and that's about 12 pages or 13 pages a day of a two panel board that you're cleaning up. But the thing is you don't have to think about it too much and it's not that bad, it's about two pages an hour. You just got stay at it. You pull up a piece of paper. You either trace it over or you use a kneaded eraser to rub it down or if it's a computer you can pop on a new layer to clean it up, or just tweak some of the lines. It depends. Everybody works differently. I have a friend that his roughs are so clean that by the time his roughs are approved, he barely has to do anything at all for the next two weeks

Have you found that with everything going digital that things are changing and that maybe you'll be asked to an animatic rather than boards on the wall for instance?

Well I can tell you I've heard of that happening, but I've never seen it happen, and I've never been asked to do that. I've just sort of heard apocryphal stories of artists having to do that. Although I know that for the Fox shows like *Family Guy* and others that they pose them out extremely detailed, and I think that the artists are drawing the boards with the animator very clearly in mind. Whereas mostly just about everything I've done we're just trying to make a board as good as possible and that the animatic is dealt with by the director separately. It wouldn't surprise me at all if more and more it gets to that point, but it's going to be very difficult for anyone to find the time to try to do both of those jobs at the same time.

Now getting back to the real grunt work and expectations, I know of different people who have different rules of thumb about how much to draw. I've heard some people say that every time there's punctuation, you draw a new panel, or every time someone stops or changes direction, you draw a new panel. Do you have any rules of thumb like that?

I've never codified that way. I can say for sure though . . . it's strange though that a lot of artists, especially in a conversation that goes back and forth between characters, might have only one panel for a line of dialog. And I would say that there's rarely any case in which you would want to have only one panel. Because animation by the very nature of the word is about movement, it's about life and you can't have any movement at all if there's only one drawing. It has to start somewhere and end some place else. So even with a character only saying a couple of words, you can start with a start-pose where the character is in a settled, normal pose and then when they say their words, they're either leaning forward, they're leaning back, they're tilting their head, they're making the expression, they're lifting the eyebrow—something. So I can say definitively that no scene has less than two panels.

Then the question comes in, "How many poses do you need to draw?" My suggestion has always been, "As few poses as possible to get the idea across." That may mean a lot of poses, but the example that I frequently give is if a character is in a scene and he's putting on a tie. Well, you could draw that with just a few poses of the character holding a tie and putting it up to his collar and then in the next panel, the tie could be completely tied and you don't need to draw all the in between things. But that scenario is only if the tie tying isn't central to the story. If it's just a little incidental action then you don't need to go into all that detail. Because it could take 50 panels to show a person tying a tie if you wanted to go on in all of that detail. This came about while I was on *Hey Arnold!* I had a character who had to put on a sweater, and it was just killing me trying to draw this because there's so many different motions that a character has to go through to put on a sweater—it was going to take me all day. So I went and asked the director for some tips. And he said, "In the first panel, he's holding the sweater like up to his head for example, and in the second panel, the sweater's on—that's all you need to do." And I was like, "Really?! That's fantastic!" But the point of that was that the scene wasn't about him putting on the sweater. The scene was about him walking out the door of a hospital with his grandson. It had nothing to do with the sweater, it was just a bit of incidental action. I always recommend that you use as few poses as possible to clearly communicate that. No scene should ever go beyond 12 or 13 panels, so if you find yourself going in that direction, you either need to find a good place to cut away to a character talking or doing something else or you've just managed to over-pose it. We had a situation recently on a show in which a character drew an object falling, and it was like 16 panels because there was all this detail of the object falling, falling, falling, hitting the ground, bouncing, bouncing. And it was like, "What are you doing? Who cares? That's like way too much work." And we just cut it down to just a few panels.

Any ways of knowing when you've drawn too much? What kinds of questions might you ask yourself?

When we're drawing on paper, for example, I just know that we had to put letters on each panel to indicate—scene numbers would be done with numbers, scene panel numbers would be done with letters. This was on Nickelodeon, it varies from studio to studio. And we just simply had a rule on SpongeBob that if you get to "n" you've gone too far. That was all. It was like, you're doing too much if you've done that, which would be about 13 or 14 panels. So it's really hard to give a firm answer to that, but one of the best things to do is to look at some of the many, many examples that you can find of storyboards on the internet and just compare it to the work that you're doing and try to consciously pull something out of that by comparing them to the actual film. A great example of that would be like on the Miyazaki DVD like *Kiki's Delivery Service, My Neighbor Totoro*—those DVDs have all the storyboards on a separate disc in animatic form. And you can see through his examples, some of the best storyboards you'll ever see and you'll also see when he's posed something out to a great degree and when he hasn't. That's a real great guideline for animation storyboards. For feature storyboards, the acting is more left to the actor to actually do, so even though action may be very posed out, conversations wouldn't really be posed out because you let the actors do all of that. So it varies from whether you're doing feature storyboards that are much more posed out, TV storyboards less so.

Is there any difference between shows done in Flash where you're dealing with assets that are already worked out, it might be a little bit different from something that's drawn out?

You know, I've only heard of one example where that was the case. For the most part, whether it's animated in Flash, or even when it's in CG, the storyboarding seems to be not effected by that. The one exception to that was a Flash show being produced at Nickelodeon where the storyboard artists were actually doing the boards with the Flash library for that production. But I've never seen that take place since then. It would make sense, I think, if studios were more organized in their planning—that would probably make sense—but with all the different shows that I've worked on, I've never experienced that.

If you're a beginner and you're in school, and you want to know what things you should study, or how you're going to make the first contact, or should I have a website, should I have a blog—if you were a kid right now in school and your goal was to do storyboards for a cartoon, what would you be doing right now?

The first thing would be to take advantage of the fact that you are in school, and make sure that you're involved in storyboarding or animating or working on a student film. By using your class experience, to take the time it requires to make a sample board, then you'll already be one leg up when you go out to show people your work, because if you want to get a job as a storyboard artist, the first thing you need is to have storyboards to show them. And a lot of artists will say, "Oh, I don't have my own boards, I don't write, so I can't create my own storyboards." But we've seen many artists who have storyboards for their student films. And so right away the have something that they've completed that we can see. And even with that, if someone can give them a critique, at least they have something to critique from. The most primary thing would be to be make sure that you're creating the work. The second thing would be definitely to have your own website. And to have a presence throughout the web, so that there are people that you'll come in contact with that you'll get to know and whether that presence comes from large communities like DeviantArt, which is an excellent place for getting a lot of feedback, a lot of encouragement, a lot of exposure, DeviantArt is very good. It's not a great professional platform because it's still primarily a venue for nonprofessionals or people that are still trying to get into the business. There's still tons of really great professionals that are on DeviantArt including myself. There's guys like Adam Hughes, huge superstars that are on DeviantArt, but there are also tons of people that are just starting out. The community is very, very supportive. Starting up a regular blog though, is essential. It's super easy, if you just want to start something basic using Google's Blogger templates, you can get a blog started in about 15 minutes and start posting things. But what you want to be able to do is if you meet somebody, then you want to show them your work. You want to simply be able to give them a website address so they can go to and look. You want to make it easy for them.

Do you think most kids are going to need to wait for the job boards, or should they aggressively try to find contacts on the inside?

That's a great comment. There's a dirty little secret about job postings I'm glad you asked me about because this can really save people a lot of heartaches if they're aware of this. The job postings that come up in animation studios or that are posted with the union or that are posted in all kinds of places—they're not always really looking for somebody. A lot of times companies are required by equal opportunity laws to post job openings, even when the job isn't open. Let's say I'm Super Duper Studios, and I want to hire somebody for a job. Now the law requires studios to make sure that they're following all kinds of legal regulations to offer that job to everybody. And later on, they make a show of, "Okay, we've offered the job to everybody, but we're going to pick this one person." So a lot of times the postings are really fake leads, and a lot of people are very frustrated by that sort of thing. The job's already gone by the time the job's been posted. That's not always the case, but it's frequently the case. One of the main ways people get work, is through people they've worked with in the past. Now this can be frustrating for someone who hasn't done any work, but that's again why student work is so important. For instance, I've seen tons of people that I've worked with that when you've dug a little bit deeper and you've gotten to know them, you find out that they all went to school together. They were all in the same class, whether it was Cal State Fullerton or it was Cal Arts, or someplace else. And it's not because it's an old boys' network, what happens is that somebody gets a job because of the merits that they have and then when they find out through their own work that let's say I find out that, "Gee, they're really looking for storyboard artists," I might mention to my friend, "Hey, they're looking for a storyboard artists, you might want to come down here and I can show your portfolio to the boss." I used to really, really hate the notion that when I started out that you have to know someone to get a good job in the entertainment field. And it is still true to some degree that it really, really helps and becomes the backbone to everything that you do. But part of the way I would recommend people do that is just to broaden their circle of people that they can as much as possible. And again, if you're in school, that's a huge, huge opportunity. Just play nice, collaborate with as many people as you can, and just make good relationships. Being helpful and friendly goes a long, long way. And everybody who's working in the storyboard field has a completely different story about how they got involved in it. A lot of guys got involved through comics because a show creator really liked their comic books. For example, Steve Hillenburg on *SpongeBob* was a really big fan of Kaz, who is a really great indie cartoonist, who had been doing fantastic comics since the eighties. He was living in New York, and Steve just always really loved Kaz's comics and he was like, "I wonder if Kaz would be interested doing a storyboard?" And he was like, "Nah, he wouldn't want to do it." And so they ended up calling him up and he was like, "Heck yeah!" He had never worked in animation before. Came out to L.A. and started working, and he's been working in animation ever since. But it's because he put his work out there. People came and noticed it and he got an opportunity. It turned out that working for the weekly newspapers that he was doing, even though he was pretty popular in that field, it's not a very lucrative field. So he was very happy to start working in animation, and consequently he's continued to work on his own print cartoons through all these years as well.

I do want to mention, backtracking a little bit, that when it came to being noticed for my writing, and how someone could get noticed for a job that way, again it happened in the screwiest way possible. I had made one of my independent comic books before I ever got into animation, it was called *Cancer Man*. I gave a copy of this comic to a friend of mine who was working on *Rocko's Modern Life* at the time. And Derek Drymon, who was the friend, apparently left the comic in the back seat of his car, and he was going out and he was going out to lunch with his friend Steve Hillenburg who later went on to create *SpongeBob*. Well Steve really loved the comic. It really cracked him up. I didn't know anything about this until a couple years later when Steve asked me to come storyboard on *SpongeBob*. And I was just like . . . I didn't even know if I could do it or not because I hadn't written for animation yet, I had just written my own comics. And he says, "Well, I read your *Cancer Man* comic, and it was really funny, so I think you could do it." And I said, "Well, if you think I could do it, then I'll give it a try." And if he hadn't seen that comic in the back seat of Derek's car, he would never have known about my writing. So the biggest, biggest, biggest thing after actually creating the work is to get that work under as many people's noses as you can.

Should you be a generalist, or a specialist starting out?

It's a tough thing to address. It is good to have a well-rounded ability, especially in storytelling. As a storyboard artist, I would say the most important thing is to be a good generalist in terms of being able to tell a story and to know what's important in a story so you know which parts of the story are important, where to emphasize the emotion, where to emphasize the action. So in that sense, it's very good to be a generalist. But in animation we are broken down into two big camps. One being the action-adventure type of show—*Batman*, or *Brave and the Bold*, or *Avengers*—and then the funny stuff. And then there's also sort of a middle-ground like *The Family Guy*, where they're cartoons, but they're not very cartoony. And among those, you're definitely going be better off being a specialist in one of those fields. Because if you're really good at drawing funny stuff, you'll have an easier time getting a job on a funny show. And if you're really good at drawing action stuff, you're going to be a shoe-in for drawing on an action show. I would never, myself, try to get work on an action show, because I know that the guys who do that kind of work could just mop the floor with me as far as drawing action-adventure and superheroes. And they probably feel the same way, about in the way they probably wouldn't feel comfortable on *SpongeBob* or on *Fish Hooks*.

You got to know your strengths.

Yeah, absolutely. You want to broaden your horizons as much as possible especially in terms of storytelling techniques. It's easy to fall into a rut of staging everything like a sitcom and that's what everybody seems to default to. But sometimes the people who stay abreast of modern trends in storytelling, whether it's television commercials or anything that's really out of the ordinary, can really pop out in a storyboard when it's done thoughtfully. And it's like, "Whoa! That's a great idea! How'd you come up with this? How'd you come up with that shot?" And that doesn't always mean the newest stuff, it can also mean the oldest stuff. By studying some of the oldest comedy works, you'll also be able to come up with a lot of innovative ideas because you'll find that 99 percent of your co-workers don't have any idea that old, classic stuff even exists. I find for example, I'll just throw this out there, that the movie *Sunset Boulevard*, directed by Billy Wilder, is I think the greatest movie ever made, and it has pretty much an endless encyclopedia of things that you could learn about storytelling. Just to focus in on that one movie. There's more that you can learn from one well-made movie just by watching it over and over again asking yourself constantly, "Why did they choose that shot? Why did they choose that angle? Why did they decide to cut there instead of afterwards? By asking yourself that question after you've placed yourself in the hands of let's say someone who's acknowledged as a master of filmmaking, whether it's again Miyazaki or if it's Billy Wilder or if it's early Steven Spielberg. But you wouldn't want to do that with Michael Bay or McG. You know, you'd be taking some risks because those filmmakers so a lot of things that are right, but they also do a lot of things that aren't necessarily good storytelling.

I'm asking all my interviewees for two tips: one that's more kind of a techie tip or kind of a hands-on tip, and maybe something that's a little more general.

They're both a little bit tied in, but the first techie tip I would say is to draw a lot on post-it notes. Draw a lot of your storyboard roughs on post-it notes and even some of the completed work on post-it notes. Post-it notes are serendipitously very similar to most screen ratios and so it's very easy to do boards on them. But what it really does, is because you're drawing on a piece of loose paper that's kind of a crappy, throwaway piece of paper, it lets you as an artist sort of loosen up a little bit and not be so precious about every drawing, because I personally have a very hard time drawing inside of a pre-printed box. A lot of storyboard paper will come to you on a sheet of paper with a nicely printed box. And I just kind of freeze up knowing that whatever I draw on this piece of paper is the final artwork, so I've had a lot of success by drawing on post-its. Because if you don't like a drawing, you just tear it up and you throw it away really quick, and you can't erase and really do a beautiful drawing. It keeps you moving at a fast pace. But also lets you rearrange the order a little bit. So if you're drawing on post-its, and then you decide that, "Oh, you know what I need a few more poses in between these two poses," and you're not cutting up pieces of paper trying to do all of those things. Now that doesn't apply to digital at all, but in terms of thumbnails, I still frequently draw on post-it notes. When I have to move really fast, I'll actually scan those thumbnails in, cut them up, and put them in the digital storyboard. For some reason, I'm able to draw on post-it notes very quickly. There was a show we did on *Kick Butowski* where we had to completely re-write the first two minutes opening, and that's like 20 percent of the show. And I had to do it in one night, and I was like, "Uugh!" Just feverishly drawing on post-its, scanned them all in, dropped them into the storyboard, and they were pretty loose, but they were there and they were good enough to ship. So that's a big one: Draw on something disposable, post-it notes are fantastic for that.

The second general note that I would give is that—I could put it in terms that my friend Robert said, "It's easier to edit crap than air." And what I would say is my suggestion is to really give yourself permission to do crappy drawings. It's very, very intimidating to try to draw a storyboard and think that you're going to be like, drawing a finished storyboard from panel one and continuing on after that because you want every drawing to look really good. But if you just start out and you just start scribbling things and getting your pencil moving and putting stuff down even when you don't have any ideas, if you have to stage a scene and your don't know where to go with it—if you just draw something horrible, then you can sort of look at it and go, "Ah well, obviously I want to have this character a little bit bigger in the frame and maybe more of an up shot on there to make it more interesting," but it can really be paralyzing to be facing either a new storyboard or a new script or a new page or whatever it is, but you have to build up a head of steam. Sometimes drawing a bunch of crappy drawings will get you through that head of steam, then you can go back later and you can fix them up. In a deadline driven industry, I try to drive this home all the time, and I need to hear this just as much as anybody else—is that "done" is the most important thing. I rarely see an artist that turns everything in on time get fired, which isn't to say it's okay to do mediocre work, but it's far better to get your work finished and not so great than it is to try to make every panel perfect and then be late on your deadlines, because in this industry, it's all about deadlines. The stakes are very high in terms of all the money that they spend, and how many people you're affecting with late boards. It's all tricks that you have to play on yourself to be able to get yourself to finish this monumental task of trying to churn out 12 pages of product every day.

One last thing I will throw into this second thing is to always keep in mind that for every single step of the way when you're drawing, what is the story about? What is this scene that I'm drawing about? And how does this scene fit into the big picture? So, it's easy to get blinders put on—you're working on this one particular scene, a mom and a daughter having breakfast in this one scene. You'll get caught up in the scene. You may be tempted to do some close ups on the cereal bowl or a cool angle—but if you've forgotten what the scene is about— you've forgotten that the scene is about a mother that doesn't trust her daughter or it's a mother who's afraid that her daughter is growing up too fast—THAT's what the scene is about. It's usually not about what it is on the surface. You need to think about what's happening. Because only then are you going to be able to do drawings that are going to communicate the real essence of the story which is always something that has to do with emotions and some sort of dramatic emotional thing rather that just what's on the surface. Always keep the story in mind.

Is there anything that you wanted to talk about that we didn't talk about? That you think is important that you want me to cover?

I'll just rattle off a few movies that I particularly like. Like I said to you before, I mentioned to you *Sunset Boulevard*. *Jaws* is another one that can be looked at as pure storytelling. Again that's a movie where you think it's about people hunting a shark, but *Jaws* is not about people hunting a shark, it's about a man who has to overcome his greatest fears to protect this family. So that's a great example of where you think on the surface, "Oh yeah, it's a movie about some guy chasing a shark." No. It's never about what you think it's about. Like *Superman*, particularly *Superman II*, it's like, "Oh, it's about some guy trying to save the world from a nuclear bomb." No, it's about a stranger in a strange place who doesn't know how to fit in. It's usually about what the people are going through. So *Jaws* is a really good example. Movies that are great to have on disc would be *Kiki's Delivery Service*, probably one of the best—there are other Miyazaki movies that are maybe more adventurous or more stylized, but in terms of pure character, plot and storytelling, *Kiki's Delivery Service* is fantastic. And I'm very fond of *The Kid* by Charlie Chaplin. It's a shorter film; it's about 45 minutes long so, it's a really good one to start off with. Others that are great from him would be *City Lights* and *The Gold Rush*, for example. And *Casablanca*! And as far as being aware of general film storytelling, I still recommend to people I work with all the time a book called *The Five C's of Cinematography* by Joseph

Mascelli because it's a straight basic encyclopedia of tried and true, tested storytelling tips and once you've learned the thought process behind using all these different techniques of storytelling then it becomes second nature and you don't have to think about it anymore.

More tips

Some of the most common things I was running into with new students was they frequently frame things way too tight. Even when you think you need to frame a character tightly, you still want to give them enough room to move their torso and their arms. And the closest that you generally want to get to a character at the extreme is usually like a head and shoulders shot. But shooting characters from the waist up is a good idea in terms of your general shooting or further away from that. It's really common when you frame characters too tightly they don't have any room to move. If they don't have room to move, they don't have room to act. In terms of screen direction, it seems to be a very difficult thing for a lot of people to catch on to. One way I try to boil it down for people very succinctly is to tell them, that if you frame a character on the left side of the screen and you have a different character on the right side of the screen, the easiest thing to remember is that that relationship should always be the same. The left character should always be on the left, and the right character should always be on the right, until you actually see them switch places on the screen. It's just one of the easiest ways to remember it without having to worry about angles and stage line and everything. It's like if Joe's on the left, Fred's on the right, then every time you show them, Joe should be on the left, and Fred should be on the right. And when characters move within a scene, you probably want to shoot that in a wider shot to give them a chance to move. And then you simply re-establish the relationship. It's an easy way to remember it.

NOTES

1   Turnaround character designs are model sheets with orthographic views of the character usually from the front, profile, 3/4 view, and back view.

2   Famous Frames is a storyboard agency.

3   The Third Floor is a preproduction studio in Los Angeles.

CHAPTER 14
Parting Thoughts

Nothing in the world can take the place of Persistence.

Talent will not; nothing is more common than unsuccessful men with talent.

Genius will not; unrewarded genius is almost a proverb.

Education will not; the world is full of educated derelicts. Persistence and determination alone are omnipotent.

Calvin Coolidge
30th president of US (1872–1933)

To be alive is to grow. To be stagnant is death. Never get comfortable and you will never get complacent with your art. I would call a guy that sweeps the street for a living and tries to do it better every day an artist before I would confer the title on a sell-out painter who cranks out the same canvas day after day. The greatest of artists always feel like they have more to learn and there is something out there they don't understand yet. That thing you don't quite understand is what keeps you driving harder and harder and makes you get better. This is what it takes for you to make it as a storyboard artist. The passion that's inside of you will have to grow and carry you through the ups and downs of a career in filmmaking.

The experience of being a professional storyboard artist is a journey of excitement and change. New tools and technologies are invented all the time, and it's up to you to break new ground in storytelling for the generations to come. Remember, it is *your* emotions that you will draw from when creating stories for others. Learn the tools well and keep up to date on the trends in the industry. But keep in mind your art is meaningless unless it has life's experiences behind it. Great art captures the truth, joy, absurdity, sadness and fear of everyday life. So along with the many hours of drawing, studying, and film history, go out and enjoy the world. Enjoy people. Fall in love. Take every opportunity possible to experience the richness this world has to offer. Your art will be better for it.

You might be tempted along the way, because of economic hardship or family pressures, to give up a life in filmmaking. No one said this would be easy, but it is much more difficult to face yourself in the mirror everyday knowing you didn't take a shot at fulfilling your dreams. We are here to tell you that it is possible and hopefully after reading this book you understand a little more about what it takes to make your storyboard career a reality. Storyboard artists are created and emerge like butterflies after long years of artistic development. Jobs will come and go, but the world will always need great storytellers. This is now your challenge. We dare you to dream and create worlds not yet seen before. This is your journey. When you discover what fills your heart and makes great stories, share it for the rest of the world to see. And when you discover what it takes to create those great stories, pass that knowledge on to those that come after you.

When it's your turn to begin the journey don't delay, and don't be scared. Mistakes and failure will make you grow. Embrace them and they will take you to the finish line. It's with a smile and a wink that I tell you the old adage is absolutely true— ". . . if you find a career you love, you'll never work a day in your life . . ."

Resources

Storyboard Artist Community

www.storyboardart.org

Promote Yourself with a Professional Facebook Page

www.facebook.com

Network with other Professionals on LinkedIn

www.linkedin.com

IATSE Local 800 Storyboard Union

www.adg.org

Drawing Books

Barbara Bradley (2003) *Drawing People*, Ohio: North Lights Books.

Andrew Loomis (1944) *Figure Drawing for All It's Worth*, New York: Viking Press.

Andrew Loomis (1939) *Fun with a Pencil*, New York: Viking Press.

Robert Valley, *Massive Swerve Books1–4*, San Francisco: RobertValley.com Anatomy Books.

George Bridgman (1920) *Constructive Anatomy*, New York: Dover Publications.

Stephen Rogers Peck (1951) *Atlas of Human Anatomy for the Artist*, New York: Oxford University Press.

Books on Story

Robert McKee (1997) *Story*, New York: Harper Collins.

David Mamet (1991) *On Directing Film*, New York: Penguin Books.

Blake Snyder (2005) *Save the Cat*, California: Michael Wise Productions.

Filmography

Battleship Potemkin (Soviet Union/1925)
Directed by Sergei M. Eisenstein

Boogie Nights (USA/1997)
Directed by Paul Thomas Anderson

Butch Cassidy and the Sundance Kid (USA/1969)
Directed by George Roy Hill

Casablanca (USA/1943)
Directed by Michael Curtiz

Citizen Kane (USA/1941)
Directed by Orson Welles

City Lights (USA/1931)
Directed by Charles Chaplin

Disney Films

> **The Gallopin' Gaucho** (USA/1928)
> Directed by Ub Iwerks

> **Plane Crazy** (USA/1928)
> Directed by Walt Disney, Ub Iwerks

> **Snow White and the Seven Dwarfs** (USA/1938)
> Directed by William Cottrell, David Hand

> **Steamboat Willie** (USA/1930)
> Directed by Ub Iwerks

> **The Three Little Pigs** (USA/1938)

The English Patient (USA/1996)
Directed by Anthony Minghella

Ghostbusters 2 (USA/1989)
Directed by Ivan Reitman

GI Joe (USA/2009)
Directed by Stephen Sommers

The Godfather: Part II (USA/1974)
Directed by Francis Ford Coppola

The Gold Rush (Germany/1925)
Directed by Charles Chaplin

The Good the Bad and the Ugly (USA/1967)
Directed by Sergio Leone

Goodfellas (USA/1990)
Directed by Martin Scorsese

Hellboy II (USA/2008)
Directed by Guillermo del Toro

The Incredibles (USA/2004)
Directed by Brad Bird

The Iron Giant (USA/1999)
Directed by Brad Bird

Jack the Giant Killer (USA/1962)
Directed by Nathan Juran

Jaws (USA/1975)
Directed by Steven Spielberg

The Jazz Singer (USA/1927)
Directed by Alan Crosland

The Kid (USA/1921)
Directed by Charles Chaplin

Kiki's Delivery Service (Japan/1989)
Directed by Hayao Miyazaki

Kung Fu Panda (USA/2008)
Directed by Mark Osborne, John Stevenson

Ladder 49 (USA/2004)
Directed by Jay Russell

Lawrence of Arabia (USA/1963)
Directed by David Lean

Little Boy (USA/2012)
Directed by Alejandro Monteverde

The Mask (USA/1994)
Directed by Chuck Russell

Men in Black (USA/1997)
Directed by Barry Sonnenfeld

The Mummy (USA/1999)
Directed by Stephen Sommers

Nine (USA/2009)
Directed by Shane Acker

The Phantom Menace (India/1999)
Directed by George Lucas

Psycho (Brazil/1960)
Directed by Alfred Hitchcock

Raiders of the Lost Ark (USA/1981)
Directed by Steven Spielberg

The Silence of the Lambs (USA/1991)
Directed by Jonathan Demme

Star Wars (USA/1978)
Directed by George Lucas

Sunset Boulevard (USA/1950)
Directed by Billy Wilder

Superman (USA/1978)
Directed by Richard Donner

Superman II (USA/1981)
Directed by Richard Lester

The Ten Commandments (USA/1956)
Directed by Cecil B. DeMille

Terminator 3 (USA/2003)
Directed by Jonathan Mostow

Thor (USA/2011)
Directed by Kenneth Branagh and Joss Whedon

Top Gun (USA/1986)
Directed by Tony Scott

Touch of Evil (France/1958)
Directed by Orson Welles

Vertigo (USA/1958)
Directed by Alfred Hitchcock

War Horse (USA/2012)
Directed by Steven Spielberg

Where the Wild Things Are (USA/2009)
Directed by Spike Jonze

The Wizard of Oz (USA/1939)
Directed by Victor Fleming

Index